DAILY
GUIDEPOSTS

YOUR FIRST YEAR OF

Motherhood

EDITED BY JULIA ATTAWAY

Guideposts
New York, New York

ISBN-10: 0-8249-4859-9
ISBN-13: 978-0-8249-4859-7

Published by Guideposts
16 East 34th Street
New York, New York 10016
www.guideposts.org

Distributed by Ideals Publications, a Guideposts company
2636 Elm Hill Pike, Suite 120
Nashville, Tennessee 37214

Acknowledgments

Every attempt has been made to credit the sources of copyrighted material used in this book. If any such acknowledgment has been inadvertently omitted or miscredited, receipt of such information would be appreciated.

All Scripture quotations, unless otherwise noted, are taken from *The Holy Bible, New International Version*. Copyright © 1973, 1978, 1984 International Bible Society. Used by permission of Zondervan Bible Publishers.

Scripture quotations marked (AMP) are taken from *The Amplified Bible*, © 1965 by Zondervan Publishing House. All rights reserved.

Scripture quotations marked (ESV) are taken from the Holy Bible, English Standard Version, copyright © 2001 by Crossway Bibles, a division of Good News Publishers. Used by permission. All rights reserved.

Scripture quotations marked (God's Word) are taken from God's Word® Translation. Copyright © 1995 by God's Word to the Nations. Used by permission.

Scripture quotations marked (KJV) are taken from *The King James Version of the Bible*.

Scripture quotations marked (MSG) are taken from *The Message*. Copyright © 1993, 1994, 1995, 1996, 2000, 2001, 2002 by Eugene H. Peterson.

Scripture quotations marked (NAS) are taken from the *New American Standard Bible*, copyright © 1960, 1962, 1963, 1968, 1971, 1972, 1973, 1975, 1977, 1996 by the Lockman Foundation. Used by permission.

Scripture quotations marked (NKJV) are taken from *The Holy Bible, New King James Version*. Copyright © 1997, 1990, 1985, 1983 by Thomas Nelson, Inc.

Scripture quotations marked (NLT) are taken from the *Holy Bible*, New Living Translation. Copyright © 1996. Used by permission of Tyndale House Publishers, Inc., Wheaton, Illinois 60189. All rights reserved.

Edited by Julia Attaway
Cover design by Georgia Morrissey
Cover photo by Corbis
Interior design by Müllerhaus
Indexed by Indexing Research
Typeset by Aptara

Printed and bound in the United States of America
10 9 8 7 6 5 4 3 2 1

Contents

Dear Fellow Mom,

There's a common misperception that having a baby is a matter of addition, the simple equation of 2+1=3. The truth is it's more like geometry, the difference between a straight line that connects two points and a triangle that connects three. Motherhood changes every dimension of our lives. It reveals our weaknesses, expands our hearts, uncovers our insecurities and casts every significant relationship we have in a new light. Becoming a mother leaves nothing—including our spiritual lives—unchanged. How could it, when we've experienced God's creative power firsthand?

This book is a guidebook of sorts, a travelogue written by those who have already gone down the sometimes rocky road of becoming a parent. The twenty moms (and one dad) you'll meet here will regale you with tales of love, frustration, exhaustion and humor. They open their hearts and lives so you can walk with them through the daily challenge of growing in faith and parenting wisdom. Most importantly, they'll help you see through the dirty diapers and new-mom anxieties to the ways God is supporting you in this tremendous new life you are entering.

Daily Guideposts: Your First Year of Motherhood doesn't sugarcoat motherhood or its challenges. We know it's tough. We know it's wonderful. We embrace the challenge, and love the Lord, and invite you to join us in the journey.

Julia Attaway, Editor

MEET THE MOTHERS

I've often thought the reason God asks us to be fruitful and multiply is because He knows it's the fastest path to humility!" writes **JULIA ATTAWAY** of New York City. At the beginning of her mothering journey, Julia was director of marketing at a major life insurance company. Today she homeschools three of her five children and is a freelance writer, newsletter editor and marketing consultant. She has written for *Daily Guideposts* since 1997. "When I had my first child," Julia says, "I wasn't sure how I was going to do it all. Perhaps the best lesson I learned that year was that it was me—not God—who had the expectation that I was supposed to be Superwoman. When I focus on what He wants instead of on my own expectations, life becomes a lot simpler."

*O*ur children have so much to teach us, if only we slow down and listen," writes **RUTH BERGEN** of Niverville, Manitoba, Canada. Seven years ago she married Brian, her knight in shining armor, and today they have two daughters, Shiloh and Eliorah. Ruth spends her days coloring with sidewalk chalk, baking cinnamon buns and cleaning toilets. She is also involved with making baby layettes for the local Crisis Pregnancy Centre. "It's true that our children need to be taught," says Ruth. "But I believe they also hold keys to freedom and joy that many of us have lost in adulthood."

*O*ne of **LIZ BISSELL'S** favorite verses is Romans 5:2, "We throw open our doors to God and discover at the same moment that he has already thrown open his door to us. We find ourselves standing where we always hoped we might stand—out in the wide open spaces of God's grace and glory, standing tall and shouting our praise." (MSG) It resonates with her experience as a mother. Liz explains: "Being a mom has been a crash course in loving when I have been exhausted, afraid and emotionally dry. It's helped me recognize my inability to control people and circumstances, and to have faith in God." Liz lives in New York City with her husband Jonathan and their two daughters Llewelyn and Julia. She and her husband are leaders in a network of house churches called The Bridge Church.

FAITH BOGDAN never wanted to have children (let alone girls) but is loving life as a stay-at-home mom of four surprises—Anna, Sarah, Rebecca and Ruth. She is completing her first book, *Oops, I'm a Mom!* Faith writes from the comfort of her log cabin in Gillett, Pennsylvania, while her two older daughters attend a cyber charter school (a live public school online) in the comfort of their bedroom. The younger two do school the old-fashioned way, by getting on a yellow bus. But life is not always comfortable, as Faith discovered when husband Dave closed his business to go to grad school full time and entered a long season of unemployment. Faith writes and speaks with a passion to help others live "well-loved" by God, and to courageously embrace suffering as His "spiritual growth hormone."

SABRA CIANCANELLI is a freelance writer and mom of two boys, Solomon and Henry. She lives in Tivoli, New York, with her husband, sons, five (yes, five!) cats, two pet rats (long story but perfect pets) and a two-year-old goldfish. When she isn't picking up a cyclone of toys, she is working at finishing her novel. "I loved working on this book," writes Sabra. "It helped me relive the many challenges and blessings of the first year with Solomon. The beginning of motherhood is a precious and tender time that I'll forever hold deep in my heart."

*P*arenting Samantha changed me in ways that nothing else could," says ELSA KOK COLOPY. "We became a single-parent family when Samantha was eighteen months old, and for twelve years we did life on our own." Elsa started writing about their adventures together, what God was doing and how He'd rescued them both. "Several of my books came out of that season of life with just Samantha and me." Today Elsa is happily married to her new husband Brian and is a stepmom to Sean, Jessica and Cassie. The former editor of the single-parent edition of *Focus on the Family* magazine, she currently works from home as a freelance author and speaker. To find out the latest, visit her at ElsaKokColopy.com.

*J*ENNIFER FULWILER sometimes can't believe that she's a passionate Christian. "The road to faith was anything but easy for me," she says. She was an atheist all her life, even in childhood. "I seemed to be missing the belief gene—God's presence was never obvious to me." But becoming a mother challenged her to open her mind to truth as never before and led her to conclude that God exists and Jesus Christ is his Son. Today she has four children under age six and writes from her home in Austin, Texas, about atheism, faith, and the joy of the Christian life. Her writing has been published in over a dozen magazines, and she blogs at ConversionDiary.com.

*M*y grandmother's favorite hymn was "In the Garden." After I became a mother, I understood why. The first line says it all: 'I come to the garden *alone!*'" laughs CAROL HATCHER of Buford, Georgia. Carol taught school until the birth of her first child, when she traded being called "Mrs. Hatcher" for "Mama." Now the mother of three, Carol writes a marriage column for a local newspaper, devotions for her personal Web site (SheeptotheRight.com) and freelance articles. You can find some of her work in the *P31 Woman* magazine and *Chicken Soup for the Soul: Devotional Stories for Mothers*. "I have to remember God can use me wherever I am in life. It's easy to think I need to wait until I have more time, extra money or a deeper understanding of the Bible," Carol says. "But when I wake up and say 'Use me today, Lord,' He always does."

A homeschooling mother of four, online magazine publisher, and entrepreneur, **DIANNA HOBBS** has a pretty full plate. So when others ask the founder and editor-in-chief of EEWMagazine.com, a top Web publication for African American Christian women, how she holds it all together, Dianna always says the same thing. "Without prayer there's *no way* I would have the strength or ability to complete any of the things I'm tasked with!" Dianna, also a sought-after recording artist and speaker, has a very specific philosophy when it comes to juggling responsibilities. "The key to balancing numerous roles is never to allow your priorities to get out of whack," she says. "There's God first, then family, and everything else comes after that." Dianna resides in upstate New York with her husband Kenya and their four children, Kyla, Kaiah, Kedar and Kaleb. You can visit her online at EmpoweringEverydayWomen.com.

It wasn't until the end of my first year of mothering that I found a MOPS (Mothers of Preschoolers) group to provide me the encouragement I desperately needed," says **ALEXANDRA KUYKENDALL** of Denver, Colorado. "As a new mom in a new city, I was looking for friends who would welcome and accept me just as I was. My MOPS group gave me a Christ-centered support network and helped me grow as a woman, mother and leader." Alexandra's passion for the MOPS ministry and what it offers new moms led her to work for the organization part-time. She now spends her time away from her three daughters as MOPS International's Ministry Strategist. In this role she scouts out trends that affect the 3,600 local MOPS groups around the world. To find a MOPS group in your community, visit www.MOPS.org.

*T*h e biggest surprise of motherhood was how much the Lord used the joys and challenges of life with children to change and shape *me* and to draw me closer to Him," writes SUSAN LABOUNTY of Oregon's Willamette Valley. "My continual prayer was II Chronicles 20:12: [I] don't know what to do, so [my] eyes are upon You." Establishing a relaxed, joyful learning environment for her four now-grown, homeschooled children was rewarding for Susan, and after a thirty-year break from college, she is again a full-time student, earning a master's degree in counseling. In her spare time, Susan enjoys being with her children, their spouses and her three grandchildren (a fourth is on the way). She loves reading, cooking and early mornings with a good cup of coffee, but Susan is happiest outdoors, especially when hiking in the mountains.

*R*eflecting on her first year of motherhood, LISA LADWIG says, "The challenges of parenting an infant pushed me to trust fully in the Lord." On many days, she found herself clinging to II Corinthians 12:9: "But he said to me, 'My grace is sufficient for you, for my power is made perfect in weakness.' Therefore I will boast all the more gladly of my weaknesses, so that the power of Christ may rest upon me." When her third child was born with special needs, Lisa was able to draw from the valuable experiences of her first year as a mom. "I knew God was teaching me important lessons, but I didn't realize how much He was also preparing my heart and equipping me for future challenges." Lisa currently lives in her home state of Rhode Island with her husband Robert and their three children.

*G*rowing up, the desire of my heart was to be a wife and mom. I had no idea that unexplained infertility would put my dreams of being a mom on hold for so many years," says DONNA MAY LYONS. Today she still marvels at the three amazing children God blessed her with: fraternal twins Ashleigh and Amanda and son D.J. III. Donna loves writing about her faith, family, parenting and the humor of daily life. She writes about parenting issues for Examiner.com from her home in Colorado Springs and was a contributing author for the book *Twins to Quints*. Donna also writes for *TWINS* magazine and is currently on the Board of Directors for the National Organization of Mothers of Twins Clubs, Inc.

*B*efore I had kids, I was *cool*," says ERIN MACPHERSON. "I had my life figured out—from my perfectly clean living room to my perfectly fitting jeans. Then God blessed me with two kids in less than two years. Suddenly, my life felt out of control—but the realness of motherhood brought me closer to Him, closer to my husband and closer to the nitty-gritty important things in life." Erin lives in Austin, Texas, with her husband Cameron, her son Joey and her daughter Kate. She is the author of "*The Christian Mama's Guide to Having a Baby*" and she blogs about her life, her kids and her faith at www.ChristianMamasGuide.com.

*T*he way each adoption happens is different, says LENORE LELAH PERSON, an editor, marketing consultant and adoptive mom of two joys, Lisbet and Kalle. She is amazed by the network of adoptive moms. "After you make the huge decision that you want to adopt a child, there are so many things you still need to decide. International or domestic, agency or independent, and then which country, which agency or which lawyer. When we were stuck at that point, several acquaintances scribbled down phone numbers and said, 'Call this person; she adopted two children and would love to talk to you about how she did it.' I would call, and a complete stranger would tell me about their path to adopting. Now I get these calls. Each time it happens, I feel honored to be part of this circle."

Growing up in a home headed by Dominican-born parents, **DEBRALEE SANTOS'** formative years were buoyed by the hopes and grounded in the struggles of the immigrant experience. Her parents taught her a profound reliance on the virtues of faith and perseverance—and an intense love of language. "Some of the happiest moments in my life were spent in our childhood church when we sang out as a chorus or time spent reading the Gospels alone. As with being a mother, the light never seemed to go out." Debralee continues to seek out the power of grace in deed and words. Aided by her delightful partner-in-arms Patrick, she is mother to Anjelica and Matthew and serves as program director for a cultural arts development initiative in northern Manhattan.

When I excel on the mission field at home, I excel on the mission field in the world," writes **RHONDA J. SMITH** of Detroit, Michigan. The challenges of being a full-time mom to three have taught her greater compassion toward the people she encounters as an ordained minister. Rhonda is a freelance writer and editor, writing for national publications including *Charisma* magazine. During the first few years of motherhood, she taught speech at a community college. "I was an ambitious academician focused on students who needed extra help," Rhonda says. "Now I dedicate my energies to my children, so they are well-prepared for life both academically and spiritually." Rhonda often blogs about her family at MusingsOfaStrongBlackWoman.com.

Christy Sturm clings to II Corinthians 5:17, "Therefore, if anyone is in Christ, he is a new creation; the old has gone, the new has come!" as she tries to start every day "new" as a mom. She lives northwest of Chicago with her husband Steve and their four children, Maggie, Steven, Henry and William. Her life changed when Henry was born with Down syndrome and Steven was diagnosed with Asperger's syndrome in the same year. Because her children don't give her enough to do, she also teaches computers at the kids' school, loves digital scrapbooking and blogs constantly at Motherhood-Unscripted.com.

*W*hen my boys are in bed after a long day, I get that same feeling I have after a grueling workout. I'm exhausted, but in a good way, proud that I got through the difficult parts and (I do hope) even managed to have some fun!" writes KAREN VALENTIN. Karen is proud of her Puerto Rican American heritage, and has authored several books, including *The Flavor of Our Hispanic Faith, Hallway Diaries* and *Allie's World*, a four-book children's series. She is a regular contributor to *Daily Guideposts* and lives in New York City with her husband and two children.

*Y*ears into parenting, SUSAN BESZE WALLACE still wakes up—often with Legos in or on her bed—marveling that she's a mom to three boys. "The journey from infertility to child loss to motherhood has shaped every inch of my heart and spirit," Susan says. A newspaper reporter coast to coast for more than a decade, Susan now lives in Haymarket, Virginia, where she focuses on the daily deadlines of her sons. She is the author of the four-book series *The New Mom's Guides* and writes for magazines and Web sites. "It's simply a privilege to be a mom. We all have our days, but when we stop and remember that this is the child meant to be yours, and you are the woman meant to be his, we can find profound honor and meaning in the most ordinary moments."

...AND THE DAD

*B*ecoming parents is the most profound thing Kari and I have ever done," writes LEROY HUIZENGA of Wheaton, Illinois. "Our family has become a school of discipleship as we've come to grasp ever more deeply what God is like through the sacrifices we've made and the love we've experienced—and given." Kari was working as a social worker when she became pregnant with their first child, Hans. Kari stays home with two-year-old Hans and their newborn daughter Miriam while Leroy continues to teach at Wheaton College and write. "Watching Kari, I see that motherhood is a huge challenge that's nourished with deep joy," writes Leroy. "I help out as much as I can, and yet I'm awed and very proud of my wife, who gives so much to our children."

First Month

~~~~~~

Father,

You created the vast heavens and the rich earth—and, unbelievably, this tender child. Thank You for this incredible gift.

Lord, You've entrusted me with so much; teach me to be a good mother, a wise and loving guide for my child. Give me an extra dose of patience during sleepless nights, and help me be patient with myself as I grow into this new role You have given me.

In Jesus' name, amen.

Tips

» It took nine months for your baby to be born. Allow yourself the same amount of time to grow into being a mom.

» Stay in your jammies and robe when people stop by to visit. It sends the subtle message that a long stay would be an intrusion.

» Your baby *will* survive if you let someone else take care of him or her while you nap. Really.

» Offer your worries daily to God. Remember that He is trusting you to do this (even if you're not so sure about it yourself).

Day One

"Stand still, and consider the wondrous works of God."
—JOB 37:14 (KJV)

~~~~~~~~~~~~~~~~

A family friend came to the hospital to visit. He'd met and studied with my father at community college, when they both sported big hair without irony, two stunned young men fresh from the Dominican Republic. A fixture at our family gatherings, a constant companion to my father, I could nonetheless not recall the last time I had seen him.

And now here he was, tucking his visitor's pass into his cap, the cold spin of winter cutting sharply into the room as he shrugged off his heavy coat and unwound his scarf.

I hadn't known he was coming and had been looking forward to closing my eyes for a bit. Anjelica had finally succumbed to a light spell of sleep, and I longed to follow her. My two-day-old daughter lived to defy the nurses' admonitions not to expect much activity in these first few days.

I turned to face my father's friend with forced cheer and reluctantly offered my daughter as I would a parcel. I knew that the moment I released her she would mewl in protest. It would not be long before I would need to start, again, the exhausting rituals of soothing her. "I am sorry," I said, equally frustrated and apologetic. "She'll probably cry."

He smiled and made no comment, his arms outstretched in welcome. How gingerly he held her! His careful fingers cradled her perfectly, and her repose was undisturbed. He chuckled softly. "You are a prisoner now."

"I know," I mumbled in exhaustion, perhaps more bitterly than I had intended.

His eyes flickered onto my own weary ones and held them. "Yes, of hope. You are now a prisoner of hope."

Lord, in this child You have given me hope I have never
known before. Thank You for blessing me this way.
—DEBRALEE SANTOS

Day Two

*"But when her baby is born she forgets the anguish because
of her joy that a child is born into the world."*
—JOHN 16:21

~~~~~~~~~~~

I spent months wondering about the person growing on the inside of me. Was it a girl or a boy? What would my baby look like? Would I be a good mother? When the moment finally came—just when I was sure I couldn't endure it any longer—my baby slid into the cold, bright world, screaming. A slimy, slightly blue child was laid on my chest as I lay there, stunned.

You are mine? I looked at this new life and blinked. Unsure what to do, I reached with swollen fingers and IVs protruding toward my child.

"It's okay, baby. . ." *Please stop crying.*

"I'm your mama. . ." *Why are you still crying?*

After several loud minutes passed, the nurse cleared her throat, touched my arm and motioned toward my still-shrieking baby. "Don't you want to know whether you had a boy or girl?" she asked.

I looked at her blankly and then laughed. This detail that had consumed me during most days of my pregnancy was now nearly forgotten. "Of course I want to know!" I spluttered, "Please tell me!" I begged, forgetting I could find out myself.

My curious nurse immediately took a peek. She smiled as I waited anxiously for her answer. "It looks to me like you have a girl!"

And to think, Father, You knew this, since the world began. . . .
—RUTH BERGEN

Day Three

*"For my thoughts are not your thoughts, neither are
your ways my ways,"* declares the Lord.
—ISAIAH 55:8

I am *not* in labor!" I declared. Water dripped from my sweatpants and onto the hospital floor. A nurse turned away to conceal a smile as I ordered Dave to take me home. He hugged me instead. We both knew the truth: I would be spending New Year's Day having a baby.

They'd told me all first babies come late. I wasn't due for two more weeks. I figured I had a month to prepare a nursery, clean the house, and pack. So we'd had a grand evening with friends, playing games and watching, ironically, *Independence Day*. I'd gone upstairs at four o'clock in the morning and fallen asleep, only to awake in discomfort half an hour later. When I went back downstairs to ask what contractions feel like, my water broke on our friends' couch. Convinced I had a weak bladder, I remained in a state of denial all the way to the hospital.

They tied me to a monitor, where a strip of paper displayed reality in jagged mountain peaks of black ink. We sent our friend Kelly (notably, a male) to our far-away house, where he packed up my nightgown and underwear. I felt like God was playing a cruel joke on me.

Fourteen hours later, I gave birth to Anna Grace. I cried at the sight of my dark-haired baby girl, nursed her and then called my mother. It was, perhaps not coincidentally, her birthday.

"Mom, I have a special present for you this year. . . ."

Lord, help me remember Your plans are always wiser than mine.
—FAITH BOGDAN

Day Four

"Now therefore fear ye not: I will nourish you, and your little ones."
—GENESIS 50:21 (KJV)

*I*t was a mere twenty-four hours post C-section of my premature twins Ashleigh and Amanda. I was in a medicine-induced slumber when an NICU nurse bounded into my room exclaiming, "Your daughters are hungry and need to be fed!" I hadn't even fully embraced the fact that I was a new mother, and already I was being called into action.

I sat in a comfortable glider with Ashleigh in my arms. I tried for what seemed like hours to get her to latch on. My baby became impatient and then agitated. So one nurse took her while another placed Amanda in my lap for a try. I repeated the ritual with even less success, and before long Amanda and I were both in tears.

I took Amanda to the NICU nurse, handed her over, and headed back to my room. The nurse called out, "What do you want us to do with them?" Brokenhearted and dejected, I responded, "I don't care. Just feed them."

The following morning I awoke refreshed from a night of uninterrupted sleep. In the light of day it was obvious that most of my frustration the night before came from exhaustion and the pain of major surgery. I was able to remember that yes, God would provide me with what I needed to nurture and care for my babies. I didn't need to despair.

That afternoon a wonderful lactation consultant, Marcia, appeared by my side. She showed me some nursing tricks and encouraged me to take nursing one day at a time. "Some days will be more successful than others," she cautioned. "And nursing twins is a monumental task. It doesn't always come naturally." Encouraged, smiling and filled with new determination, I believed her.

Jesus, give me courage and confidence, and most of all trust that You will be with me in this adventure of mothering.
—DONNA MAY LYONS

Day Five

"I sought the Lord, and he answered me; he delivered me from all my fears."
—PSALM 34:4

Solomon's cries flooded the hospital room. My husband had run home to feed our cats, and here I was two days after my emergency C-section, alone with my new little boy for the first time.

I shimmied myself up, bracing myself as I went to pick him up. He needed a new diaper and as I began to change him, he quieted.

I sighed with relief. *This isn't so bad,* I thought.

As I fastened his diaper, I noticed the bandage that had been on his belly button wasn't there anymore. *Wait! The end of his umbilical stump. It's not there anymore either!* My heart pounded from my temples to my toes as I found the remote and called the nurse.

In seconds the nurse opened the door. "What's up?" she asked.

"His belly button," I said. "I think it fell off."

"Couldn't have," she said. "Not yet."

I had worried about the belly button since I read about the care of it in one of my many baby books. I thought I remembered there was not much to do other than keep it clean and dry. Had I somehow done something wrong? I felt overwhelmed: there were so many new things to learn. I still remember the look on my co-worker's face when I confessed I'd never changed an infant's diaper.

The nurse looked at Solomon's belly button. "Would you look at that! You're right. It did come off. It looks great. No problems."

I picked up Solomon and got back in bed with him in my arms.

In a few minutes a group of nurses came in the room. "We just had to come and see your good little healer ourselves," one of them said.

I smiled with newfound mama pride.

Dear Lord, thank You for everyday miracles, for healing belly buttons and solace for new-mom worries.
—SABRA CIANCANELLI

7

Day Six

*"Honor your father and your mother, as the Lord
your God has commanded you. . . ."*
—DEUTERONOMY 5:16

I feel like wolf-boy!" my husband exclaimed as we giddily devoured the succulent Asian-style pork ribs my dad made for our celebratory return home. Our fingers and mouths covered in sauce, we spent the evening joking about our exhaustion, the miraculous painless labor I had (until I needed a C-section) and our relief to be home after five days in the hospital with Llewelyn.

That night my parents opened up to us in a new way. Stories about having kids and being parents flowed freely as we reveled in the exhilaration of Llewelyn's birth. As one of five kids from a Japanese American family, with both parents working, I'd often wondered how my mom and dad did it. Finally my dad shared a secret with us:

"When you have one child, it's two to one. When you have two, it's one to one. When you have three, you're outnumbered. When you have four . . . they form their own tribe and run wild!" We hooted and laughed so hard my stitches hurt. It was truly one of the best nights I have ever had with my parents.

As a mother, my appreciation and admiration for my parents is deeper and fuller. I see things in them I never saw before. I understand the sacrifices they made for me and find myself looking to them and to the way I was raised for wisdom in raising my daughter.

*Thank You, Father, for my parents. Help me honor
them in a way that is pleasing to You.*
—LIZ BISSELL

Day Seven

"My grace is sufficient for you, for my power is made perfect in weakness. . . ."
—II CORINTHIANS 12:9

~~~~~~~~~~~~~~~

We rode in silence, neither of us attempting to talk. I didn't dare look at Alan; I couldn't bear to read his thoughts. I didn't want to see his hurt. It was night; we'd left late, not wanting to admit we had to go. His hand reached across the space between us and spoke what neither of us could voice.

I strained my ears, wanting to hear a baby in the car seat behind me, but it sat empty, straps flopped open. I thought of my baby girl and my heart screamed "Turn around!" as we placed more miles between us. How could we leave her?

No nurse pushed my wheelchair toward the car with a pink bundle in my lap. We pushed our cart of luggage to the car alone and loaded it easily. No excitement. No fanfare. No photos.

No baby.

Traffic was heavy as people scurried about eating dinner, going to movies, shopping. I wanted them to stop. Didn't they know my world was off-kilter? How could they sit and laugh over cheesecake and cappuccinos?

All I wanted was to hold my baby and make everything all right. And I wished God would do the same for me. I breathed in deeply—the one simple act my newborn couldn't master—and remembered the verse. The one God gave me months before she was born. I kept repeating it. *His grace is sufficient. His grace is sufficient.*

Lord, Your grace is sufficient. Help me know that.
—CAROL HATCHER

Day Eight

*"Love the Lord your God with all your heart and
with all your soul and with all your mind."*
—MATTHEW 22:37

~~~~~~~~~

A s I waited for the doctor to take Tyler away for his circumcision, I felt like Abraham preparing to sacrifice Isaac. I held my newborn close to my body, tears baptizing his head. I didn't *have* to put him through this pain. The doctor made it clear there were no health benefits, that it was strictly for cosmetic, cultural or religious reasons. My husband was clear on his motives—the locker room and the girl—but what were mine? *Circumcision is so Old Testament*, I argued with myself. *We're not bound by the law. Is it relevant today?*

Before I could finish the debate, it was time. The doctor came in with a sweet smile on her pretty face, but she might as well have been wearing a black hooded mask and carrying a hacksaw.

"He'll be right back," she said. And with that she rolled my baby away, leaving me in postpartum hysterics.

A week later, after the wound healed, I finally relaxed. I no longer had to change Tyler's diaper with shaky hands or squeeze tons of Vaseline onto the sore spot. I didn't have to wonder if my baby was in pain every time he cried. This issue I'd thought about since I found out I was having a boy was over. Tyler now matched his big brother, and perhaps I'd saved him from a little ridicule in the future. Perhaps it didn't make any difference. But this is certain: If another baby is in my future, I'll be praying really hard for a girl!

*Lord, I have enough trouble with the commandments You've
ordered me to follow. Help me focus on the first one.*
—KAREN VALENTIN

Day Nine

Accompanied by trumpets, cymbals and other instruments,
they raised their voices in praise to the Lord and sang:
"He is good; his love endures forever."
—II CHRONICLES 5:13

I sent my husband out this morning to buy sanitary pads. I gave him detailed instructions: brand, size, price. Eager to help in any way he can (he's still feeling guilty about my long labor; the other day he threatened to walk up to complete strangers to demand, "Do you *realize* what you did to your mother?"), my dear Andrew went off to execute a task that I, as a woman, still find mildly embarrassing.

He came back a while later, breathless, and tossed me the bag. "I did it, but I was so flustered that I left my wallet at the store!" he called as he left again. Fortunately the checkout girl had seen the wallet and set it aside. She returned it, suppressing a smirk.

Our marriage ceremony included no vows promising to do mortifying things for your spouse, but having a baby sure pushes the envelope. Seeing Andrew in this giddy state is kind of fun. He glows. He holds Elizabeth just so, fearful of breaking her. The tenderness with which he looks at her is divine. He startles as easily as the baby does, the Moro reflex of fatherhood kicking in each time he has to do something new.

I laugh with delight at this view of my husband, just as I chuckle at the ridiculousness of God's grace in giving me such a phenomenally dependent and delicious baby. *Elizabeth, Elizabeth,* I want to sing. *Your life has changed everything! God knew His world wouldn't be complete without you!* It's true, of course. The thanks that bubbles up is too big for my soul to contain, a sure sign that it's meant to be offered to Someone Whose heart is bigger.

Ah, dear Father! How good You are! How good You are!
—JULIA ATTAWAY

Day Ten

*"Blessed be the God . . . of all comfort . . . who comforts
us in all our affliction."*
—II CORINTHIANS 1:3–4 (ESV)

I was nervous the day I brought Joshua home. I struggled to remember all the discharge orders: If his stool is runny and green, call the doctor. If blood from his circumcision is larger than a dime, call the doctor. If you are unsure, call the doctor. I settled a little; at least I could always call the doctor!

My husband Flynn called in my sister Sharon to stay with me while he went shopping. He knew that Sharon (I call her Mama Two) would be able to calm me. She's my best friend and has been my defender ever since third grade, when Henderson Alexander tried to pull my jumper zipper down on the playground. (She made him apologize and promise never to do it again.) Sharon had no children of her own, and she'd pledged to have Joshua calling her Mama Two as soon as he could talk.

She walked into the nursery just as I was starting to change Joshua's diaper. I opened it and screamed. Sharon rushed over. There was blood.

"What did the doctor say about blood?" Sharon demanded.

"Call if it's bigger than a dime!" I whimpered.

We looked in anguish at the stain, debating whether this was a ten-cent worry or something more. Mama Two began to pray. I joined her. Joshua fell asleep. Then Sharon began to croon "It Is Well with My Soul." Slowly, slowly the words seeped in, and our racing hearts became calm. When Flynn, the mathematician, finally arrived home, he took a look at the diaper and declared the blood spot to be smaller than a dime.

*I praise and thank You, Lord, for making
everything well with my soul.*
—RHONDA J. SMITH

Day Eleven

"Even to your old age I am he, and to gray hairs I will carry you.
I have made, and I will bear; I will carry and will save."
—ISAIAH 46: 4 (ESV)

*I*t's our very first appointment with the pediatrician. We present our beautiful Geneva to Dr. Rosenberg for examination. Our daughter is weighed and measured, and after what seems like several minutes, Dr. Rosenberg removes her stethoscope from the baby's tiny chest. She smiles at us kindly. "Geneva has something called a heart murmur. It's probably nothing major, but we'll need to do some tests just to make sure." Bob and I stare at the doctor and then at each other. My own heart seems to have stopped beating.

We write down the name of the pediatric cardiologist the pediatrician recommends. Then we're off to the hospital to get an EKG. I manage to keep my emotions in check as the technician puts stickers, clips and wires all over Geneva's teensy shoulders, chest and thighs. Everyone is friendly, everything goes smoothly, but I keep thinking, *This is all wrong. This is not the way it's supposed to be.*

We leave the hospital, and in the privacy of our pick-up truck, Bob and I look down at our sweet girl. We pray. We remember the truths we need to cling to: that God is sovereign over all, and He is good. He does not make mistakes. We belong to Him, and our daughter belongs to Him.

And then we drive home. Together, with God in charge.

Lord, I love You, even when—especially when—things
aren't going the way I think they should.
—LISA LADWIG

Day Twelve

Sarah said, "God has brought me laughter, and everyone
who hears about this will laugh with me."
—GENESIS 21:6

~~~~~~~~~~~~~~~~

My father paced the baby superstore. My mom and I sat in its nursing lounge, trying to feed thirteen-day-old Zachary into a euphoric milk coma for his first pictures.

Just me, my mom, my breasts, my shaky mothering/nursing/burping skills, my dad hovering nearby and an hour wait.

Someone wisely told me to bring the "picture outfit" instead of dressing Zachary in it. I laid his little body on the changing table, and within seconds my dad was pounding on the door: "It's our turn!"

At that moment, diaper open, a fountain of pee sprang two feet in the air and splashed down right on Zach's own head. No more milk coma. He cried. Dad pounded. I shouted, "He peed his head!" while laughing uncontrollably. More crying. My mother stared in disbelief.

My parents raised three daughters. The idea of having a boy still made me giggle. And now I cackled at the sheer wonder of Zach's trajectory. How will I ever teach him to aim? He needs to know how to change the oil in a car . . . we have to make sure he has a chance to try every sport . . . how can I ensure he loves reading? . . . I hope he'll cook with me . . . *How in the world does a woman teach a boy to be a man?*

It was all I could do at that moment to snap a onesie correctly. So that's all I did. I had prepared the best I could, and now I had to roll with it. And dry his hair.

Lord, I'm overwhelmed with hopes and
dreams for this life You've entrusted to me. Help me
take it all one step at a time, with laughter.
—SUSAN BESZE WALLACE

Day Thirteen

"In his heart a man plans his course, but the Lord determines his steps."
—PROVERBS 16:9

A blanket of diamond-like snow covered the slumbering farmlands of Gillett, Pennsylvania. Thirty women laden with frilly packages crowded into the living room of my log cabin. I sat cradling Anna Grace, a tiny bundle wrapped in pink plaid. Freshly painted faces beamed at her. We were all as "put together" as the rose corsage pinned to my sweater.

But on the inside, my emotions threatened to spill over and water the rose. Motherhood had not been in my plans. I loved the baby in my arms and was as fiercely protective of her as any doting new mom would be. But her entrance into the world had raised a dead-end sign on the road I'd mapped out for myself. This would-be career woman was now and forever a tied-down mom. Could I pack away my knowledge-hungry mind and adventure-loving spirit to embrace a quiet life spent nursing and sleeping? What kind of mother would I make?

Cake was served and a stuffed-bear diapering game played. Afterward, my cousin sat at the piano and sang:

Because He lives, I can face tomorrow,
Because He lives, all fear is gone;
Because I know, He holds the future. . . .

My lips trembled as I watched Anna's sleeping face. *He holds the future.* I had believed *I* held my future in my hands, but it was not mine to hold. I closed my eyes, letting a tear escape, and opened one hand, palm up. There was no more need to fear, wonder or regret. Only surrender. It was an act I'd repeat for years to come.

Dear Father, I seem to forget that You hold my future in Your able hands.
—FAITH BOGDAN

Day Fourteen

"Everyone should be quick to listen, slow to speak. . . ."
—JAMES 1:19

~~~~~~~~~

*B*rian! Don't forget her hat!" I hollered from the bathroom.

"Got it," Brian responded as he sat on the floor, dressing Shiloh for her first trip to church. It was January and we live in the middle of Canada, so we made sure our sweet bundle was layered and warm. After fifteen minutes preparing her for the great outdoors, we exited our home with our arms covered in pink fleece. We couldn't wait to get to church and show off our beautiful girl!

Fortunately, we live in the same town as the church and the trek took only a few minutes. Brian parked the car close to the church door and carried the car seat containing Shiloh while I ran on ahead.

"Hurry! Hurry!" I waved to Brian to get him to move faster, "We're late!" I was concerned that we'd miss our friends.

I needn't have worried. It didn't take long for us to be mauled by a small gathering of admirers, which quickly grew as word spread that "baby Shiloh" had arrived. Everyone was smitten.

However, after about ten minutes of baby talk, the crowd gradually tapered off. Conversations changed to the weather, the hockey game that afternoon and what people were planning to eat for lunch.

Brian and I looked at each other, perplexed. How could the conversation revolve around anything other than our little girl? Surely the details of Shiloh's first days were more interesting than news of a threatening cold front! Wasn't our world the center of everyone else's? Wasn't it?

*Father, not everything is about me. In my excitement over this
new life You've given us, help me continue to listen to others.*
—RUTH BERGEN

Day Fifteen

Behold, children are a gift of the Lord, the fruit of the womb is a reward.
—PSALM 127:3

~~~~~~~~~~~~~~~~~

I was standing alone in the doctor's office as Henry was examined. I watched the doctor turn, lift, pull, move, poke and prod Henry all over. Then out of the blue he said, "Has it crossed your mind that Henry has Down syndrome?" Before the words even registered, I said, "Funny you should say that, because I thought it in passing when I was looking at him one day."

That's all I remember of the conversation. A dull roar began filling my ears, and my insides started to roil. Slowly, very slowly, the knowledge crept into my consciousness. I heard a voice inside me trying to keep tears at bay; I didn't want the doctor to think I was a bad mother because I was sad about the news.

Then I had to go out and tell my mom, who was with my son Steven in the waiting room. She let out a noise, raw and guttural, animal-like, a wounded moan. My heart knew exactly what she meant. The weight of this cross was more than I could comprehend. It would be weeks of testing, reading, researching, and doctor's appointments before I could accept that the dreams I'd had for my child would never come true. Henry would never be president. Henry wouldn't be a doctor. Henry might not go to college. Henry might not ever even live on his own.

It was bitterly hard to accept. Yet one thing was not hard, that I knew in my heart: This child, regardless of his limitations, was a gift from the Lord. And even though I didn't understand—couldn't understand—why this was happening, I chose to trust that God knew what He was doing.

*Lord, no matter what difficulties arise, my child
is a gift from You, and I praise You.*
—CHRISTY STURM

Day Sixteen

Don't run from suffering; embrace it. Follow me and I'll show you how. . . .
—LUKE 9:23 (MSG)

~~~~~~~~~~~~~~~

*M*y mom looked at her watch and then at me, her expression part determination, part apology. It was time to feed Gabriella again. I held back the tears and started into my new nursing ritual.

Easing my sore bottom onto the inflated doughnut on our living room sofa, I leaned forward. My mom pressed pillows behind my back and then on either side of me. Finally she nestled the half-circle nursing pillow on my lap, wrapping it around my belly until I became a walled-in lactation fortress.

Modesty disappeared at the hospital. Now I sat topless as Mom retrieved my sleeping baby. We tickled Gabi and washed her face with a cool washcloth, trying to awaken her. When her little eyes fluttered open, I held her in one arm and used my free hand to shove my breast into her mouth. It was an unnatural move for what was supposed to be a natural process. Mom swooped in and gently massaged the baby's jaw with her index finger, trying to jump-start the suckling process.

After what seemed like an eternity, Gabriella finally clued in and began moving her jaw on her own. Relief flooded through me: We'd done it! That was quickly followed by what I'd been dreading: stinging pain that shot from my nipple out through my entire body.

"Do you want to stop?" Mom asked. But now *my* determination kicked in. If I pushed through the first couple of minutes, the sting would lose its intensity. I relaxed just enough to remember the gift of nutritious milk that lay on the other side of the pain.

Jesus, You are proof that great good can come from suffering.
Help me embrace the crosses motherhood brings.
—ALEXANDRA KUYKENDALL

Day Seventeen

Joshua said to them, "Do not be afraid; do not be discouraged. Be strong and courageous. . . ."
—JOSHUA 10:25

There had to be a mistake: I was alone. My mom left after ten days, and now my husband was back at work. I was solely responsible for Samantha's care.

I walked to Samantha's bedroom door and listened for a sound, even as I held the baby monitor up to my other ear. I shook the monitor and checked the battery light. She had been sleeping for an hour; wasn't that too long at this time of the day?

Everything I'd been taught was gone from my mind. Every prebaby, postbaby, first-year nugget of wisdom was chased out of my thoughts by worst-case scenarios. I imagined a stray cat climbing though the vents and finding a way into Sam's crib. I pictured the soft rain falling outside begin to flood her little room. And did I wrap her too tightly in the blanket? What if she moved around? Were the slats in the crib *really* a safe distance apart?

Finally I cracked the door and peeked inside. Samantha was there, sleeping quietly, her little lips suckling the air.

She was fine.

I shut the door and forced myself to go out into the living room. I picked up a book and read a few lines without understanding a word.

How was I going to survive the next eighteen years?

Oh, Lord, help me to find peace in You today.
—ELSA KOK COLOPY

Day Eighteen

For you created my inmost being; you knit me together in my mother's womb.
—PSALM 139:13

~~~~~~~~~~~~~~~

People used to give me their baby stuff. After all, Dave and I had been married ten years, and we'd certainly be having a baby soon. But we didn't. I gave my sister the crib back and told my friend I was donating her changing table to the church attic sale. We were actively working on adopting, but I didn't want baby things around, just in case.

That's why we had to borrow a car seat when our lawyer called to say "The baby was born this morning."

Excited and a bit scared, Dave and I drove the few hours to the hospital the next day. We explained our situation at the front desk. After several hushed phone calls, an administrator told us that they could not be responsible for letting the baby into our custody. We should go out to the parking lot, where the birth mother's lawyer would meet us.

We went back outside. In about thirty minutes the lawyer walked out of the hospital holding a bundle in her arms. We walked over.

"She's a beautiful little girl," the lawyer said as she let us take a look. The baby was sleeping, wrapped in a white hospital blanket. All we could see was her face: pink cheeks, eyelashes curved in arcs, a little turned-up nose and puckered lips. Then the miracle: The lawyer handed the baby to me.

It wasn't until we were home that I noticed that the baby was wearing a pink hand-crocheted cap and matching booties. Who made them? We never found out. Some gentle soul who knew this child was going to be adopted and sent a little bit of love with her on her journey.

Lord, You handled this child with care before she ever became mine; grant me the grace to care for her even half as tenderly.
—LENORE LELAH PERSON

Day Nineteen
A Dad's View

"Everyone to whom much was given, of him much will be required. . . ."
—LUKE 12.48 (ESV)

~~~~~~~~~~

The nurses rolled Kari gently back and forth, as the alarm on the fetal monitor sounded. The baby's heartbeat rebounded, silencing the beeping alarm. The nurses left; my wife wept, worried.

I tried to comfort her. *This is life and death*, I thought. *This is for real.* Cold sweat ran down the back of my neck.

Beep! The alarm sounded again. I backed away as a team of nurses rushed in. Bile built inside me as the doctor explained we should take the baby by C-section instead of waiting any longer. Kari was whisked away while I put on the scrubs an orderly handed me.

Now is not the time to puke. I entered the operating room and sat by Kari's head, the rest of her body shielded by a curtain. My wife was anesthetized from the neck down, crying, trying to breathe; I tried to console her, stroking her hair. *This is for real.*

A doctor said, "We're going to take the baby out, so if you want to watch. . ." I stood, looked over the curtain, and bit my lip hard to avoid retching. And then . . . then . . . someone . . . a doctor? . . . reached in and pulled out another human being, our son Hans, covered in blood and mad as spit. The room spun around me. *This is for real*, I thought, as the medical team worked on Hans and Kari. Five minutes of emotional terror: *I am responsible for this child's body, soul and spirit. His food and shelter, his moral and religious formation, his emotional well-being. It's on me.*

"Would you like to hold him?" A voice jolted me back to reality. A smiling nurse brought our clean, swaddled, now-quiet son and placed him in my arms. I knelt so my wife could see him too. I smiled; Kari wept joy. *This is real, and by God's grace we can do this.*

Thank You, Lord, for entrusting us with Your child.
—LEROY HUIZENGA

Day Twenty

~~~~~~~~~~

I feel defeated," I wrote in my journal, and tried not to cry. Around me beeps, chirps, and bells sounded, alerting the nurses to check on the sick babies lined up in beds along the wall. I counted the wires, tubes and cords coming from Grace's small body: *one, two, three, four, five.* She was bigger than the other preemies in the unit, but she was dependent on oxygen and monitors just the same.

Grace's nurse kept encouraging me to leave, reminding me my older children needed me. Like I needed a reminder. In desperation, I sent up a prayer. *Oh, Lord, I can't take much more.*

Seconds later, I felt a hand on my shoulder. "Are you okay?" one of the receptionists asked.

"Yeah," I drawled unconvincingly, trying to muster a smile.

"Are you sure?" she probed again. That one little push started the tears. She hugged me tight and whispered in my ear, "God is *still* good. All the time."

I was shocked—and thrilled. I knew the hospital employees weren't supposed to share their faith, because they might offend someone. My God-sent messenger hugged me a little longer and then, with a grin and a wink, she disappeared in the cacophony of sounds.

*Father, you see my hurt and long to fix it as much as I long
to fix what's wrong. You* are *still good, all the time.*
—CAROL HATCHER

Day Twenty-One

Be patient, then, brothers, until the Lord's coming. See how
the farmer waits for the land to yield its valuable crop and
how patient he is for the autumn and spring rains.

—JAMES 5:7

I worried about bringing home the baby with our four cats and researched the best way to make introductions. Some suggested putting a screen door on the baby's room to keep the cats away.

"Let's just wait," my husband Tony said. "We'll see how they do."

While we were in the hospital, Tony brought home a blanket we had wrapped around Solomon. The books suggested letting the cats get used to the smell of the new baby.

"They didn't seem to care about the blanket at all," Tony reported back to me.

After we brought Solomon home, despite our best efforts, the cats avoided us. Our oldest cat, Toad, had always slept at my feet, but since we'd come home from the hospital she rested on the kitchen floor in front of the refrigerator.

One night, I was rocking Solomon to sleep. It had been a rough day and I was beginning to think he had colic. Rocking seemed to help, but it took a lot of patience. I had to move the chair exactly the same way, rhythmically back and forth, slowly stopping on the bump of the carpet's edge.

Solomon's cries stopped. I could feel him relax in my arms. His eyes had a beautiful faraway look that meant sleep was coming.

Toad rounded the corner of the doorway. "Come here," I whispered. Toad eased her way into the room. She rubbed her head against my legs. As Solomon slept on my shoulder, Toad sat on my lap and purred.

Dear Lord, transitions aren't always easy. Help me to remember
that patience and love get us through the tough times.

—SABRA CIANCANELLI

Day Twenty-Two

Love is patient, love is kind . . . it is not self-seeking.
—I CORINTHIANS 13:4–5

My husband Kenya slowly hung up the phone with a dazed expression. I noticed his dark cheeks glistening and his lips quivering and braced myself for bad news. "Mama Callie's gone," he said in a small voice before collapsing onto my chest, sobbing uncontrollably. The day after we brought our new baby boy home, Kenya's grandmother, Callie J. Myles, made her transition. Sadly, she never would meet her great-grandson Kedar.

It was a challenging time for me, both emotionally and physically. The previous day, walking up the stairs to our wooden front porch was a nightmare. "Ouch!" I cried involuntarily with each step. I was in severe pain from a dislocated pelvis that came with delivering an eight-pound, six-ounce baby boy. My heart was joyful as I watched a very proud dad carry our new bundle into the house, but my body felt awful. All I wanted was to lie down in bed and enjoy my time of rest and recuperation.

But after that call Kenya was in and out of the house for nearly two weeks, handling arrangements and spending time with his grieving family. To be honest, part of me wanted to scream, "Where do you think you're going? I just gave birth, and I'm in a lot of pain!"

But I didn't, because I wasn't the only one hurting.

Father, please help me consider the needs of those
I love, even in my own time of need.
—DIANNA HOBBS

Day Twenty-Three

"And if by grace, then it is no longer by works; if it were, grace would no longer be grace."
—ROMANS 11:6

*I*t was (another) "mommy brain" moment. Joey had (another) dirty diaper and I had forgotten (again) to refill his diaper bag. So there I was (again) in the middle of church with a stinky baby and no way to change him.

I slid over two rows and whispered into my friend Beth's ear (again) and she pulled a fresh diaper out of her always-stocked bag (again) and saved me.

As I changed my son in the church bathroom, I chastised myself for being disorganized and unprepared, wondering why I couldn't remember to restock my diaper bag. It really isn't that hard. Apparently, God had me in mind when He said that our value doesn't come from what we do, but by grace alone. Because when it came to performing mom duties, I got an F–.

Just then, Beth came into the bathroom and gave me a hug. "You know," she said, "you don't have to be completely organized to be a good mother in God's eyes. Joey could be naked at church on Easter Sunday and God would *still* extend His hand of grace to you."

Her words made that nearly empty diaper bag languishing under the pew a little less important. I made a mental note to pick up extra diapers at the store to replenish Beth's supply (again) and walked back into the sanctuary. I may be forgetful, but I can be a pretty good mom, anyway.

Father, thank You (again) for Your abundant grace.
—ERIN MACPHERSON

Day Twenty-Four

*You were taught, with regard to your former way of life, to
put off your old self, which is being corrupted by its deceitful
desires; to be made new in the attitude of your minds.*

—EPHESIANS 4:22–23

"How is your day going?" my husband asked.

I sighed into the phone. "Terrible! Lucy cried on and off all morning, and then we had an awful trip to the store—it was hot, and it took forever to carry in all the groceries." I went on to detail every single thing that had inconvenienced me since he'd left for work.

After we hung up, my litany of complaints echoed in my mind. I felt a sting as I remembered: *I promised myself I wouldn't do this.*

When I was pregnant, I'd developed a deep vein thrombosis in my right leg, a life-threatening and severely painful blood clot. I was effectively disabled. I couldn't get to the bathroom without assistance. In those moments of leaning on Joe as I hobbled through the house, trying not to scream from the pain, I'd promised that if I ever went back to being a healthy, able-bodied person, I would not bemoan the inconveniences of daily life. And yet here I was, the phone still in my hand, having done exactly that—and it wasn't a rare occurrence.

That afternoon I took my lousy attitude to prayer. The Lord showed me there would always be an infinite number of things to complain about—if that's what I wanted to do. We live in a fallen world, where things are not perfect. So if I wake up each morning asking "What's wrong with today?" I'll have no trouble creating a long list. It's better and wiser and undoubtedly healthier to focus my energy on creating a different list: one based on what's going right.

*Lord, teach me to pay attention to what is good about
each day, and fill my heart with thankfulness.*

—JENNIFER FULWILER

Day Twenty-Five

After the earthquake came a fire, but the Lord was not in the fire. And after the fire came a gentle whisper.
—I KINGS 19:12

She starts at about four thirty and winds down around ten. White noise, walking, football hold, music, swaddling, simethicone—there's no colic cure we haven't tried. I'm ready to buy earplugs to take the edge off the crying. Elizabeth is fussy during the day too. But the evening hours are the marathon.

Now that I am breast-feeding, I'm supposed to stop eating all dairy products. No yogurt, milk, cheese (how can I live without cheese?), not even butter. I'm supposed to check the ingredients on packaged food to make sure there aren't any milk solids hidden away. We don't eat much meat, so I'm suddenly protein-challenged.

"How long do I have to not-eat like this?" I skeptically asked our pediatrician.

"Oh, most kids grow out of colic by five months," he replied. Five-and-a-half hours of night crying times 120 days is 660 hours of squalling. I weighed my despair on one side and creamy brie on a baguette on the other, and decided dairy-free was the way to go.

It *does* help. Within forty-eight hours on my new diet I had a different baby. She still fusses all day, but we only get two hours of full-scale sunset shrieking now. Other things are getting better too. I've learned that somewhere just to the right of that voice in my head that shouts "I can't take this!" is a smaller voice that whispers "Yes, you can!" I'm trying to pay attention to the little one, because now that I've discovered I have less patience than I thought, the whisper guides me to dig deeper and find patience I never imagined I had. Perhaps, just perhaps, my baby will cry me into becoming a better person.

Keep whispering, Lord. I'm listening.
—JULIA ATTAWAY

Day Twenty-Six

The Lord [is] gracious, and full of compassion;
slow to anger, and of great mercy.
—PSALM 145:8 (KJV)

~~~~~~~~~

My first impression of Flynn was in ninth-grade government class, where he and his buddy Vojo couldn't shake the sillies. If the wind blew, they laughed, and the only thing I thought was funny was that they thought they were cool. My second impression was at a high school class reunion committee meeting. Flynn's jokes were jovial, his smile was smooth and he handled all his reunion business well. That take-charge man became my husband.

Flynn initiated our meals. He planned our dates. He bought me flowers and jewelry I didn't know I wanted. He washed the dishes and the clothes. He took responsibility and took care of me.

After four years of marital bliss we had Joshua. Flynn-the-dad helped whenever I asked him. But surprisingly, I had to ask. It began to annoy me. Then came a day I was busy with laundry and Flynn commented, "I think I smell the baby's diaper." I paused to process the comment. What needed to be done was obvious, but Flynn didn't get up to do it.

"Well, aren't you going to change it?" I snapped. He complied; I worried. Where was my take-charge man? Was I becoming a married single mom?

Later that day we talked about my fear of Flynn's in-home abandonment. It turned out he thought I'd adjusted well to having Joshua and that I knew when to ask him for help. What he hadn't figured out yet was where his fatherhood fit. I looked at my husband, usually so confident, and decided it was okay to claim the role of married single mother for a time so that Flynn could navigate his way into fatherhood.

Remind me, Father, to ask for Your guidance when my husband and I disagree.
—RHONDA J. SMITH

Day Twenty-Seven

Count it all joy. . . .
—JAMES 1:2 (KJV)

~~~~~~~~~~

When I held Michelle in my arms for the first time, wrapped in a soft blanket, I was overcome with a deep sense of the holy nature of mothering. I had a beatific vision of myself moving about my daily tasks with steady, joyful benevolence. But reality came home with the baby. Saintly visions of my mothering self faded. I was more like a gerbil on a wheel running round and round through cycles of feeding, sleeping, waking, fussing, and colic. Laundry mounted. Stacks of dishes grew. Diaper-changing seemed endless.

I loved mothering my baby, but where, oh where, was the joy in the accompanying tedium?

Then one day some friends inadvertently offered me a way to find it. Their baby had had a heart transplant, and though the surgery was miraculously successful, afterward their little guy's kidneys didn't function. In one update, the father wrote, "So we're praying for pee. And when it comes time to change his wet diapers—preferably very heavy, very often—we won't complain. They could never be as full as our hearts."

Ah! I was looking at the mundane aspects of motherhood the wrong way, and joy was being hidden by my perspective. Instead of focusing on the repetitiveness of my chores, I decided to look at routine work as a chance to humbly serve and grow. Stacks of dishes became evidence of God's provision of food. Piles of laundry meant we had sufficient clothing. Dirty diapers meant working kidneys. And looked at from the perspective of gratitude, even the most dreary tasks made joy grow.

Lord, teach me to see the joy You hide in the mundane
and repetitive parts of motherhood.
—SUSAN LA BOUNTY

Day Twenty-Eight

A good name is more desirable than great riches; to
be esteemed is better than silver or gold.
—PROVERBS 22:1

~~~~~~~~~~~~

S itting in the doctor's office making faces at my baby, it happened again.
"Zachary Todd?" the nurse queried.

Something inside me moved every time I heard his name. The name I
scribbled dozens of times when toying with the idea of motherhood and then
craving its reality. The name that made my hand shake in the hospital when
I wrote it on the Social Security form. The name I will eventually yell thou-
sands of times: in love, in discipline, in hopes of a goal, a hit, a basket—or a
quick arrival at the dinner table.

His name initially went with huge blue eyes and toes so sweet you could
eat them. I thought a "Z" name—and nickname—would be unique and strong.
I wanted his middle name to be his dad's. And after years of infertility, I loved
that Zachary meant "the Lord remembers."

With each ounce of growth, the name is becoming something else. A
personality. A promise. A being who is no longer inside me but able to affect
his world. Just *how* he will have an impact on his world—*that* is his name. Not
some notion I doodled in my planner.

I admit, at one early check-up I let a pediatric nurse call out twice, just so
I could hear his name again. He was finally here. Making a name for himself.

Jehovah, Yahweh, Adonai—may your mighty names inspire my child
to make his own name stand for more than sounds and letters.
—SUSAN BESZE WALLACE

Day Twenty-Nine

But the Helper, the Holy Spirit, whom the Father will send
in My name, He will teach you all things, and bring to
your remembrance all things that I said to you.
—JOHN 14:26 (NKJV)

T he swollen, slightly bloody welt that spanned Kedar's right cheek matched the fiery one on the side of my neck. With little control over his flailing limbs, my son had used his fragile but sharp fingernails to badly scratch his own face and mine.

I tried using baby scratch mitts to keep my infant from tearing into his tender face. But my little warrior managed to wriggle his fingers right out. I hated hearing his tortured screams whenever he mauled himself. I felt so sorry for him, this helpless little person who had no idea how to stop hurting himself.

Suddenly, I had a random *aha!* moment. It came in the form of a flashback from ten years prior, when my dad was a pastor. Sometimes Dad took my siblings and me on in-home visits to church members. I vividly recalled a home where we saw the cutest baby girl in her bouncer with *socks* on her hands. Bored and silly, my sisters, brothers and I cracked up, hysterically.

But on this particular day, I saw things differently. "What a novel idea!" I thought as I slipped a pair of blue and white cotton socks onto my newborn's hands. And Kedar never did manage to claw his way out of those.

God, I appreciate how You bring back simple and helpful
memories to guide me along this path of motherhood.
—DIANNA HOBBS

Day Thirty

"The Lord does not look at the things man looks at. Man looks at the outward appearance, but the Lord looks at the heart."

—I SAMUEL 16:7

~~~~~~~~~~~

I'd just finished breast-feeding Joey when I heard the doorbell ring. I quickly covered up, scanning the room as I ran to answer. The house was a disaster. There was a pile of dirty clothes and receiving blankets in the corner. The baby's bouncy seat sat haphazardly in the middle of the living room. Dishes filled the kitchen sink and spilled out onto the counter. And that didn't even account for the baby paraphernalia that had made its way into every nook and cranny.

I looked through the peephole and saw my sweet friend Kristen, holding a foil-covered pan.

In my prebaby days, my house was superclean—wait, strike that—my house was *immaculate*. Well-vacuumed. Well-dusted. With scented candles on the coffee table and potpourri in the bathroom. Now it smelled like spit-up and dirty diapers and looked like a tornado had hit it. What would Kristen think?

I opened the door, mortified. Kristen didn't even notice. She thrust a pan of homemade manicotti into my hands, made her way to my toy-strewn couch and put her feet up on my dusty coffee table. She'd come to see me, not my housecleaning. Before long, the dirt and grime faded into the background. I was spending time with my friend.

Lord, thank You for friends who care about me just as I am.

—ERIN MACPHERSON

Second Month

~~~~~~

Jesus,

I give You what I have right now: my weariness and limitations and not-knowing-what-to-do. My exhaustion is the cross You have asked me to bear today, and I ask You to give me the courage to take it up willingly. Help me when I stumble; pick me up when I fall. Comfort me when I fear I cannot do this mothering thing well, and whisper again in my heart Your certainty that I can.

Amen.

Tips

» Keep extra, packed diaper bags in your car and your stroller. Re-pack them whenever you go grocery shopping.

» Make a list of specific things people can do to help: laundry, dusting, dishes, dinner. A list makes it easier to accept help when God sends it.

» Don't check the time when your baby wakes up. You'll feel less frazzled if you're not as focused on how long it's been since the last time you woke.

Day One

"Trust in him at all times, O people; pour out your heart before him; God is a refuge for us."

—PSALM 62:8 (ESV)

We had to wait over two weeks for an appointment with the pediatric cardiologist to see about Geneva's heart murmur. How could I maintain my sanity that long? It was hard not knowing what was wrong, but the wait was harder. My imagination pulled me toward worst-case scenarios and "what ifs," and I didn't like feeling that the level of control I had over my daughter's life was much less than I'd thought it would be. I could do absolutely nothing to help her little heart.

The one thing that lay in my power was a choice: I could worry, or I could wait on God and trust Him. I did both. But worrying made it difficult to enjoy my sweet girl. It made me focus on her breathing patterns instead of getting lost in her beautiful eyes. I had to relinquish my desire for control almost hourly and remind myself that Geneva belonged to God. She was safer in His hands than in mine.

When the cardiology appointment finally arrived, we learned that Geneva had two small holes in her heart. The doctor thought, however, that the holes would close on their own as she grew.

Did my worrying change the outcome? Not at all. But learning to put Geneva's life in God's hands changed me, so I could become a better mom.

Lord, You are so trustworthy. Help me trust You today with my life—and my baby's.

—LISA LADWIG

Day Two

*"Now what I am commanding you today is not too
difficult for you or beyond your reach."*
—DEUTERONOMY 30:11

<hr />

I can't take it! I can't *do* this any more!" I sobbed over the phone at my husband. Andrew made startled there-there noises on the other end, clearly taken aback by a level of hysteria he'd never witnessed in me before. The baby—I couldn't even call her by name I was so blubbery—had fussed all morning. Nothing helped, I was out of patience and I had no emotional reserves left.

Shortly after I hung up, with the assurance that Andrew was leaving work and on his way home to help, the phone rang. It was my sister. I hiccuped out my incompetence and fragility. Beth was immediately sympathetic. "Oh, five weeks is the *worst*! The adrenaline has worn off, exhaustion has set in, and you're still two weeks from a smile." She nailed my situation in a single breath, and I immediately felt better. *This is normal. It's awful, but it's normal.*

Andrew arrived. I handed him Elizabeth and went into the other room to—well, I don't even remember what I did. Cry, maybe. Sleep a little. Recover. I loved my baby. I loved my hero of a husband. And I loved the good Lord who made every day, even the worst ones, come to an end.

God, make tomorrow a better day. And if You don't, make it anyway.
—JULIA ATTAWAY

Day Three

"Spread your protection over them, that those who love your name may rejoice in you."
—PSALM 5:11

~~~~~~~~~~~

They say your first love can be intense. It was. At sixteen, I found him all kinds of dreamy—but he couldn't hold a candle to my new baby girl. This love, this child, takes me to a whole new place. I would give anything for her. Do anything to protect her. Leap over high buildings, fight off dragons, lay down my life.

She has no clue. She has no idea as she eats and sleeps and dreams and burps. She doesn't know how I listen at the doorway to make sure she's asleep, how I check to make sure she's breathing in the middle of the night. She has no notion that I spend half my day removing hazards from her life, wondering how on earth I will be able to parent her toward adulthood. If only she knew how unprepared I feel. If only she understood that her mom is sometimes crazy, halfway goofy and often misdirected. But no, she is blissfully ignorant of all my shortcomings and adores me with infant abandon.

Heavenly Father, I'm oh-so-grateful, but still . . . oh, I am scared!
—ELSA KOK COLOPY

Day Four

Direct me in the path of your commands, for there I find delight.
—PSALM 119:35

~~~~~~~~~~~~~

"Come on, sweet girl. Turn your head," I coaxed my newborn. I gently tried to shift her to the left, and she tensed up and held herself in the opposite direction. I sighed, envisioning her head permanently formed in its current lumpy shape.

It wasn't Grace's fault. While in the NICU after birth, she was strapped facing to the right. It became comfortable because it was familiar.

Unfortunately, her head was now flat on one side. The doctor said she should look left as much as possible. No amount of persuasion could get her to turn. When I tried to force Grace to change direction, she fought back. "Lay her so when she turns right, she faces the wall," the pediatrician told me. "That way she'll turn left to look out into the room."

I instinctively understand Grace's resistance to change; I'm stiff-necked in my own way. I tend to tell God how I want my path to go, and I keep my head turned in that direction. *God, two children is plenty; we are done*, I told Him. He obviously had other plans, and they involved stretching myself in new ways.

Like Grace, I'm comfortable with what's familiar. I dislike doing things differently, so I don't always recognize when I'm not following what God has planned for me. It's work to turn my head. But I'm trying.

Lord, turn my head and heart in the direction You would have me go.
—CAROL HATCHER

Day Five

*"Let your speech [be] always with grace, seasoned with salt,
that ye may know how ye ought to answer every man."*
—COLOSSIANS 4:6 (KJV)

Jim and I took Ashleigh and Amanda to the mall for the first time. They were so tiny they could lie side by side in a single stroller. We delighted in the opportunity to dress them up and parade them about. Beaming, we watched the reactions of passersby when they realized there were two babies in the stroller.

"Are they twins?"

"How old are they?"

"Which one's older?"

"Is it a boy and a girl?" This last question perplexed me, for the girls were dressed in pink and had frilly headbands on their heads.

There were also some classically insensitive questions:

"Did you use fertility drugs?"

"Are they double trouble?"

"Which one's the bad twin?"

And then came the most unbelievable question ever, "Which one do you love more?"

Appalled, I wanted to come back with some equally appalling response. But as I gaped and stammered and searched for words, it dawned on me that though I couldn't stop people from asking silly or insensitive comments, I *could* still respond graciously.

It took me a few days to come up with an all-purpose, friendly and respectful reply. From then on, whenever someone asked an insensitive question about my twins, I smiled and said, "My girls are double the blessing."

*Lord, give me words that are graceful, wise and filled with
love; ones that build others up, not tear them down.*
—DONNA MAY LYONS

Day Six

*"My people will live in peaceful dwelling places, in
secure homes, in undisturbed places of rest."*
—ISAIAH 32:18

~~~~~~~~~~

Horrified, my mother gasped and leapt to her feet. "Ay, no!"
She'd come by to lend a hand in the late afternoon, leaving her
office in a rush to make better time crossing the city, bringing some fruit
and yogurt. She was tired, her eyes drawn, her bandaged hand clearly aching.
She'd cut open her finger while making breakfast just before I'd given birth,
and although she'd thought it minor, she cut a vein and needed an ER visit
and stitches. Now she struggled to hold Anjelica and change her. My own
wounds from my unexpected C-section kept me in pain and at a remove. I
was annoyed—unfairly, I knew—at my mother's limitations just when I needed her to be at full capacity.

Now the bottle of breast milk I'd just pumped lay upended on the floor,
spooling into a perfect oval of cream. My mother had leaned back for a moment in her chair, and her elbow connected with the bottle I'd thought I'd
put away. There it lay between us, precious milk that should have been better
cared for and secured.

Faint, angry thoughts rose and crashed in my weary head. I caught sight
of my daughter tucked into her small seat, curled fists rising with each breath,
at peace and oblivious to loss or distress. She wanted for nothing.

"No, no es nada; no te preocupes." *It is nothing; do not worry.*

I wrapped my arms around my mother, my sides and center throbbing,
and she held me, her arms and hands surely aching from the strain. We two
mothers, staggering and hobbled, striving to care perfectly for my child.

Lord, spilt milk is spilt milk. We can work through these things together.
—DEBRALEE SANTOS

Day Seven

*"Where no counsel [is], the people fall: but in the
multitude of counsellors [there is] safety."*
—PROVERBS 11:14 (KJV)

*Y*ou're fine, Dianna," Mom assured me, flashing a grin that lit up her dimpled cheeks. But I didn't *feel* fine. Actually, I didn't feel *anything* other than depression, irritability and emotional detachment from everyone, including my six-week-old. But I was too embarrassed to say that.

So on a cloudy August day in Buffalo I drove home from my mom's house, grappling with even more confusion than I had before. Although I had hugged and thanked her for listening to my venting session, truthfully, I didn't think my mom understood *at all*. It was my fault, though. I'd only revealed a little bit about the sadness I was struggling with. I didn't want this euphoric new grandma, who had just told me what an awesome mom I was, to know how conflicted I felt deep inside.

I pulled up to our green-and-yellow Victorian home and sat in the driveway, thinking. *Why wasn't I strong like my mother?* She made having eleven kids, staying in great shape and being married to my impossibly stubborn dad look deceptively easy. But how?

Once inside the house, I unstrapped the baby carrier and gently placed my baby in the crib. I picked up the phone and began dialing. Mom's singsongy hello was met with my quivering voice. "Mom, I really need some advice," I said, as hot tears washed over my face.

*God, let me never be ashamed to request and
receive trusted counsel when I need it.*
—DIANNA HOBBS

Day Eight

He who walks with the wise grows wise,
but a companion of fools suffers harm.
—PROVERBS 13:20

When Zach was several weeks old, my husband's sister Lori flew across the country to meet him. She was a parenting powerhouse, a font of creativity and always encouraging. That day, she was also hungry.

As we went from airport to upscale restaurant with my in-laws, it dawned on this brand-new mom that Zach would need to eat too. I started to sweat. Going back to the car was too awkward. Not exactly sanitary to go into a bathroom stall. That left right there, at the table.

I'd figured out nursing, but not in public. Out came the big blanket. I feigned interest in the conversation and managed to order something, but all I could think was *Do you people know what's going on under here?* I managed to switch sides without flashing anyone and brought out a sweaty, red-faced baby in a happy milk stupor.

The next day Lori wanted to go shopping. I wanted to stay at home. But with little sleep and great trust in this woman who had raised my niece and nephew, Zach and I rolled out. I stopped often to feed, change and soothe him, and Lori always stopped with me. I felt sort of clunky and slow for a while, like a muddy bike tire. But as we rolled, chunks of uncertainty began to drop away. Lori knew what I needed when I didn't. Perhaps she even knew that I might have stayed in the house for weeks if it weren't for her can-do spirit— and that *doing* was the best way to start learning how to master the art of motherhood.

Praise God for mothers who have walked before
us and still want to walk with us.
—SUSAN BESZE WALLACE

Day Nine

But he said to me, "My grace is sufficient for you. . . ."
—II CORINTHIANS 12:9

~~~~~~~~~~~~~~~

Something had to be wrong with me. I don't know why, but my girl just wouldn't latch on to nurse anymore. She stopped—out of the blue—at six weeks. I tried to force it, but she just cried and turned her head. I talked to friends, looked up research, but Samantha still wouldn't take the breast.

It wasn't until I'd had her on a bottle for a few weeks that I found out about a group of midwives nearby that could have helped me. Apparently it isn't unusual for some moms to have my problem.

I couldn't believe it. I knew how important it was for babies to be on breast milk for as long as possible. Had I already messed up everything? I looked at my baby, sucking contentedly on a bottle.

"I'm sorry, honey," I whispered. "I'm just so new at this. I didn't know. . . ." A few tears spilled out; one dropped on Samantha's cheek. She opened her eyes and our gaze held. "I'm sorry," I said again, wondering how often I would have to say those words.

Sam looked at me seriously, her eyes deep and blue. Then she released the bottle and grinned around the nipple. I couldn't help but smile back. Maybe I'd ruined her for life, but in this single moment, she seemed perfectly fine. That was enough.

Father, help me do the best I can and leave the rest to You.
—ELSA KOK COLOPY

Day Ten

But be glad and rejoice forever in what I will create, for I will
create Jerusalem to be a delight and its people a joy.

—ISAIAH 65:18

~~~~~~~~~~~~~~~

I can't kiss him enough, squeeze him enough, tickle him and hear him laugh enough. This sweet, gentle, chubby baby is worth the world to me. I'd endure every pain, emotion, tension or discomfort, and even double it for the honor and blessing of calling Tyler my son.

And yet, when the plus sign appeared on the pregnancy stick, I'd burst into tears. I already had my hands full with my first baby, Brandon. I barely had time for a shower, let alone another child. My resentment grew with my stomach. I wasn't fascinated or curious; I already knew *What to Expect When You're Expecting*—and I hated every bit of it. I didn't want to eat green vegetables. I didn't want to hear people chide, "You shouldn't eat that candy bar; it's not good for the baby." I didn't want to wear frumpy maternity clothes, feel tired, sleep uncomfortably or waddle like a penguin.

My marriage grew tense, and I grieved the relationship I would lose with my older son. I was sure it would never be the same after I gave birth. My new baby wasn't even born yet and he was already getting in the way! Joyless . . . I was completely joyless as I waited for Tyler to be born.

Yet today my son fills me with so much joy my heart wants to explode. No, I didn't rejoice over the pregnancy test telling me he was coming. But every day I'm grateful for the little plus sign that gives me a reason to rejoice today.

Jesus, teach me to trust that there are positives
hidden even in what seems most negative.

—KAREN VALENTIN

Day Eleven

"My lover is mine and I am his; he browses among the lilies."
—SONG OF SOLOMON 2:16

~~~~~~~~~~~~~~~~

My six-week postpartum check-up had gone well, perhaps a little too well. My doctor gave me a clean bill of health and the clearance to go about my normal daily activities. Which meant—much to my chagrin—that I was cleared to do you-know-what.

It wasn't that I didn't want to have sex. Oh, who am I kidding?—I had no desire for sex *at all*. I was exhausted. And I felt so frumpy. And to be completely honest, I was terrified about what havoc marital relations could wreak on my still-tender nether parts.

Just as I got in the car, my sister-in-law called. She said she had a surprise for me, and asked me to drop by her house on the way home. I walked in to a brightly decorated room and found my sisters on the couch yelling "Surprise!"

My sisters knew that getting back in the, *er* . . . swing of things can be a bit rough on a new mom. So they did what been-there, done-that women of wisdom do: they threw me a postpartum lingerie shower.

As I pulled tummy-hiding baby dolls and red, lacy nursing bras out of gift bags, I remembered my husband Cameron waiting at home. He had been so patient with me—so tender, so loving and so willing to give me all of the time I needed to adjust to motherhood. And suddenly, the idea of going home and being with him didn't sound so terrible after all.

Lord, thank You for my husband and for the way he became a father.
—ERIN MACPHERSON

Day Twelve

"How many times shall I forgive my brother when he sins against me? . . ."
—MATTHEW 18:21

~~~~~~~~~~

I grabbed my diaper bag and tried to sneak out of the service as unobtrusively as possible with a howling baby. Ignoring the looks of fellow churchgoers, I breathed a sigh of relief when we reached the back door. As we entered the foyer, Shiloh began to settle. "That figures!" I smiled at my little girl. "You didn't like the message?"

Rather than risk disturbing people again, I sat in a corner of the large room and began to visit with another mom. "You had to leave too?" I asked, as Courtney nodded.

Suddenly I felt we were being watched. Looking up I saw a gray-haired man walking toward our small gathering. "Hi—" I began, only to be cut off.

"Shh!" Mr. Thomson said, holding his finger to his lips and gruffly shaking his head. "You need to be quiet in here!" he bellowed. I apologized; Mr. Thomson shook his head in disgust and stomped off.

"Wow," I whispered to Courtney, suddenly aware of every squawk from Shiloh. Then anger set in. *But there's nobody in this room!* I fumed inwardly. *Who can we possibly disturb?*

A few weeks passed, and my memory of the incident didn't. Resentment began to build a wall thicker than Jericho. *He needs to apologize,* I thought when I saw Mr. Thomson at the end of one service.

Turning to walk out of the building, I was suddenly aware that the door was being opened for me. Grateful for this gesture, I turned to thank my benefactor—and came eye to eye with Mr. Thomson. Surprised, I stumbled over my words. "Uh, thanks. . . ," I said, cautiously reaching out to shake his hand. And as I did, I felt the walls begin to soften.

Thank You, Jesus, for the freedom of forgiveness.
—RUTH BERGEN

Day Thirteen

*In this way they will lay up treasure for themselves as a firm foundation
for the coming age, so that they may take hold of the life that is truly life.*
—I TIMOTHY 6:19

I didn't grow up watching much TV, but somehow 1960s television affected my view of what a home should be. I liked those perpetually clean houses where the ever-kempt mother never lost her smile. Where beautiful dinners appeared like magic on the table. Where evening meant family reading before the fire or pleasant, quiet games on the floor.

It was picture perfect and perfectly sweet. Problem is, real life isn't. My vision of family life worked well enough until a baby entered the picture. I thought she would ease into my schedule, but four hours of hair-tearing colic every evening doesn't fit in any schedule, anywhere. My lovely, placid atmosphere began to unravel, along with my nerves.

Then I visited a friend who had a baby and a toddler. Sue was relaxed, and her home was inviting. It was orderly, but not immaculate. As Sue sat on the floor with her girls, a few dishes waited to be washed. Crumbs were scattered beneath the high chair. Toys were strewn about. A stack of diapers sat on the couch alongside a basket of half-folded laundry.

I almost laughed out loud as the utterly obvious became an epiphany: I'm living real life in a fallen world where everything tends toward disorder. I can work cheerfully, if not perfectly. And what isn't done today will wait just fine for tomorrow. God doesn't measure mothers on a scale of TV-show perfection. So first things first. Relax. Love God and love my family well. And worry about the house afterward.

Lord, may Your gentle love and grace be the foundation of my home.
—SUSAN LABOUNTY

Day Fourteen

"Let us fix our eyes on Jesus, the author and perfecter of our faith, who for the joy set before him endured the cross. . . ."
—HEBREWS 12:2

She needs a shot? But didn't she get all of them already?" I nervously asked our pediatrician. I was desperately anxious to spare Llewelyn pain. "Can't she get it next time? Please?" I begged, recognizing the absurdity of my request.

"Oh no," Dr. Canieso replied matter-of-factly. "Next time she needs four shots."

"Four!" I cried, pricked to the heart.

I couldn't bear to watch as the needle slid into Llewelyn's pudgy thigh. My sweet baby let out a wrenching wail. The doctor took one look at my horrified expression and said calmly, "Go ahead. You can nurse her. She'll be okay." And in fact, Llewelyn was fine. But I wasn't.

I felt sad. Guilty. Scared. As our next appointment neared, I became increasingly fearful and pleaded with my husband to come along. I dreaded hearing my daughter cry in pain. I was sure four shots were simply too much for her to bear.

The night before our doctor's visit I sat down to write in my journal. Thinking about what Llewelyn would face the next day, I somehow got around to pondering how God allowed Jesus to suffer for us. Christ knew the night before he died that his anguish on the cross would be too much to bear. But He looked beyond that to the joy set before Him: an eternal relationship with us! I thought of the joy set before me: Llewelyn, a healthy and inoculated baby. Yes, I could endure the short-term pain of hearing her cry.

Lord, when I want to say, "Keep her from pain," help me say, "Hold her in Your love" instead.
—LIZ BISSELL

Day Fifteen

Let the wise listen and add to their learning,
and let the discerning get guidance.
—PROVERBS 1:5

Zach just wasn't settling in his cradle, and we were at wits' end. My husband Todd threw out an idea: "He sleeps so well in his car seat. Why don't we put him in there?" Seeing my reaction, he added the infamous words, "Just tonight?"

Strapped in like he was going to the moon, Zach felt secure enough to conk out. Maybe it helped his gassy tummy, maybe his need to be cozy. Whatever the key, one night became every night. It felt increasingly weird, but not as weird as putting Zach in the seat and then putting the seat in a dark *bathroom*, with the fan on. That trick worked when he'd fallen asleep in the car and I didn't want to break the spell, or when he couldn't settle down.

My baby sleeps where people pee. I was too embarrassed to admit our crutch. I never shared it with the pediatrician or a single friend. Then one day a girlfriend told me how she'd rolled her jogger stroller right in the front door and into the bathroom to prolong the nap her son had started on their walk. I was stunned. And comforted beyond words.

I wasn't crazy.

There's virtually nothing about parenthood that someone else hasn't experienced. I could have saved myself so much angst by just sharing. From that (thankfully early) moment on, when I had an issue, I talked about it freely, diving into the maternal pool of been-there-done-that, hoping someone would throw me a rope. Amazingly, someone always did.

I can parent better by being authentic and admitting my
uncertainties—to You, Lord, and to other moms.
—SUSAN BESZE WALLACE

Day Sixteen

*And my God will meet all your needs according
to his glorious riches in Christ Jesus.*
—PHILIPPIANS 4:19

I always knew I would have a girl. I felt it deep in my bones from the time I played with baby dolls. So at our ultrasound appointment, as the technician was about to confirm what I already knew, I felt my breath leave me when she said, "Boy."

"Boy?" I asked, "How sure are you?"

"Well, we're not allowed to say 100 percent, but in your case I'll say 99.9."

In my heart, I knew the news was fantastic. Our baby was healthy, perfect, a little big even. But part of me was confused to learn it wasn't a girl growing beneath my heart.

As we drove home my husband said, "It's a boy. We're having a boy."

"A boy," I echoed.

I looked at the open road ahead and pictured my husband and son playing in the backyard. I imagined a sweet little boy in plaid flannel pajamas with a well-loved teddy in his arms. I looked down at the black-and-white ultrasound in my hands and traced my baby's profile with my fingertip. Yes, I was already in love.

Sometimes when Solomon sleeps in my arms and I'm overcome with the depth of my love for him, this prayer comes to my lips:

*Dear God, thank You for knowing and giving me
what I need. Thank You for this baby!*
—SABRA CIANCANELLI

Day Seventeen

"For I know the plans I have for you," declares the Lord, "plans to prosper
you and not to harm you, plans to give you hope and a future."
—JEREMIAH 29:11

~~~~~~~~~~~~~~~

At Henry's doctor's appointment, just checking in at reception got me
started. "How are you doing?" came the cheery question. I was tired of
pretending I was okay. I was depressed, panicked and questioning ever having
had a child in the first place. I replied, "I've been better. I'm struggling."

The nurse called me in, and she asked how I was doing too. I told her. I
held Henry and paced and cried, talking about my disappointment and fears
about having a Down syndrome child. What I hated was that as much as I
loved my son and truly trusted in God's plan, part of me wanted to leave my
child at a fire station. It was a horrible way to feel—and it was even more horrible to admit it.

I was mortified that although I had older children, I wasn't sure of my
ability to parent Henry. I was ashamed that I claimed to trust in the Lord but
couldn't muster a serene Christian face or attitude. I was angry at God—and I
felt bad about that, too, until a wise friend said, "You think God's big enough
to handle the running of the universe, but too small to handle your anger?"

It was hard to pray. It was hard to have faith or see God's promises.
Thankfully, I was able to trust in one thing: that He believed in me, even
when I didn't believe in myself. And perhaps that was all He asked of me right
then.

Father God, Your hope surrounds me, holding me up even when I feel
hopeless. Help me trust in You, even when I don't feel Your presence.
—CHRISTY STURM

Day Eighteen

"Sovereign Lord, as you have promised, you now dismiss your servant in peace. For my eyes have seen your salvation."

—LUKE 2:29–30

I walked in the door, tightly gripping my baby, feeling as though I was presenting a gift to the queen.

"Grandmother," I called. "I've brought someone to see you." I offered my tiny pink bundle, almost forgetting Grandmother's eyesight had failed long ago. I placed the baby in her outstretched arms. A smile lit that warm, wrinkled face as Grandmother traced over Grace's features with her fingers. Her lips moved. I knew she must be praying over my sleeping daughter.

Grandmother had asked for me all morning, wondering when I was bringing the new baby to meet her. At ninety-four, she'd been hovering close to death for three months. It was obvious for weeks that she was waiting to meet the newest member of our family. She wanted to hold Grace. Her wish was granted.

It was a Simeon moment. I believe my grandmother even uttered the same words. *You now dismiss your servant in peace.* One week after meeting baby Grace, Grandmother went to be with the Lord.

God, thank You for all the people of faith who have been part of my life.

—CAROL HATCHER

Day Nineteen

Do not fear, for I am with you . . . I will strengthen you and help you. . . .
—ISAIAH 41:10

~~~~~~~~~~~~~~~

I had just fallen asleep after Lucy's second night, waking only to hear her cries pierce the silence once again. I trudged into her room and began my usual litany of inner complaints: *Tomorrow is going to be terrible! I'll be way too tired to pay those bills, and I might as well forget about that meet-up with my girlfriends! The whole day is going to be misery.*

As I heard my own grouchy words for the zillionth time, it finally dawned on me: This is all about fear. Almost all of my stress about new motherhood came down to a complete lack of trust that God would give me what I needed to get through the next day.

At that moment I decided to take a leap of faith—I would choose to have just one day without fear. For the next twenty-four-hour period alone, I would embrace a childlike confidence that my Father would not give me more than I could handle.

The results were amazing. Each night-feeding was transformed into a chance to practice radical trust. Each challenging moment of the day became an opportunity to marvel at the ways the Lord took care of me. I was given exactly what I needed to remain peaceful. I had nothing to fear. Thrilled, I decided to try it again the next day. And then the next. And then the next. . . .

Lord, today I will live in a spirit of trust in You.
—JENNIFER FULWILER

Day Twenty

And ye shall know the truth, and the truth shall make you free.
—JOHN 8:32 (KJV)

~~~~~~~~~~

How do you like motherhood?" asked my friend Carla a while after I came home from the hospital with Joshua.

"It's all right."

She laughed.

"Why are you laughing?"

"Cause I'm not used to hearing anyone say how they really feel about motherhood, and your answer surprised me."

"Well, you asked. . . ."

Carla later told me how freeing my honesty was for her. She felt she didn't have to pretend anymore to be having a good day. My sister Sharon had a similar reaction when I gave the same answer a few months later. "Girl, I always remember your, 'It's all right.' That was too funny—but it's helped me often when I'm having a rough day."

Honesty's important in being a mother. When I was pregnant, my mama told me not to feel bad if I ever felt like throwing my baby out the window. I was aghast at the time—but thanked her later. Knowing that I *might* feel that way made it easier to deal with frustration and ambivalence when it appeared later on. So when people ask me how I feel, I tell them. A good dose of someone else's reality sometimes helps a mom know she's not alone.

Thank You, Lord, for truth that creates a supportive motherhood community.
—RHONDA J. SMITH

Day Twenty-One

"Share each other's burdens, and in this way obey the law of Christ."
—GALATIANS 6:2 (NLT)

*I*t was 3:00 AM. I had just changed and nursed Kedar by the light of the small blue lamp and the silently flickering television. He was so peaceful when he first fell asleep in my arms, but as soon as I laid him down in the bassinet next to my bed his little body began squirming. My fleeting hopes that he wouldn't wake up were dashed ten minutes later, when a piercing scream jolted me out of an exhausted sleep.

"Shh. Mommy's here." I stroked his back with one eye open, trying to calm him. He cried even louder until I picked him up again.

"What's the matter? Is he okay?" Kenya asked groggily.

"He's not hungry or wet. I think he just wants me to hold him," I whispered. "He's fine. Try to get back to sleep. You have to work in the morning."

But Kenya sat up and extended his arms. "Here, let me take him for a little while. You get some rest." Pleasantly surprised, I carefully handed Kedar over to his dad, slid underneath the covers, and conked out. When I awoke to the bright sunlight streaming through the blinds, I couldn't believe I had slept for more than a half hour. And there, over to my left, was Kedar lying on Kenya's chest, resting as comfortably as his dad.

God, thank You for those who share the load when it gets too heavy.
—DIANNA HOBBS

Day Twenty-Two
A Dad's View

"Therefore encourage one another and build one another up, just as you are doing."

—I THESSALONIANS 5:11 (ESV)

have so many thank-you notes to write. I'm so fat."

Coffee shot up my nose as Kari's two statements hit me back-to-back. I felt like the defensive end in football facing the option play: I could take the quarterback or the running back, but not both.

I went for the easier option: "Well, it's really considerate of you to do thank-yous. People appreciate them."

"Yeah. I haven't lost any weight yet," my wife replied, dicing some vegetables.

Option reverse! I wasn't getting out of this one. I drew a breath, tensed, put my shoulders down and prepared for the running back to level me.

"Well," I ventured, "I think you look good." I did mean it.

Tossing her salad, she stated, "You *have* to say that."

What do you do when the truth is also convenient? I went low: "Really, Kari, you just gave birth, so you look like you've given birth, but you look good. And you're eating healthy, and soon you can get back to the gym." Having wrapped up, it was time to drive: "I find you attractive. Sexy, even."

My wife smiled and giggled as I gave her a hug: a tackle for a loss.

Lord, help me give and receive encouragement as I adapt to a new normal.

—LEROY HUIZENGA

Day Twenty-Three

"From now on I will tell you of new things, of hidden things unknown to you."
—ISAIAH 8:6

~~~~~~~~~~

Transition isn't easy. Not when you're seven weeks old. And certainly not when you're thirty-six.

We've spent the first eon of Shiloh's life trying desperately to comfort a lovely little person who has a very large voice. Something about screaming shrieks from a panic-stricken newborn makes even the calmest person feel like a total shipwreck. And I was never very calm to begin with.

It makes sense, though. I mean, everything Shiloh has ever known has changed. She is learning to trust a totally new system. No more snug little cocoon. No instantaneous food supply. Suddenly she lives in a world of cold fingers, indigestion and parents who can't get it right every single time.

I'd be screaming too. In fact, lately I have.

I find transition uncomfortable too. That doesn't stop life from thrusting changes into my lap. It's scary to discover that I have to learn new things and figure out how this new world of motherhood works. People and things I used to lean on aren't there in quite the same way. Life doesn't feel quite so cozy or safe; I'm out on my own.

I'm learning that the womblike comfort of my old life was not created to hold me forever. But there's new freedom to be had once the "cord" disappears and I begin to walk the path I have not known before.

Dearest God, help me trust You on this road, even
when I can't see how it will turn out.
—RUTH BERGEN

Day Twenty-Four

Blessed are those who have learned to acclaim you, who walk in the light of your presence, O Lord.

—PSALM 89:15

~~~~~~~~~~~~~~~

It was another end-of-the-day checklist:

Samantha fed, cleaned and sleeping? Check.

Billy fed and smooched? Check.

Laundry done? Check.

Time with God? Umm, no. *Again.*

I'm sorry, God. I glanced toward the ceiling of our small apartment and imagined God looking down in disapproval. *I'm so sorry. I know I should put You first in the day; it just feels like I don't have a second to spare.*

My excuses felt lame as I sat drenched in guilt for a few minutes.

Suddenly a memory of my morning hours popped into my brain. I recalled how when I scooped up Samantha from her crib, I'd thanked God for her—right there in her room. And then another memory flashed of the worship song I sang as I cradled Sam before her nap. And then God's gentle spirit reminded me of the beautiful sunset we'd seen out on the back balcony and the fleeting whisper of gratitude I'd expressed to God.

I glanced again at the ceiling, this time with a smile. *You weren't looking down with disapproval, were You? You were with me all day. You were with Samantha. You were in the sunset and in the worship music and in my whispers. Oh, Lord, I want to be intentional in my time with You, but when I can't, help me to remember that You are with me each step. That You love me in every moment.*

Thank You, Lord, for making Your presence known; help me to see You, enjoy You and rest in Your love.

—ELSA KOK COLOPY

Day Twenty-Five

Blessed be the Lord, Who daily bears us up; God is our salvation.
—PSALM 68:19 (ESV)

I'm still getting up every three hours, every night," I complained to my older sister Maria. She'd raised three children; I knew she would understand.

The worst came when Solomon stayed up all night and slept all day. "He's got his days and nights reversed," Maria explained. "Those are hard times. You need to sleep when he sleeps."

I'd never been able to sleep during the day. On days that Solomon thought were nights, I just stayed awake.

One day after I had been up all night, I had a terrible exhausted and shaky feeling. I called my sister. "I don't know how people live through this," I complained.

"Oh, it's hard, but it goes fast," Maria said. "You'll see; some of my favorite moments are those late nights when it was just me and the baby. Go rest your eyes. You'll be okay. We all get through it."

I got off the phone and lay down on the couch as Solomon slept in the bassinette beside me. I woke up hours later with Tony coming through the door.

"Look at you," he said. "I'm so glad you could sleep."

Later that night, in the blue light of the television, I held Solomon in my arms and looked down at his wide-awake eyes. I found a good old movie on the classics channel.

"Well, it's just you and me, kid," I said.

Dear Lord, thank You for the advice that gets me through, and for helping me find beauty in the most challenging times.
—SABRA CIANCANELLI

Day Twenty-Six

*Like the coolness of snow at harvest time is a trustworthy messenger
to those who send him; he refreshes the spirit of his masters.*
—PROVERBS 25:13

~~~~~~~~~~~~~~~~~

*T*he baby shower was lovely, but I kept checking the clock. I was ready to get back to my own newborn, who was alone with Dad for the first time.

They needed me by now, I was sure.

As I turned the knob and walked into the living room, I saw father and son lying on a blanket, just gazing at each other. I felt like an intruder. I asked how they spent the morning, and Todd told me he'd taken Zach to the library—and gotten him his own library card.

Part of me wanted to dismiss what he did as silly. Just like in the days after Zach's birth when my husband pushed the bassinet down the hospital hallway yelling "Road trip!" on the way to the nursery. In a few seconds, though, my condescension softened into awe and gratitude for the man I married.

He said it felt like the right thing to do. He didn't read it in a new parent guide, ask a friend's opinion or consult another soul. He just held our little guy while he talked him through checking out his first books. He went with a loving impulse. And from the calm little body lying next to his six-foot dad, I'd say Zach felt it.

It wouldn't be the last time I'd second-guess a Dad decision, but it would be the time that would always humble me into remembering that the beauty of a team is that we do things together, with a shared goal, even if we're not always alike.

Lord, help me fulfill my role and uplift—not judge—my husband in his.
—SUSAN BESZE WALLACE

Day Twenty-Seven

Instead, speaking the truth in love, we will in all things grow up into him who is the Head, that is, Christ.
—EPHESIANS 4:15

Car seats are supposedly like sleeping potions for babies, but it didn't work that way with Michelle. She hated the car seat from the minute she sat in it and was relentlessly vocal in communicating her displeasure.

Driving on a long trip, we thought Michelle's car-seat resistance was intensifying—until we realized she had a fever. We took her to a doctor. Diagnosis: ear infection. Prescription: an antibiotic and an antihistamine that the doctor said would make her sleepy. Sleep sounded good to this fatigued mother.

If only it were that simple. After taking the antihistamine, Michelle fussed even more, screeching and writhing in my arms into the night. I tried to calm her. I prayed. I worried about her. I pitied my tired self, especially as I watched my husband sleep while I paced the floor. I reminded God that He says He gives His beloved sleep.

My willingness to stay up shriveled as fatigue and frustration grew. But wishing I could go to bed wouldn't make it reality. *These things happen with babies*, I thought. *I may as well try to see it as a chance to grow in patience.* I began to pray. "Thank You, Lord, for precious Michelle. Help me to care for her like You care for me—gently and patiently." I was surprised how quickly acceptance and prayer changed my heart and attitude.

By morning, Michelle slept soundly.

I phoned the doctor, who chuckled and said that antihistamines sometimes cause agitation instead of drowsiness. Sleepy as I was, I had room in my head for one more thought: I immediately threw that medicine in the trash.

Lord, help me look at seemingly impossible challenges as opportunities to grow.
—SUSAN LABOUNTY

Day Twenty-Eight

And in the church God has appointed . . . those able to help others. . . .
—I CORINTHIANS 12:28

~~~~~~~~~~~~~

I'd been cooped up long enough. Folks and food flowed through my house at a rate rivaling the local soup kitchen, but I no longer wanted to feel like a charity case. I needed to get away to a place with less noise and advice. Surely I was ready to handle my baby by myself outside my neighborhood! This outreach ministry to Rhonda could rest for a season.

The breezy fall air had touches of warmth, so I dressed Joshua in a short-sleeved shirt, crocheted sweater and matching cap. We headed to the United Assemblies Conference, a sedate gathering of churches affiliated with my congregation. Joshua fell asleep in the car. We sat quietly among meditative worshippers, until suddenly Joshua squelched the silence with successive shrills. I'd forgotten that this slumberous baby babble might happen. At home we ignore it, accepting that my son has inherited talking in his sleep from my husband.

I knew Joshua would be quiet in a few moments, but the monklike prayer warriors around us didn't want to wait. Someone shouted, "Give him a bottle!" and all eyes directed me to the door. I searched my bag frantically, and just as I touched the bottle to his lip, Joshua sighed and fell silent.

After service I rushed out to avoid ridicule. Joshua cried the whole time home; no singing or hush-babying quieted him. When I took him out of the seat, he was drenched because I'd overdressed him. I sighed, and entered my house. Perhaps that outreach ministry to Rhonda wasn't such a bad idea, after all.

Thank You, Lord, for help even when I don't think I need it.
—RHONDA J. SMITH

Day Twenty-Nine

"Lord, teach us to pray, just as John taught his disciples."
—LUKE 11:1

~~~~~~~~~~

Pat, pat, pat. Rub, rub, rub. Elizabeth was a good eater, but a lousy burper. I walked up and down the dark hallway of our apartment, guiding myself by sliding one shoulder along the wall. Whenever I felt a doorjamb, I opened my eyes; it was my system to ensure I didn't fall asleep on my feet.

Pat, pat, rub, rub. In addition to being a reluctant burper, Elizabeth was a heaver. There was a cloth diaper over my shoulder, and one strategically placed on the floor every four paces. That way when the milk flew I didn't have to bend down to clean it up; I reached out with my foot, rubbed the cloth diaper over the mess, and shoved it out of the way. Once the baby slept, I'd come back and clean up for real. Or maybe that could wait until morning.

Pat, pat, pat. Half an hour of burping to get up one tiny pocket of air. I wondered how many miles I'd walked. I tried to think of something to do to stay awake. I didn't have the cognitive ability to pray. Or did I? I named someone on my prayer list. And then,

Our	Father,	who art	in Heaven...
Pat	*pat*	*pat*	*pat*
Hallowed	be	thy	name...
Rub	*rub*	*rub*	*rub*

I lost track of where I was but restarted quickly. When I finished, I named someone else and began again.

Lord, make my every step a step toward You.
—JULIA ATTAWAY

Day Thirty

Into your hands I commit my spirit; redeem me, O Lord, the God of truth.
—PSALM 31:5

I sat in the restaurant with my sister-in-law Lindsay. I watched from across the table as she held Gabriella. I didn't know if it was exhaustion or motherhood, but I felt removed from the moment, as though I was watching this very put-together woman through a fog. Lindsay seemed so confident in the way she talked to the baby and held her. Even the way she'd ordered lunch showed a self-assurance I desperately wanted but didn't know where to find.

I watched as Lindsay put her face inches away from Gabi's, waited for the baby to focus on her and gave Gabi a big smile. Gabi returned the smile, and Lindsay cheered. My heart sank a little deeper. Gabi had only given a few little smiles in her lifetime. I had never made her smile like that. I felt defeated.

Later that day, I sat alone on my bed. Tears rolled down my cheeks, crying eventually moving to sobbing as I admitted my fear: I was a bad mom. I couldn't even make my baby smile. Lindsay would do a better job at being Gabi's mom.

Unable to seize the perspective that time and balanced hormones would later offer, I was sure this was my new norm: failing as a mom. I had no idea that what I was experiencing fell somewhere between normal baby blues and postpartum depression. A fog really was clouding my thinking, preventing me from seeing my life and myself clearly.

Lord, give me understanding to know if I am experiencing
something more than normal baby blues, and if necessary,
give me the courage to search out the help I need.
—ALEXANDRA KUYKENDALL

Editor's note: Need help distinguishing postpartum depression from the "baby blues"? See page 394.

Third Month

———

Oh, Father,

A smile makes all the difference in the world! It brings me hope and delight. In the blur that my brain has become, remind me that the joy I find in my child's smile is only a feeble reflection of the joy You want me to find in You.

I give You my longing for quiet time this month. It is hard to find time to worship You the way I used to; show me new ways to honor You in this new phase of my life. You are with me even when I feel nothing but exhaustion. Turn my heart to You whenever I see my baby smile.

In Christ my Lord, amen.

Tips

» Bring the baby into the bathroom when you take a shower. He can cope with almost anything as long as he knows where you are.

» Walking outdoors is great exercise, and the baby's crying will seem far less intense when it's not bouncing off your own four walls.

» Temporarily remove the word *should* from your vocabulary, at least as it relates to chores. Focus on what God has given you to do instead.

Day One

*"Can a woman forget her nursing child, and not have
compassion on the son of her womb?"*
—ISAIAH 49:15 (NKJV)

From the moment Grandma Rosie laid eyes on Kedar, the two were inseparable. Every Thursday when we brought "Dar" over, Rosie's deep brown face radiated love beneath her perfectly groomed silver hair.

"There's Grandma's baby!" she squealed with delight. It was the sweetest thing to see a clearly enraptured grandma coo and ooh over her beloved grandson. From day one she gave him *everything*: toys, clothes, books, and above all else, her heart.

"Twinkle, twinkle little star," she sang in a faint voice as Kedar lay snuggled on her chest. The old wooden rocking chair with the peach cushion creaked as Rosie moved back and forth rhythmically. Kedar's eyes opened and closed drowsily.

"Okay, we'll be back," I whispered, not wanting to interrupt Rosie's one-on-one time. Kenya and I waved good-bye, leaving baby Kedar alone with grandma for the very first time.

After about twenty minutes of strolling around Delaware Park hand-in-hand with Kenya I blurted, "Do you think Kedar's okay? I mean, I nursed him before we left, but maybe I should call to make sure he isn't hungry or crying." Hastily, I grabbed my phone and began dialing Rosie's number.

"He'll be fine, baby," Kenya said slipping my cell phone out of my hand and sliding it into his pocket before I could complete the call. "It's okay," he reassured me. And when we returned an hour later, the rocking chair sat perfectly still as Kedar and Rosie silently slept, together.

*Father, help me know the difference between
healthy concern and needless worry.*
—DIANNA HOBBS

Day Two

*Samuel took a single rock and set it upright between Mizpah
and Shen. He named it "Ebenezer" (Rock of Help), saying,
"This marks the place where GOD helped us."*
—I SAMUEL 7:12 (MSG)

~~~~~~~~~~~

"Junk, junk, junk, bill, bill, junk. . . ," I muttered, sorting through our pile of mail. "Making sense of all these medical bills and insurance statements is a full-time job!"

Opening an envelope, I glanced at the contents. It was a bill for $706. In a panic, I called Jonathan. "Hey. We just got a bill for $706 from some doctor who attended my C-section. Did they expect me to ask in the middle of an emergency if each doctor was in-network?"

"Liz, calm down. Don't worry. Call the insurance company and find out what they say."

I called, and the news was not good. "I'm sorry, ma'am. This doctor was out-of-network and you will have to pay the bill."

Money was tight since we went down to one income, and we'd already spent far more than we anticipated. Now this! *Where would we get $700?*

"Liz, let's pray about the bill." Jonathan said that night.

"Okay," I responded, somewhat doubtfully, and bowed my head. "God, we praise you! Thank you that You promise to provide for all of our needs. Help us find a way to deal with this $700 bill. . . ."

Several days later, Jonathan was talking with his sister Sarah on the phone and mentioned the bill. "You should appeal it," she said, reminding him that she used to work in the insurance industry. "Send a letter to the insurance company, stating that you did not give consent to have this physician see you."

And guess what? It worked!

Thank You, Lord, for being our Rock of Help.
—LIZ BISSELL

Day Three

I guide you in the way of wisdom and lead you along straight paths.
When you walk, your steps will not be hampered;
when you run, you will not stumble.
—PROVERBS 4:11–12 (NIV)

~~~~~~~~~~~~

I had the baby monitor on, positioned as close to my head as the length of the cord and location of my pillow would allow. Even though Gabi's bedroom was across the hall, I wanted to make sure I heard her if she needed me during the night. Hoping the monitor would give me the reassurance I needed, I lay in bed awake, listening to the whirl of the humidifier transmitted through the monitor.

We had just returned from two nights at Denver's Children's Hospital. Gabi had been diagnosed with RSV, a virus that inhibited her breathing. Exhausted, I didn't think I'd ever relax again. Mostly, I didn't trust my instincts. We'd visited the emergency room a week earlier, only to be sent home, feeling like overprotective parents. When Gabi was quickly admitted days later, she needed oxygen.

Now we were home, and I was in charge. There were no nurses to walk in and make the professional assessment. I listened. Was Gabi wheezing? Coughing? How would I know if the oxygen tubing was still in her little nose? I strained to catch any sound that would indicate distress, fearing I would need to make medical decisions I felt unprepared to make.

I only had the hospital nurse's discharge instructions, which included a lot of "Trust your instincts." I had lost trust in those instincts. I wanted someone else to be the boss, to tell me what to do. So I prayed:

Holy Spirit, give me the eyes to see and the ears
to hear what my child needs tonight.
—ALEXANDRA KUYKENDALL

Day Four

". . . A time to weep and a time to laugh,
a time to mourn and a time to dance."
—ECCLESIASTES 3:4

My newborn invaded every crevice of my being, except one. May 3 is her day, not his.

Two of my babies died before I conceived Zachary. One, a gut-wrenching blank ultrasound at sixteen weeks. The other, a long journey of tests, both home and hospital bed rest, and ultimately the birth at twenty-six weeks of a dead daughter. May 3.

My blood thickens when I'm pregnant, preventing the sustenance of new life. Olivia Grace had stopped growing. Back then we didn't know the why, just the what. She was starving to death. The day of her birth and death changed my husband and me forever. I was broken. I had to take one day of tears and questions and hoping at a time.

Perseverance, gifted physicians, and a litany of tests and ultrasounds resulted in a "normal" pregnancy and labor two years later. I somehow embraced Zach's journey here fully, despite constant thoughts of Olivia. I cried tears of happiness over my new son often, but many of them were for her too.

And so, May 3. Zach was two months old. Olivia would have been two years. He likely wouldn't be here if she'd lived. She could have been a shell of a person if she'd survived. Thoughts swirled as I visited the cemetery.

I held Zach tightly while walking the grass to her headstone. The convergence of emotions overwhelmed me. The two pink balloons I'd brought, representing her would-be age, beat against each other wildly in the wind, much like my thoughts. I loved *her*. I have *him*.

When released, the balloons instantly quieted but floated together. And it made sense. I loved *her*. I have *him*. I can do both.

You gave me so much, Lord, when You took her home.
Thank You for new beginnings.
—SUSAN BESZE WALLACE

Day Five

My heart grew hot within me, and as I meditated, the
fire burned; then I spoke with my tongue.

—PSALM 39:3

~~~~~~~~~~~~

Brian and I were at a community fundraiser when I bumped into an old friend I hadn't seen in years. "Sheila!" I screamed as I hugged her.

"How's the new mommy?" she asked. Her question sent me off on a tangent as I gushed about the wonders of my child. Sheila interrupted me to mention that she'd just received Shiloh's birth announcement in the mail.

"I have to say," Sheila shook her head and chuckled, "my daughter and I were laughing when we saw the picture on the announcement." I looked at her, perplexed. Sheila waved her hand in the air, "I mean, only a mother could think that photo is cute!"

The blood drained from my face and my fingers grew ice cold. I couldn't even fake a smile. Another friend who stood next to me nervously folded and then unfolded her arms.

"*What?*" I sputtered. I'm usually reluctant to confront others, but this comment made my passive nature completely disappear. "You know what?" I tapped my foot, unsure of what to say, as the mother bear in me emerged. "I think you should get your eyesight checked, because it's obvious to me that there are some issues!" Growling, I stomped off.

I crawled into bed that night and lay silently in the dark, reflecting on the conversation with Sheila. The fury inside me tapered—a bit. Though still annoyed at my friend's forthrightness, I was most surprised by the strong reaction it had stirred within me.

"God, I *need* your grace to walk this parenting journey," I desperately prayed while twisting the corner of my blanket in my fingers, "Because I have a hunch it's going to be an uncomfortable ride."

Oh, Father! What do I say? And when should I say it? And when should
I be silent? And what do I do with this Mama Bear inside me?

—RUTH BERGEN

Day Six

But if we walk in the light, as he is in the light, we have fellowship with
one another, and the blood of Jesus, his Son, purifies us from all sin.
—I JOHN 1:7

To bare my breast in front of my Bible study friends or not—now *that* was one dilemma I'd never thought I'd face! Yet here I was, contemplating the predicament. Joey would be due for a feeding smack-dab in the middle of my Bible group's prayer time. Would it be appropriate to feed him discreetly in front of everyone, or should I excuse myself to find a private corner to nurse?

And there was more. How many diapers would he need for our two-hour outing? And where would I change him? What would I do if he started crying while someone was reading Scripture? Suddenly the idea of going felt overwhelming. Maybe I should just skip it until I had this mothering thing figured out.

But . . . but this was my one chance to get away each week and spend time intensely studying the Word. I said a quick prayer, packed the diaper bag and left.

Things did not go perfectly. Joey cried when he woke up in his car seat. I had to change his diaper on the floor of the bathroom. I was only sort-of discreet when I nursed him, but no one seemed to notice. It wasn't ideal, but it wasn't awful. My sense of refreshment and renewal far outweighed the stress of mastering baby logistics. We'll do it again.

Lord, help me overcome the obstacles that seem to stand
in the way of fellowship with other believers.
—ERIN MACPHERSON

Day Seven

"Blessed are those who recognize they are spiritually helpless. The kingdom of heaven belongs to them."
—MATTHEW 5:3 (GOD'S WORD)

O n Tuesday I figured out how to get out of the apartment and down two flights of stairs with the laundry *and* the baby. It was ridiculously empowering. Thursday I got through a nonautomatic door with the stroller; I swung it open, did a funky little hip thing to catch it on my rear, and rolled the stroller in backward. Pretty clever, eh? At this rate I'll be able to buy groceries by the time Elizabeth is six.

What is it about the management of life with a baby that's so overwhelming? Have I truly become incompetent, or am I just a little slow on the uptake? I've organized conferences and trained employees, and yet making a peanut butter sandwich, left-handed, with my baby on my shoulder, at 2:00 AM, feels like a major accomplishment. In fact, I think it is.

It's an accomplishment on the order of remembering where I left the wipes box, a feat as profound as getting out of the house having forgotten only three things. This new world of motherhood is a bizarre blend of junior-high insecurity and early-onset amnesia. It's uncomfy. I'm used to being the master of my life, accustomed to having things under control. I don't like drinking from this fire hose of new things to learn. I have to resort to shrugging my shoulders, laughing at myself, and accepting that I don't know what I'm doing. I have to acknowledge that I'm not the One in control of my life, and I can't always make everything better.

Huh. Maybe that's the point.

Okay, Lord. You're in charge.
—JULIA ATTAWAY

Day Eight

"The people will no longer quote this proverb: 'The parents eat sour grapes, but their children's mouths pucker at the taste.'"
—JEREMIAH 31:29 (NLT)

My mama stayed home with us until we went to school. She made up songs to teach us whatever she decided we needed to know before kindergarten. She took us to fancy restaurants far from home, and we caught the bus or a cab to experience others' way of life. My mama laughed *with* us and not at us, lovingly redirecting our mistakes. She was beyond generous with her time and treasures, and fabulous about affirming our talents.

I loved my mama, and always knew I wanted to raise my children the same way she did. She did so much so well that I was sure there was no hope for me in the one area where she didn't excel: physical affection. How would I ever be able to hug and kiss Joshua with abandon if even my almost-perfect mom didn't do that with me?

My mother's mother didn't hug or kiss much either. Perhaps it was something genetic, a blip on the physical contact gene. But wait . . . my grandma never took my mother to a fancy restaurant. She didn't do a lot of the things my mother had done with us. A light bulb went on in my head: My mom had imitated her mother in some ways, but followed her own path in others. I had that freedom too. If I wanted to hug and kiss my baby, I could. I didn't have to do everything just like my mother. I didn't have to *be* my mom. I could imitate her best aspects and be myself in others.

Thank You, Lord, that You ask me to be myself,
not my mother or anyone else.
—RHONDA J. SMITH

Day Nine

The Lord God formed the man from the dust of the ground and breathed
into his nostrils the breath of life, and the man became a living being.
—GENESIS 2:7

We're praying for God to heal Henry," a well-meaning acquaintance told me. I didn't know how to respond. I'd been hearing many sentiments like this: people expressing sympathy, promising prayer, saying there must be something exceptional about me to have been given a Down syndrome child. Whatever the sentiment, my feelings were the same: They didn't get it.

No one said *Congratulations!* when they met my son. There was no talk about how cute he was, or how he was getting so big, or how he was a perfect addition to our family. *Find one thing nice to say about my child*, my heart pleaded. *See him as a person, not a liability!* Henry deserved more positive reactions, and I was his defender. I wanted to scream, "He's not sick, he has Down syndrome!" and "He's a *person*, acknowledge him!"

I knew people meant well. But their sympathy made it seem that they thought God made a mistake in creating Henry. I fumed—and then felt like a bad Christian for being angry. I loved my son; I hated my situation. I appreciated that others prayed for me but resented that they didn't understand what I needed. I loved God, and felt like a deficient Christian. Not knowing what else to do with my emotional tornado, I had long pour-my-guts-out talks with God about my feelings. He might not make them go away, but He could help me sort them out, put them in perspective, and help me live through them.

Heavenly Father, when my head swirls with conflicting emotions,
help me accept that having negative feelings is normal. It's
what I do with them that is either sinful or holy.
—CHRISTY STURM

Day Ten

"But Martha was distracted with much serving."
—LUKE 10:40 (ESV)

~~~~~~~~~~~~~~

I don't know who was more radiant: the bride marching past or me, sitting there watching. My arms were baby-free—perfumed, adorned in fine fabric, and wrapped around a husband. A wedding was a good place for this hopeless romantic to have a sleeping infant; I could cry sappy tears and offer cheers without interruption.

Anna's nursery nap continued past the ceremony. I traded in my diaper bag for a camera case and shot photos of a rosy cake and velvety bridesmaids. Freedom was as delicious as the punch I sipped as I savored adult conversation.

Someone asked if I could travel across town and help decorate the banquet room for the private dinner reception. Anna was still sleeping. Void of all reason, I answered, "Yes." For the next two hours I trimmed tables in Martha Stewart fashion. Only with a tingling in my breasts did I finally remember my baby. I drove back to the church and dashed to the nursery.

There was Anna, wide awake, being burped on the shoulder of another woman.

"Dave said I could nurse her," Catherine (not her real name) confessed, with the face of a criminal before a firing squad. "She was so hungry."

I stood there, processing the situation. Anna turned a grief-stricken face toward me and her lips quivered before erupting with a cry of hurt. I grabbed and held her tightly against a shame-filled heart.

Soon enough, I laughed and all but prostrated myself in gratitude before my heroine. And the only table I served for a while afterward was my family's.

Lord, help me to be a minister to my family first. Amen.
—FAITH BOGDAN

Day Eleven

"Put your hope in God, for I will yet praise him, my Savior and my God."
— PSALM 43:5

~~~~~~~~~~~~

Lisbet was napping when our lawyer called. "I have good news," he began. "The birth mother signed the relinquishment papers."

I began to shake. Knowing everything was okay brought all of the anxiety I'd buried to the surface, and I had to sit down.

Every adoption has milestones. This was a big one: when the birth parents terminated their rights—and could no longer ask for the baby back.

I remembered a phone call six months earlier from this same lawyer, when a different baby napped in my living room. "I'm sorry. The birth mother has changed her mind," he said. Mercifully, we'd only had that baby one day. We hadn't even named her yet. The next morning, with the awkwardness of new parents, we placed that tiny brown-haired girl into a car seat and drove four hours north to transfer her back into the lawyer's custody and back to her birth mother. And then we were no longer new parents.

This time I hung up, picked up my daughter and cuddled her close. What a gift! The horrible thing that I couldn't bear to think about . . . didn't happen. I held Lisbet, marveling at her and at the powerful lesson I'd just learned: in all things I must proceed, day by day, with faith and hope. If I want to live in peace, I can't dwell on what *might* happen—illnesses or accidents or troubles. I have to carry on, keeping my focus on what I can give, doing what I can do and trusting ever more in God.

Lord, teach me to hope constructively, instead of just hoping bad things don't happen.
—LENORE LELAH PERSON

Day Twelve

"When I was a child, I talked like a child, I thought like a child, I reasoned like a child. When I became a [woman], I put childish ways behind me."
—I CORINTHIANS 13:11

The appointment went easily into the calendar. Lasik eye surgery for my husband Todd was going to open up a new career path, not to mention give him twenty-twenty vision, something neither of us had ever enjoyed.

When the day came, I realized I was going to spend hours—including the ones known in many circles as the *witching* hours—in a waiting room with baby Zach. I could feel the edginess start to creep in.

I became nauseous listening to the doctor describe the procedure, and left the room. Zach and I made faces at each other. We both attempted a fitful nap. And we went outside to bounce out the grumpies (mine) and gas (his) beyond the earshot of nervous patients.

I drove weary Zach and a foggy-minded and goggle-eyed Todd to Waffle House for a quick bite and then home. I was exhausted and feeling put-out to be in charge of all this when I'd just become in charge of a baby. When I'd tucked both my guys into bed, I breathed deep and really looked at my husband. My heart softened.

He had done what he had done that day to better lead our family, never complaining once. I *was* in charge of much, with a beautiful man who had chosen me to be his copilot on this awesome ride of marriage and parenthood. Any burden with him is a blessing. Even when I have trouble seeing it.

Lord, help me make gratitude and respect for my husband a theme throughout each day.
—SUSAN BESZE WALLACE

Day Thirteen

Even the sparrow has found a home, and the swallow a
nest for herself, where she may have her young. . . .
—PSALM 84:3

I looked up from nursing and scanned our little fixer-upper house. We'd moved in only a few days before Gabriella was born, and now the unpacking was just getting started. Boxes still taped shut were stacked in our dining room, walls were bare, furniture was scattered haphazardly around the room.

I didn't have to venture down the wooden staircase to know the basement was an even greater disaster. Paint cans, drop cloths and tools covered the floor. We'd moved into the only house in our neighborhood we could afford: one that needed lots of love.

Although Gabriella was only an infant, maternal guilt was already becoming a frequent visitor. I hadn't pictured bringing my newborn baby home to a setting like this. Where's the peaceful sanctuary for our sleepy bundle of joy? The lullabies around here were power saws and nail guns. Where's the doting husband at my beck and call? On his back, installing the kitchen sink.

This guilt is justified, I thought irritably. God gave mothers an instinct to make homes for their babies. He even made birds feather their nests, flittering about retrieving tufts of straw to make a safe, special place. Why couldn't I give my baby something as simple as a quiet, put-together home?

Then I remembered why we first liked this house. It was the one on the block that obviously needed lots of love. We knew we could care for its wounds and transform it into a home. The chaos of construction was still in full swing, but the end result, a love-filled home, was already complete.

Lord, make love the defining ingredient of our home.
—ALEXANDRA KUYKENDALL

Day Fourteen

May the favor of the Lord our God rest upon us; establish the work of our hands for us—yes, establish the work of our hands.
—PSALM 90:17

~~~~~~~~~~~~~~~~~

I tugged hard at the jacket. No, it would not fit. The buttons strained, not delicately, across my chest. My fingers flailed at the task.

I stole a glance at the clock; I had no time to spare. My first in-office meeting since Anjelica was born was in an hour, and it would require a real suit jacket, the kind I donned easily before, wavering only between color and style. I sank onto the edge of my bed.

My hands fell into my lap. I winced to see my nails, once tended and manicured, now plain and short, unadorned. My fingers, worn from housework, seemed to have narrowed into long shoots.

I remembered my grandmother Isida, whom we all called *La Vieja* ("The Old One"), washing reams of clothing and bedding and towels every day, by hand, in the yard of her small home in Santo Domingo, while I watched, seated beside her during my long summer visits.

I remembered her long, tapered fingers picking out tiny brown grains and leaves from the basins of rice and beans she'd wash for the large noon meal she'd prepare for over a dozen people, packing up containers to send throughout the neighborhood of dusty, uneven streets.

I remembered her laying her cool palms on the top of my head in an offering of quiet affection, and her fingers holding the rosary early in the mornings, praying in a small murmur, seated on the edge of her own bed, her head bowed.

La Vieja raised seventeen remarkable children, my mother the eldest among them, with her nimble, worn, beautiful hands. I stared at my own hands and raised them, again, to my jacket. I must hurry. There was work to be done.

Into Your hands, Lord, I trust my life and my day.
—DEBRALEE SANTOS

Day Fifteen

A generous man will prosper; he who refreshes others will himself be refreshed.
—PROVERBS 11:25

~~~~~~~~~~~~~~~

Shortly after the twins were born, my friend Noreen told me to get out my calendar and schedule a date with my husband for three months down the road. "I'm coming to babysit so you can have some time away," she said. At the time, the idea of leaving the house for a date night was unimaginable.

The days and weeks crept by, and I thought I'd never feel human again. I'd become a nursing machine, a pumping station, a laundress. When I wasn't doing anything, I daydreamed about the date night. Every now and then Noreen reminded me the offer still stood, and that brought hope to my days.

As the much-anticipated time approached, I made reservations at a restaurant and a hotel. I secretly planned a romantic dinner and anticipated that we'd relax together for a while before I told Jim to stay overnight so he could get some well-deserved rest.

Noreen and her daughter arrived promptly, as promised. My husband and I enjoyed an uninterrupted dinner and relished our time relaxing in the hotel room. But we made one mistake: We talked about the babies instead of zoning out. Before long, we were both missing the girls terribly. Jim wouldn't hear of staying over. He told me I should use the room, but I was nursing and that simply wasn't possible. So we checked out and headed home. Our date night lasted five glorious hours. And that was enough.

Lord, it takes You surprisingly little time to refresh my tired soul.
Nudge me to carve out space in my life to allow You to refresh me.
—DONNA MAY LYONS

Day Sixteen

"Have I not commanded you? Be strong and courageous.
Do not be terrified; do not be discouraged, for the Lord
your God will be with you wherever you go."
—JOSHUA 1:9

One day while I was complaining about the seemingly endless monotony of motherhood, Jonathan said, "Liz, why don't you visit my parents?"

"Drive up by myself?" I answered incredulously. "But I don't know how to get there! And what if Llewelyn cries?"

"So you'll print up directions. We've driven up there tons of times. You'll be fine."

My husband's parents live three-and-a-half hours away, and although we'd visited often, Jonathan always drove. Though we were on friendly terms and I liked them, I felt anxious about going alone. *But these are Llewelyn's grandparents*, I reasoned. So I made arrangements to go.

Traffic was surprisingly good, and Llewelyn fell asleep almost immediately. As I drove, my mind wandered to thoughts of Jonathan's parents, Torre and Jean. They were people of deep faith, who had served as missionaries in Pakistan, Liberia and Nigeria. *What could I learn from them?* I wondered. Suddenly I was eager to engage with them on a deeper level about their faith and to use this trip as a new beginning in our relationship.

When I finally turned onto their street, I was filled with elation and relief. *Thank you God!* I cried, jubilant as the "Hallelujah Chorus." I scooped Llewelyn out of her car seat and climbed the steps to my in-laws' house. Jean immediately met us at the door. "Hi, Liz! Hi, Llewelyn!" she exclaimed, opening her arms for a big hug. "I'm so glad you're here!"

So was I.

Lord, help me forge past my insecurities, finding the courage to try new things.
—LIZ BISSELL

Day Seventeen
A Dad's View

"Not that we are competent in ourselves to claim anything for ourselves, but our competence comes from God."
—II CORINTHIANS 3:5

Okay, have fun!" my wife said as she headed out the door for a rare evening with friends.

"Will do . . . you too!" I replied, feigning enthusiasm in the midst of stark terror. Our baby was now dependent on me alone for care and comfort. On me, who once pinkified an entire load of laundry through ignorance compounded by carelessness. On me, who once mangled the side of our car and a bicycle in the garage in the same unpleasant incident. On me, who once left our apartment windows open while on a trip, during which the blizzard of the century hit. *On me.*

I had helped a lot with the baby before—diapers, baths, comforting him, and so forth—but always with Kari present somewhere in the house. Now I was in charge, alone, with our first and only child.

Although Kari had briefed me on everything—where items were, what to do if he wouldn't settle down, how to reach her in case of disaster—I did a quick review. List of important numbers: on counter; check. Diapers, wipes and changing table: in living room; check. Bath supplies: in the tub already; check. Mama's milk, bottled and ready; check. Baby Hans himself: uh. . .

I panicked for a moment as I tried to remember where we left him. Not on the floor in his baby gym, not resting in the car seat, not in the bassinet . . . Fortunately, I discovered him moments later in the playpen, sound asleep. *I can do this,* I thought.

The evening proved uneventful and indeed rewarding; Hans was changed, bathed, fed and cuddled without incident. Unlike that fateful load of former whites, unlike the unfortunate meeting of Sentra and Schwinn, unlike the snow bank that once greeted us in our kitchen. *I can do this.*

Lord, thank You for this child—and the miracle of being able to care for him.
—LEROY HUIZENGA

Day Eighteen

*And let us not be weary in well doing: for in due
season we shall reap, if we faint not.*
—GALATIANS 6:9 (KJV)

"For crying out loud, can't I have even one minute to myself?" I muttered, tossing the magazine aside. The house was quiet, and just as I'd settled in to thumb through glossy pages of home decor, the baby began to cry. I walked up the stairs to the nursery, attempting to muster feelings of maternal warmth.

Fatigued, nerves frayed, I struggled not to resent this endless work of mothering. Was it selfish to want some time to myself? Must my senses be so relentlessly attuned to the needs of my child? What about *me*?

Settling into our old wooden rocking chair, I began to think and pray. As the chair creaked back and forth, I studied my daughter's face. What a gift she was! Completely helpless, her ability to thrive was in my hands. I squeezed her closer. God had entrusted me with this life.

I was struck by how easily the temporal distracts from the eternal. Magazines—and whatever else hinders my desire to respond willingly and warmly to my child—can wait. The way I can find joy in mothering is to *be* a mother, wholeheartedly.

Lord, give me vision, strength and joy for doing Your work.
—SUSAN LABOUNTY

Day Nineteen

"If any of you needs wisdom to know what you should do, you should ask God, and he will give it to you. God is generous to everyone and doesn't find fault with them."

—JAMES 1:5 (GOD'S WORD)

W hat does that one say?" I asked Kenya, as we stood reading labels on skin creams and lotions during a late-night trip to Walmart. We were on a mission: Baby Kedar had developed painful, itchy and unsightly dark patches on his skin, caused by a recurring condition called eczema. I've struggled with the disorder my whole life, and unfortunately passed it along to our baby boy.

"Hand me that one. That one too."

"Hey, what do you think about this?" We stood in the aisle comparing the prices and active ingredients of moisturizers our doctor said were safe to use on the baby. The prescription ointment he'd given Kedar wasn't working, and I was determined to find something that would. *Lord, show me how to help my son*, I prayed. Two hours later, we left the store with a bag full of products and an eagerness to develop our own skincare regimen for Kedar.

From then on, I lathered up my baby two to three times a day with the special "potion" Kenya and I mixed together with prayer. To our surprise, after a week of consistent applications, Kedar's skin began to smooth out, and soon the irritating rash was almost imperceptible. Though incurable, his eczema was now controllable. *Thank You, God!*

Father, I know problems are going to arise in life. Remind me to apply a mixture of prayer, determination and creative thinking whenever they do.

—DIANNA HOBBS

Day Twenty

I will instruct you and teach you in the way you should go; I will counsel you and watch over you.

—PSALM 32:8

~~~~~~~~~~~

I looked out the window at the perfect spring day. It had been a long winter and I was itching to go outside. I dressed Solomon in a light-blue jacket with a teddy bear and a matching fleece hat with bear ears. I loved getting him ready to go out. Looking at his adorable clothes and choosing what he would wear was so much fun.

"We're going for a long walk, buddy," I told him. "It's gorgeous outside."

The sun was shining through puffy white clouds. "Solomon, this is spring," I said.

We weren't four steps out the door when I looked down and saw Solomon's eyes closed. He was sound asleep.

Should I just bring him back inside? I thought. *There's a huge pile of laundry to get done and the living room needs to be vacuumed.*

Purple crocus bloomed at the edge of the driveway. I felt the warm breeze on my face. Neighbors were outside gardening. The village was busy. People were drinking coffee in front of the bakery. As I passed, a man stood up and looked in the carriage at Solomon. "Now, that's the life," he said. "Don't you wish you were him?"

I smiled and thought, *Nope, I'm pretty thrilled being me.*

Dear God, thank You for glorious days and helping me remember this is the time to enjoy my beautiful new baby. And the laundry can always wait.

—SABRA CIANCANELLI

Day Twenty-One

*As I was with Moses, so I will be with you; I will
never leave you nor forsake you.*
—JOSHUA 1:5

~~~~~~~~~~~~~~

Tyler looked at me with panic in his eyes. He was crying, but softly, because he didn't have the breath to express the level of distress he was in. He wasn't gasping for air or turning blue, but as I looked at my baby I found myself breathing extra hard, as if helping him along.

Gary was working, so I called my neighbor Marcie to come down. "I don't know what's going on," I said, packing a small bag in a frenzy, "I can't tell if he's really having trouble breathing, or if I'm just imagining things, but something doesn't feel right." She looked at Tyler and couldn't tell either.

"If you think something is wrong, it probably is," Marcie insisted. "Never question your instincts as a mother." I ran out the door, leaving Brandon with her. It was late, and I felt bad for bothering her. What if nothing was wrong? Am I just a neurotic mother?

I wasn't. Tyler's oxygen levels were extremely low, and at his delicate age, that was serious. We were admitted, placed in isolation, and Tyler was hooked up to an oxygen tank. He had respiratory syncytial virus (RSV). After two very tense days, Tyler was discharged.

"But his stomach is still pushing out when he breathes," I said, pointing out one of the signs they'd shown me as a symptom of respiratory distress.

"Yes," the doctor said, "He's going to do that. He still has the virus. But his levels are much better."

I was uneasy about leaving. How will I know if he's in trouble again? I bundled up my baby and took him home. But just five hours later, I found myself breathing deep again as I watched him struggle to breathe—just as I had done the first time.

Oh, Lord Jesus, be with me when I am scared.
—KAREN VALENTIN

Day Twenty-Two

"If any of you lacks wisdom, let him ask God, who gives generously to all without reproach, and it will be given him."

—JAMES 1:5 (ESV)

I was alone again; Gary had just left for work. Marcie rushed down for the second time. Once more, I questioned myself.

"I know the doctor said to expect some distress since he still had the virus," I said in tears. "But I really think he's having trouble again."

"Then he probably is, Karen," Marcie replied.

"But they just discharged him!" I said, as I guided Tyler's tiny arms through the sleeves of his snowsuit. "They're going to think I'm crazy."

"Who cares?" she said softly, rubbing my back. "You are his mother. Trust yourself. You know what's best for your son."

I hailed a cab, and in minutes we were back in the emergency room. Tyler's oxygen levels were lower than before. They admitted him once again.

We were back in our room. I cradled my baby, who was sleeping peacefully, oxygen tubes in his little nose.

Then I broke down. So many emotions poured out: I was scared for Tyler—he was still so new. I was angry with the doctors for discharging him early and angry with myself for letting them when I had felt uneasy about leaving. I felt foolish for questioning myself, but proud and relieved that despite my doubts, I took action anyway.

The words of my neighbor and friend echoed in my ear. "You are his mother, trust your instincts. You know what's best for your son." In that moment, I owned those words. God put this little life in my care and placed a gift of intuition in my heart's core. I promised myself—and Tyler—that I would trust in that gift as never before.

Holy Spirit, You do give me the wisdom I need. You do.

—KAREN VALENTIN

Day Twenty-Three

The pride of your heart has deceived you. . . .
—OBADIAH 1:3

⁓⁓⁓⁓⁓⁓

Thank you so much, but I couldn't let you do that," I told my neighbor Patty when she offered to cook a few meals for me. I'd declined dozens of similar offers since my daughter was born. I was sure I was doing my well-wishers a favor: they didn't *really* want to go out of their way to help me. Undoubtedly they breathed a sigh of relief when I said no.

Then a friend had her first child. I went to her house one afternoon to hold the baby while she got a much-needed nap. I sat on her couch with babe in arms, and it felt good to do something to help. I was fulfilled and energized knowing I was serving someone in need.

That realization was followed by the memory of all the times I'd declined offers of help. If I like to give others a hand, why wouldn't they want to do the same for me? I was so startled by how backward my thinking had been that I laughed out loud—and startled the sleepy baby. My pride had been talking when I refused the generosity of others. Thinking they didn't genuinely want to help was the same as thinking I was more saintly than everyone I knew.

The next day I called my neighbor and told her I'd take her up on her offer for meals after all. And sure enough, when she arrived with a steaming dish of chicken casserole, we were both blessed.

Lord, remind me that I bless others by accepting their help.
—JENNIFER FULWILER

Day Twenty-Four

So God created man in his own image, in the image of God
he created him; male and female he created them.
—GENESIS 1:27

~~~~~~~~~~

S
he looks just like me," my mother-in-law commented as she inspected her newest grandbaby for telltale family signs. She was pleased when she found a little divot on the baby's bottom lip just like hers.

Don't tell her, but baby Grace *really* looks like me. More often than not, friends and strangers alike tell me, "She looks just like you." I grin and say, "You think?" secretly knowing she does.

But why is it that each of us wants to see ourselves in the baby? God made us in His image, but He doesn't look down and say "Carol has my green eyes" or "Alan is tall just like me." He looks at our hearts, and in the depths of our souls, where He hopes to find a little piece of Himself. And when He finds it, He is pleased—just as I am when I see myself in my baby girl.

The more I see of myself in my daughter, the happier I am. I bet God feels the same. I wonder how much I look like Him today.

God, help my heart to reflect You so others see You in me.
—CAROL HATCHER

Day Twenty-Five

Every good and perfect gift is from above, coming down from the Father of the heavenly lights. . . .
—JAMES 1:17

~~~~~~~~~~~~~~~

O h. My. Goodness." I gaped as I looked into the gift box. "You're not going to believe this." I held up the outfit for Andrew to see. His eyes widened.

In theory, it was a one-piece sweat suit. What had been done to it was jaw-dropping. There were ribbons and lace and fake jewels and dangly things. There was fabric paint. There was the word *sugar* embroidered in a place that, on a baby, often smells anything but sweet. This was the sweat suit to end all sweat suits, the pinkest, frilliest, most-filled-in-spaces sweat suit in the world. Fortunately it was size nine months, and Elizabeth weighed only fourteen pounds.

"We have to keep it, you know," Andrew commented. "So Rita sees." Rita was our landlady, the woman who'd given us the gift.

"Do you think we could put Elizabeth in it once and bring Rita a picture?" I asked. "I'm not sure I can take her anywhere in this with a straight face."

My baby is round-cheeked and solemn, and even in pink is often mistaken for a boy. I held the outfit up against her, and Andrew and I burst into laughter. It looked awful. "I guess when she's big enough, we'll have to dress her up in it and bring her down to show off," Andrew said. "Once, before we give it away."

I carefully repacked the amazing outfit in its box. Someone, somewhere will be thrilled to discover this in a thrift shop.

Lord, thank You for people who care enough to give us gifts, even if they don't give what we want.
—JULIA ATTAWAY

Day Twenty-Six

I have set the Lord always before me. Because he is
at my right hand I will not be shaken.

—PSALM 16:8

~~~~~~~~~~~

Gingerly I laid sleeping Zachary into his carrier during church and draped a blanket over to keep out the noise and light. Sleep-deprived and on my own for the day, I longed to join him in his cocoon.

Up and down stairs after the service. Click seat in car. Stop by the store for quick grocery run. Car seat back out. Hurry across parking lot, seat bumping my hip. Ba-dum bump, ba-dum bump, ba-dum bump, ba-dum *whoaa*.

The seat got instantly lighter and nearly ba-dum-bumped me in the head. There on the grocery store sidewalk, in front of a bank of pay phones, lay three-month-old Zach, on concrete, soon to be wailing. I'd never buckled him in.

As my cruddy luck would have it, there were three men on those pay phones and they looked at me with such disdain I thought I might throw up. I cuddled Zach, forgot the errand, and ran back to the car, assuring the men my son was fine—no blood, no apparent injury. I had no clue what to do.

At home, nursing him seemed appropriate, or at least comforting. I called Children's Hospital begging for someone to call back, wondering if you could be arrested for stupidity. I held Zach tightly and sobbed, "Please God, let him be okay."

Zach dozed, and so did I, phone in hand. I never let go. We slept two hours. The hospital never called back. Or so I thought. In my confusion I never hung up the phone. Zach was fine.

Lord, learning lessons the hard way hurts. Keep my
baby safe and help me remain calm in trauma.

—SUSAN BESZE WALLACE

Day Twenty-Seven

What I'm trying to do here is get you to relax, not be so preoccupied with getting so you can respond to God's giving. . . .
—LUKE 12:29 (MSG)

~~~~~~~~~~~~

Gabi looked at me, smiled and started kicking. Kicking! My baby-milestone radar perked up. I was excited for about two seconds before the stress crept in. What could I do to encourage this new skill? Surely every good mother had a developmentally appropriate toy to help. A quick scouring of the toy basket left me empty-handed, and we were off to the store.

Later that day my sister-in-law Kendall came over to visit. We waited for Derek to arrive home from work before presenting Gabi with my new purchase: a keyboard that lit up and made music when kicked.

I set the toy up in the crib, just as the picture on the box indicated. Eager to show off Gabi's new skill to dad and aunt, I put her in the crib with her feet just inches away from the magic keyboard. She looked up at the three adult faces floating above her and smiled.

Sure that Gabi was simply unaware of the potential fun at hand, I pressed the keyboard buttons to show her the lights and sounds. My daughter looked up at us, and smiled. Finally, Kendall picked up Gabi's foot and used it to push the keys. When she let go, Gabi's foot thudded to the crib mattress. Obviously unmotivated by the toy, Gabi looked up again at the three adults who loved her. She smiled, and seeing us smile back, she finally kicked!

Lord, help me remember that people are more important to my child than purchases.
—ALEXANDRA KUYKENDALL

Day Twenty-Eight

Do not despise your mother when she is old.
—PROVERBS 23:22

I stood in the blazing Florida heat with Anna on my hip. A figure approached with hungry arms extended toward my baby. I presented Grandmamma with her first grandchild and watched a middle-aged woman plunge into a tear-filled fountain of youth.

Anna performed satisfactorily in all areas of cuteness as she fulfilled the duties of a grandbaby: She gaped, grinned, squealed and rolled over for a captive audience.

The next morning all three generations of girls set out to go walking in the cool tropic air. As I buckled Anna into the stroller, a piece of "motherly advice" came unbidden to my ears. It was delivered in the same southern drawl that had advised me for nineteen years under this same roof.

"Don't you think she needs a sweater?"

I stood and stared at my mother as she commented on the risk of getting pneumonia from being underdressed in temperatures of less than eighty degrees. I opened my mouth to eject some common sense, but stopped short, as if I'd swallowed a mosquito. My counselor was half a century old. She'd given up the last two decades of her life to raise children. Part of her heart had left the nest with us, and part of it remained there, for the grandchildren. That heart still pulsated with the same mothering instincts that had helped us survive—hats, scarves and all.

I draped a windbreaker over Anna (ever so lightly), and we walked into a gleaming sunrise. Soon enough, Grandmamma whisked away the jacket. Anna was still alive. I smiled; so was love.

Dear Father, help me to see the love in my
mother's advice, and respond in kind.
—FAITH BOGDAN

Day Twenty-Nine

*And Mary said, My soul doth magnify the Lord, And
my spirit hath rejoiced in God my Saviour.*
—LUKE 1:46–47 (KJV)

Every year a carnival visits our town for one weekend in June. Friday and Saturday are filled with cotton candy and rides, while Sunday brings all the churches in town together. We gather on Main Street, surrounded by Ferris wheels, and share a community worship service in the open air.

My family and I arrived at the church event just before the music started to play. Brian went to find a seat, but I decided to keep walking with Shiloh in her stroller. I was hoping she'd fall asleep.

This was when I noticed him: a middle-aged man, wearing a white tank top, smoking a cigarette. He leaned lazily against his car, scowling as he stared toward the crowd. He wasn't happy; it didn't take a psychologist to discern that.

My suspicions skyrocketed as I saw him open his trunk and stare angrily at something inside. *A drug dealer?* I wondered, remembering a news article I'd recently read. For thirty minutes, I kept a careful eye on him while I nervously paced the opposite side of the street. When the church service finally ended and people began to leave, I chewed my nails as I watched the man in the white tank top inch his way toward the crowd. *What should I do?*

When he reached the risers, the man put his hands on his hips and slowly bent down. I drew a deep breath—and watched as he began to pack up the chairs.

This man was here to work! He was a carnival employee who had been waiting (impatiently) for the service to end so he could continue his job.

*Lord, help me use my imagination to magnify You,
instead of magnifying my worries.*
—RUTH BERGEN

Day Thirty

"Every good gift and every perfect gift is from above, coming down from the Father of lights with whom there is no variation or shadow due to change."
—JAMES 1:17 (ESV)

~~~~~~~~~~~~

I tried to change my dentist appointment so Tony would be home to watch Solomon, but Mom insisted, "Solomon's never been without one of you. It's time he had a babysitter."

I watched from the window as my mother pulled into the driveway. She came in and sat down beside Solomon.

"Oh, we're going to have fun!" she said to him.

"If he cries," I said, "bounce him gently. He likes to look out that window. If he gets upset, you can try music. I have it tuned to Golden Oldies. That's his favorite. If that doesn't work, turn on the TV to one of the higher channels that doesn't come in. He likes the fuzzy sound of static."

Mom widened her eyes, taking it all in. "It's just a check-up, right?"

"Yeah," I nodded. "I should be back in less than an hour."

"Don't worry," she said. "He'll be fine."

I was half out the door when I remembered Solomon's favorite blanket. I ran up the stairs to his room and got it. "Here," I said. "He might need this."

"He sure is particular for a little guy," Mom said.

I thought about Solomon. He had only been in my life for a few months and yet it felt like a lifetime. He had favorites, likes, dislikes. Miraculously, he wasn't just a baby: he was his own little person.

Dear God, my child is a mystery. As he grows and shows me who he is, I remain in awe of You and Your handiwork.
—SABRA CIANCANELLI

Fourth Month

~~~~~~

Lord,

Give me an open mind so that each challenge I face in motherhood drives me to look for new ways to grow closer to You. Use it all, Lord: my frustrations, crazy dreams, deepest hopes, and frenzied struggle to hold it all together. I give You everything, knowing that You alone can make sense out of it all and bring order to my heart.

In Jesus' name, amen.

Tips

» When transferring a sleeping baby from your arms, wait five minutes longer than you think you need to. No, make it ten.

» Start a morning ritual of singing praise songs with your baby to get your hearts set on the right path for the day.

» Ask an older mom to pray for you as you go through this exhausting phase of life.

Day One

Thy word is a lamp to my feet and a light for my path.
—PSALM 119:105

~~~~~~~~~~

*I*t was 6:30 AM and not only was I up, but I'd already downed two cups of coffee and a leftover cream-cheese Danish. Why does Joey insist on getting up at such an ungodly hour?

The funny thing is that I'm a total morning person—or at least I was, before I had a baby. I used to wake up before sunrise, brew a strong pot of coffee and sit on the back patio while the sun came up, reading my Bible and praying. It was a wonderful and peaceful way to start the day.

Now my morning routine was anything but peaceful or prayerful. I was awakened by a screaming, hungry baby who was raring to go and who wasn't going to allow me five minutes to brush my teeth, much less twenty minutes to spend with God. How could I start my day prayerfully when my baby seemed to think 5:00 AM was an acceptable time to get up?

I tried setting my alarm to get up before Joey did, but his wake-up time was unpredictable. I tried praying and reading my Bible at night, but I sometimes fell asleep. I even tried doing a quiet time immediately after I put Joey down for his morning nap. None of these were the perfect, start-my-day-off-with-God-and-a-gorgeous-sunrise solution, but all of them gave me *some* time with the Lord. Which is what I needed to stay sane, and focused, and happy, and to be the mom that Joey needed.

Lord, help me find time—somehow—to read Your Word and pray.
—ERIN MACPHERSON

Day Two

Blessed are the merciful, for they will be shown mercy.
—MATTHEW 5:7

~~~~~~~~~~~~~

Kedar was all smiles after his bath. I pulled his little white T-shirt over his head and snapped it across the bottom. Almost immediately, the snaps began unsnapping. I tugged at the fabric more firmly and re-snapped the onesie. Nope. Didn't work. The tee was too small.

Now wait a minute, I thought to myself. *I just bought these last week!* Could Kedar be going through *another* overnight growth spurt like the one a month ago? I remembered trying to dress him for church one Sunday and he didn't fit half the things in his wardrobe anymore. How did he keep sprouting like a beanstalk?

"I think my breast milk has growth hormones in it or something," I joked with Kenya about the too-small-tee after work. But I noticed he didn't seem amused. Instead, dear hubby had the "oops look" on his face.

Uh-oh. I knew that look. And whatever he was about to say wasn't good. "What?" I asked dryly, narrowing my eyes to slits.

"Well," Kenya responded slowly, "I, uh, kinda forgot to tell you that, um, the whole load from yesterday kinda shrunk in the dryer. I'm sorry."

I paused and then said, "It *kinda* shrunk, huh? Oh, well. Guess we'll just have to get some new stuff." He smiled, knowing I was repeating the words he said to me when I made the same mistake a couple of weeks earlier. I could kinda relate.

Father, help me view the missteps of others the way I want them to view mine . . . through eyes of love and compassion.
—DIANNA HOBBS

Day Three

My comfort in my suffering is this: Your promise preserves my life.
—PSALM 119:50

~~~~~~~~~~~~~

I hung up the phone and looked wistfully at Elizabeth. Andrew called to say he'd submitted his resignation letter at work. Back while I was pregnant we'd agreed that one of us would stay home to raise the baby. I had the bigger salary and the better benefits, so when my maternity leave was up, the plan was that Andrew would quit his job and I'd go back to work. It was logical, practical, sensible. But I didn't want to go.

I didn't want to go back to office politics and three-hour meetings. I wasn't interested in writing brochures and training employees. I wanted to be with my baby. "Oh, you'll get used to it once you're busy in the office," my friends advised. "And babies adapt. Besides, at least your husband's taking care of her, so you won't have to worry!"

I wasn't worried. I was sad. A cry wrenched itself from my heart and wound itself viscerally through my body. How could I leave my sweet Boo?

The first day back at the office I had two meetings, spoke with my boss, and was briefed on the status of projects that began in my absence. I changed my voice-mail message and took my e-mail off of automatic forwarding. It felt familiar, even if it didn't feel right. I called home three times, maybe four.

"We're all right," Andrew reported. "We're doing just fine."

I hung up the phone, and cried.

Jesus, be with me as I do hard things.
—JULIA ATTAWAY

Day Four

. . . Being strengthened with all power according to his glorious might so that you may have great endurance and patience. . . .
—COLOSSIANS 1:11

～～～～～

Every fiber of my being was on edge. The cat got under my feet and I fought the urge to sling her across the room. My husband tried to smile and I accused him of smirking; he disappeared down the hallway. What was happening? It was as if I stood outside myself, watching a nice gentle woman become She-Ra, the Evil One. My daughter's piercing cries echoed in my ears. I'd tried carrying her, rocking her, cooing, giggling, singing and humming. I'd put her down, picked her up, changed her diaper, offered milk, held her close and finally put her into her crib so I could take a few deep breaths and pull myself together.

As I sat on the couch, head buried in my hands, the cat came up and rubbed her body against my leg. I patted her head. "I'm sorry for wanting to throw you, kitty." She purred. I sighed and went to my husband. "I'm sorry, honey. This is not your fault." He smiled. I went to my girl, still crying in her crib. I scooped her up. "I'm sorry, Sam," I said. "Mommy is going to get through this." Just for a moment, she stopped crying and hiccuped at me; then she grinned with tears and slime all over her face.

I smiled.

She started crying.

Here we go again. . . .

Lord, grant me patience.
—ELSA KOK COLOPY

Day Five

Show hospitality to one another without grumbling.
—I PETER 4:9 (ESV)

~~~~~~~~~~~~~~~

I walked into the bathroom and saw a horrendous sight: the bar of soap, drowning in its own dish. Submerged in a pool of water, it was slowly being transformed into a blob of slime.

We all have our pet peeves, and one of mine is slimy soap. I rescued the bar, took a deep breath and tried to convince myself it wasn't a big deal. I was the hostess, after all. As soon as they became grandparents my folks started doing crazy things like flying halfway across the country to see us, even if only for a few days. Now they were visiting for the weekend. I loved having them, and I was trying hard to be hospitable, but in my mind I was grumbling about everything they were doing the "wrong" way. All that inward griping was making me irritable and unkind.

I went into the living room with the best false smile I could muster. Geneva was there, delighting in her Grammy and Poppy. The three of them were laughing and smiling genuine smiles. The contrast between my grumbling heart and the love and joy on my daughter's face told me all I needed to know. Geneva knew what was important in life, and it was time for me to learn a thing or two from her.

Lord, help me to overlook things that are not
important and to value the things that are.
—LISA LADWIG

Day Six

May the Lord answer you when you are in distress; may
the name of the God of Jacob protect you.
—PSALM 20:1

I'd been dreading it for weeks: the day my husband was going out of town. I'd grown used to having Jim's help and feared the thought of going it alone.

I prayed a lot on day one and two and asked God for endurance. The twins were a little fussy, but both days went fairly well. I didn't forget to feed anyone, and I managed to get a few hours of sleep. Day three was more difficult, because both girls came down with colds. They were crabby; I was anxious. I began counting the hours until my husband's return.

That night I put the girls to bed at a decent hour. As I folded laundry, I heard a noise outside the house. What was it? A robber? I sat for what seemed like hours listening for more sounds, letting my mind play what-if games and wondering what to do if someone tried to break in.

I called my friend Noreen. She asked if all the doors were locked. *Yes.* Was the house alarm set? *Yes.* "I want to pray with you," she said. I'd never prayed on the phone before, but I was ready to try anything. Noreen began, "Lord, I ask You to send your loving protection to my friend Donna. . ." She prayed; and I gave my hearty amen. When I hung up I knew God was with me, and I was able to sleep peacefully.

I awoke at six thirty the next morning, again in a panic. But this time it was because my girls had slept eight hours straight—something they'd never done!

Jesus, use my every fear to increase my certainty of how secure I am in You.
—DONNA MAY LYONS

Day Seven

And why do you worry about clothes? See how the lilies
of the field grow. They do not labor or spin.
—MATTHEW 6:28

I slid the white door open and stood still, not wanting to enter. Only a few patches of carpet peered through the maze of fabric on the floor. That's what my wardrobe had become: taunting heaps of cloth.

Deep breath. Grab a shirt. Squirm into it. *Too tight on the belly.* Try a sweater. *No way I can nurse in that.* And so it went.

We were on our way out, precious Zachary in tow. But nothing was precious about the bloated middle that kept me from zipping or snapping anything I owned. I no longer merited maternity tents, but my bosom and belly prevented most other clothes from fitting. My frustration bubbled to a boil.

Whose body is this, anyway? I want the old me back!

Tantrums and tears over clothes felt a little more like a seventh-grade menstrual cycle than motherhood. My watery eyes flitted over a navy-blue work dress. And dress pants. And a sheer blouse that a nursing bra would never have any business inside.

It wasn't just my clothes that didn't fit me. There was a lot of *me* that didn't fit either. My new life was full of ripples and rolls—of the flesh and my identity. Motherhood was shifting *everything*.

I settled on a forgiving top and forgave myself the tears. The new me was going to need more patience. And a shopping trip.

God, I know clothes don't make the woman, but my
body is making me crazy. Help me persevere.
—SUSAN BESZE WALLACE

Day Eight

*Be careful that you do not forget the Lord, who brought
you out of Egypt, out of the land of slavery.*
—DEUTERONOMY 6:12

New-baby days flew by in a blur of chaos and excitement, until one day I realized that Brian and I hadn't been alone in a very long time. Once I mentioned it, Brian wasted no time fixing the problem. He promptly made arrangements for child care and then booked an afternoon off from work so we could go on a date.

Our sitter arrived and we hopped in the car. I tried guessing our destination but couldn't figure it out until Brian pulled up in front of a small coffee shop. "Second Cup Coffee!" I squealed and gave him a hug. We hadn't been back here since our first date, two years earlier.

"You buy the drinks and I'll find us a spot." I commanded, as I scanned the crowded room for an empty table. Eventually I found a small table in the corner. Brian arrived with our treats: coffee for me and hot chocolate with whipped cream for him. "Remember our first date?" I asked as I took my coffee. Brian nodded, with an undeniable twinkle in his eye. "You were late!" I teased.

"And you wouldn't stop talking!" Brian shot back. He tried to grab my hand and whispered, "Kind of like today. . ."

"One of my best qualities!" I teased. It's funny: We live together and spend most of our days under the same roof, but in this undistracted moment, I realized how much I missed him. I guess even the most treasured relationships can slip out of my mind if I don't make an effort to sustain them.

Dear Lord, when I begin to forget You, give me a nudge.
—RUTH BERGEN

Day Nine

An anxious heart weighs a man down, but a kind word cheers him up.
—PROVERBS 12:25

~~~~~~~~~~~~

Solomon was up all night with a fever and the stomach flu. "Call the pediatrician immediately," my book on caring for infants advised.

Immediately is the word that set me in a panic, so I was a little confused when the doctor's office seemed so casual about it.

"Oh, I bet it's just a bug," the receptionist said. "You can make an appointment or wait a day or two."

I took the earliest opening, two hours away. Solomon had gone through three diapers by the time of our appointment. The last one was right as we were about to leave. Thinking the pediatrician might need a sample, I put a dirty diaper in a plastic bag and shoved it in my purse.

Our pediatrician examined Solomon. "What's his dirty diaper look like?" he asked.

"Wait," I said fumbling for my purse. "I have one here."

"One what?" he asked.

"A diaper," I answered.

"Stop!" He held up his hands in the classic freeze pose. "I don't need to see it. You just take that home with you. He's fine, just your average stomach bug."

"Sorry about the diaper," I said feeling my face turn red.

"No worries," he said. "It's not the first time. New-mom love mixed with worry is powerful stuff."

On the way home I kept picturing the doctor raising his hands like it was a hold-up. I laughed and looked back at Solomon. He was fast asleep in his car seat.

Dear God, it feels so good to laugh. Help me worry less and laugh more.
—SABRA CIANCANELLI

Day Ten

You intended to harm me, but God intended it for good
to accomplish what is now being done. . . .
—GENESIS 50:20

~~~~~~~~~~~~~~~

I wondered from the start if Carol disliked me. When we met at church, her arms embraced me, but her eyes pushed me away with suspicion. She later told me, "You know we were checking out who this girl was that Flynn brought around."

Carol was one of Flynn's mom's friends. I totally understood why she wanted to make sure Andrina's only son wasn't dating some floozy. But after Flynn and I were married and I joined their church, Carol still watched me. She wondered about me when I sought equity for the women, questioned whether Flynn and I were experienced enough to colead a married couples' ministry, and thought we were trying to do too much.

What really told me what Carol thought was her reaction when she found out I was heading back to work. She said, "Don't you be leaving that baby with Flynn and Andrina and go do what you want to do. You raise that baby." Didn't she see that Andrina was overjoyed to be a grandma and thrilled to care for Josh? Or that Flynn was a hands-on dad? And that I didn't have a history of abandoning my baby so I could be free to do what I want?

Perhaps Carol thought my sense of righteousness seemed stronger than my motherhood sense, or that my career goals were clearer than my goals for Joshua. Or perhaps she just stereotyped what a working mother with my personality would be like. I don't know why Carol thought I wouldn't be a good mom, but her comments made me continually take inventory about my motherhood priorities. And that was a good thing.

Thank You, Lord, for accomplishing Your will
in me, even through unlikely ways.
—RHONDA J. SMITH

Day Eleven

Evening, morning and noon I cry out in distress, and he hears my voice.
—PSALM 55:17

I pushed the double stroller through the apartment door, ready to collapse. Our playgroup that morning was twenty blocks away, and after chasing my toddler and carrying the baby while there, I had to walk the mile home too. Money was too tight for a cab, and my side-by-side stroller is awkward to maneuver on the subway or bus.

Tyler fell asleep during the walk, and my husband Gary had passed out on the couch. My body twitched with envy, aching for rest. First I had to fix Brandon's lunch, though, and get him ready for a nap. I made a batch of macaroni and cheese and poured it into two bowls—I was starved too. As I opened the fridge to get Brandon some milk, Tyler awoke, demanding a bottle with a frantic scream. My lunch was uneaten, but that didn't matter: I was last on the list.

Tyler had his bottle. Brandon ate and went down for a nap. Gary was still curled in a snuggly ball, snoring lightly. I wanted to wake him to take care of Tyler so I could nap, but I didn't want to get into another debate over who needed more sleep.

My head ached, my macaroni and cheese was cold, and Brandon's cup of milk had spilled on the floor. As I got on my knees to clean up the mess, my self-pity was overwhelming. *What about me? Don't I matter too? Who cares about what I feel and what I need?*

Being on my knees was a good place to ask those questions, because as neglected as I felt in that moment, I already knew the answers.

*Lord, I know You care for me beyond all measure. Help
me use that knowledge to keep self-pity at bay.*
—KAREN VALENTIN

Day Twelve

*When they measure themselves by themselves and compare
themselves with themselves, they are not wise.*
—II CORINTHIANS 10:12

~~~~~~~~~~~~~~

As mothers of little ones do, we sat on the living-room floor with our babies. I held Michelle and looked around, eager to get to know the cheerful women in this weekly moms' group. And then it started.

"Hang a black-and-white mobile over her crib—it will stimulate her brain."

"We listen to Baby Mozart."

"He's already doing baby flashcards, and he's *so* good at it!"

"My son was crawling all over at five months."

"Her baby says twenty-five words, and she's barely one!"

I started to squirm. This kind of conversation made me uncomfortable. So did the parallel track of mothers who chimed in with concerns about whether they'd already hampered their child's future:

"My baby doesn't smile much. Do you think he could be autistic?"

"Maybe I didn't nurse her long enough."

"Perhaps I'm not nurturing enough."

All I could think was, *How can I politely escape?* Waiting for an opportune moment to leave, I reminded myself that Jesus didn't use flashcards or have a black-and-white mobile over his crib, yet He grew in wisdom and stature in the sight of God and man. The Lord says my daughter is fearfully and wonderfully made. He says He knows the plans He has for her and they are good. I'm pretty sure we'll be okay, Baby Mozart or not.

*Lord, help me rest in the knowledge that You hold
my child's future securely in Your hands.*
—SUSAN LABOUNTY

Day Thirteen

I will lie down and sleep in peace, for you alone,
O Lord, make me dwell in safety.

—PSALM 4:8

Lack of sleep can endanger lives. I listened to the news report and let out a laugh. The story was about new attempts to shorten the hours doctors work in their first year of residency. Instead of twenty-four-hour shifts, it was suggested that newbies should only have to work sixteen. I tried to count the hours of sleep I'd had the night before, but I didn't have the mental capacity.

Grace is my third child, but I still struggle with lack of sleep. Everyone else—doctors, pilots and truck drivers—seem to have rules about how long they can work, but there are no regulations on mamas. We can put the keys in the fridge, wash our hands with lotion, forget to shampoo in the shower, and draw a blank on when the baby ate without getting fines or pink slips.

There is compensation, though: We learn to send up countless pillow prayers. *Lord, thank you for this fluffy pillow. Thank You that I'm lying down. Thank You for this break.* And then there's the most important pillow prayer of all:

Lord, please let the baby sleep. Please let the
baby sleep. Please let the baby sleep.

—CAROL HATCHER

Day Fourteen

Love one another deeply, from the heart.
—1 PETER 1:22

~~~~~~~~~~

*I*t wasn't one of our more romantic moments. Billy and I climbed into bed after an exhausting day with Samantha. She'd been crying in fits, and her baby temper had us both undone. I felt I'd been sucked dry by her needs—all I wanted to do was sleep.

Billy reached over to touch me. My thoughts were less than kind. *Is that all you think about? Can't you tell I'm worn out?* I tried to keep my irritation from showing, "Not tonight, honey. I'm tired."

"You said that the last two nights!"

"Well, I've been really tired. This mom thing isn't easy, you know."

"What about the wife thing? I need you too. . . ."

Anger boiled up as a full-blown pity party kicked off in my brain, but before I could really get going, God nudged my heart. I remembered how just that morning I read about the differences in men and women and how men were wired to experience love through physical touch. I turned to my man and softened my tone.

"I'm sorry, Billy. I am very tired tonight, and I do love you. Can we wait until tomorrow? If you get Samantha ready for bed so I can take a warm bath and refresh for a bit, I'll get some candles going and we'll enjoy some time for you and me."

He wrestled with his thoughts, seeming to go through the same process I'd just gone through. Finally, he kissed me. "It's a date."

Lord, pour love through me to my husband. Help us to be creative in finding ways to meet each other's needs.
—ELSA KOK COLOPY

Day Fifteen
A Dad's View

Bear one another's burdens, and so fulfill the law of Christ.
—GALATIANS 6:2 (ESV)

~~~~~~~~~~~~~~~

I can't do it anymore," my wife sighed as she came down the stairs, exhausted from an hour of trying to get Hans to sleep. "I am going to go crazy if something doesn't change." Her face was full of intensity and tears as she stood there staring at me.

I winced, because I felt powerless to fix it. Powerless to speak the right words, powerless to restore her strength and, above all, powerless to make the baby fall asleep quickly and soundly for her. And of course I made the mistake of telling my wife these precise things. I made it about me, when the moment was about her.

With great patience mixed with exasperation, she said, "Honey, I don't want you to fix it. Right now, I just want you to *listen*." I didn't necessarily believe her, but listen I did, for about an hour while she poured out her frustrations.

The baby's voice rose like a siren through the monitor. We looked at each other with tired resignation.

"I'll go," I said.

"Are you sure?" my wife said. "You've got so much work to do."

It was true that I had papers to grade and classes to prepare for, but my wife needed a break. I kissed her on the forehead, went upstairs and rocked Hans for a couple of hours. *Time spent on my wife and my son*, I thought, *is never wasted.*

Lord, help me keep my priorities in order.
—LEROY HUIZENGA

Day Sixteen

*"For my thoughts are not your thoughts, neither are
your ways my ways," declares the Lord.*
—ISAIAH 55:8

~~~~~~~~~~~~~~~

I call home from work every morning. "Hi honey, how's it going?" I ask Andrew.

"We're doing okay," he usually reports.

One morning I add, "How was your walk?"

"Umm, we didn't get out yet. She cried every time I tried to get her dressed."

"What?!" I sputter, "It's nearly lunch time, and she's not even dressed?"

Silence, as we both try to figure out how to handle this. *How hard is it to get a baby dressed?* I wonder. I consider informing my husband that he can let Elizabeth cry if he's quick about putting on her clothes. I consider other, less charitable thoughts. I send up a little prayer to the Holy Spirit for guidance. It occurs to me that Andrew is probably thinking, *She thinks I'm incompetent.*

"It would do you both good to get outside," I venture. "The weather's nice and crisp."

"I'll try again," Andrew sighs. I realize with a start that although getting Elizabeth dressed is not hard for me, it's hard for him. He thinks of taking her out as a chore, not as freedom and fresh air and a mind-broadening break. *My ways are not your ways, says the Lord*—and Andrew's ways aren't always my ways either. It's okay that he's not me; his job is to be Elizabeth's Daddy. He can do things differently.

"I love you," I say into the phone, and mean it. There are things father and daughter are going to have to figure out about each other, without me.

*Lord, I guess if You'd wanted my child to have two parents
just like me, You would have arranged that. Help me let my
husband be the parent You are leading him to be.*
—JULIA ATTAWAY

Day Seventeen

If any of you lacks wisdom, he should ask God, who gives generously to all without finding fault, and it will be given to him.

—JAMES 1:5

A week ago, we thought Henry had a cold. When his temperature registered at 102.9, I took him to the doctor. The pediatrician examined Henry as I tried to fill him in on what had been going on.

"Henry's not eating, he's coughing, he's droopy and he's had a fever," I began.

"Why did you stop breast-feeding?" the doctor replied. "It's really important for his health, you know."

"His muscle tone is too low to nurse, and I pumped for three months," I replied, "I think Henry just isn't acting like himself with this bug. He's having a hard time breathing."

The doctor said, "I knew he'd get sick if you stopped nursing. You ought to get in touch with La Leche League to find out where to buy breast milk."

Was it my sleep-deprived, Mommy-worried brain that was the problem here, or was the doctor not listening? Normally I accepted my pediatrician's opinion as gospel. But Henry was truly sick, and it was clear the doctor hadn't heard my concerns. I glumly packed up my boy to go. Then I stopped, realizing that even if it meant I was being a pushy mom, I *had* to speak up. I repeated, with emphasis, "Henry's not right. I don't think it's a cold. He's *so* lethargic, and with that high fever last night. . ."

The word *fever* finally registered with the doctor. He reexamined Henry. Suddenly he said, "I want you to take him to Children's Memorial right away." We rushed to the car, drove downtown, and in front of my eyes, the ER went into overdrive: Henry's fever was 104, his oxygen saturation was in the sixties, and they rushed to get him on oxygen.

Lord, give me the strength to act on my convictions,
even if others might tell me I'm wrong.

—CHRISTY STURM

Day Eighteen

"These things I command you, that ye love one another."
—JOHN 15:17 (KJV)

I paced the living room, fuming. I'd just started reorganizing my desk and was knee-deep in boxes of papers when Lucy unexpectedly woke from her nap. It was the third time in three days she'd derailed my plans with her unpredictable schedule, and I was getting sick of it.

Ever since I'd become a mother, it seemed hard to get anything done. I set Lucy in her bouncy seat and gave her a bottle, hoping she didn't sense that I was about to explode with frustration.

I huffed over to the day's to-do list on the kitchen counter. *Organize desk, clean out fridge, reply to e-mails*—wait. Something was missing. I'd planned the day but left out an important item: I'd never planned to love. I'd assumed the most important thing to accomplish was the to-do item ranked highest on my list. Then if people got in my way (say, by not taking good naps), I was frustrated and felt like a failure.

The next morning I stood in the kitchen, reviewing the new day's tasks. I pulled a bright red pen from the drawer, and wrote *LOVE* at the top of the page. If that came first, the rest would follow.

Jesus, help me remember what You put first on my to-do list.
—JENNIFER FULWILER

Day Nineteen

Be still, and know that I am God. . . .
—PSALM 46:10

~~~~~~~~~~~~~~~~

"Bye, hon," I mumbled to Jonathan as he kissed my forehead and left for work. Rolling wearily off my bed, I shook out my arms, which were cramped and stiff from encircling Llewelyn as we coslept. I picked up my daughter and shuffled to the changing table. Though exhausted, I gave her a weary smile as I laid her down and replaced her soaked diaper. Quietly I began singing our morning song: "Good morning to you! Good morning, dear Llewelyn. Good morning to you!" I carefully placed Llewelyn in the baby swing. *Please, God, help her sit here for just a few minutes!*

As I entered the kitchen, my heart dropped. Dishes were piled in the sink and overflowed onto the counter. Dirty pots and pans encrusted with sauce and strands of spaghetti sat on the stove, and a bowl of leftover pasta was sitting on the counter. I sighed, suddenly overwhelmed and discouraged.

"Oh, Lord!" I cried, instinctually looking up at the ceiling. I exhaled, closing my eyes for a few seconds to let the disappointment wash over me. *Right now I need a few minutes with God and a cup of coffee*, I thought.

I sat down at the table with my steaming mug. I opened up my journal and stilled my mind by focusing on my senses. I focused on the feeling of warmth from my sweatshirt. I heard the sounds of a descending airplane, chirping birds, and people talking outside on the street. I admired the coziness of our apartment. I tasted the creaminess of my coffee. And I sensed something else too: God's quiet presence.

Thank You, Father, for rare moments of quiet and peace.
—LIZ BISSELL

Day Twenty

For we who live are always being given over to death for Jesus' sake, so that the life of Jesus also may be manifested in our mortal flesh.
—II CORINTHIANS 4:11 (ESV)

A few years back I had a miscarriage. Several eyes pitied my loss—looks being the only thing people knew to give beyond prayer. They had no words to make me all right. The truth is I was more all right than not. My quiet was consumed with loud thoughts of what type of mother I would have been. Being a mother scared me. My loss gave me time to prepare my heart.

When I became pregnant with Joshua, I started with prayer. "Lord, I ask that my child be wise, full of understanding, receptive to the things of You and obedient to those in authority over him." It began as a preparation mantra, became routine and then one day I began to understand why God placed it upon my heart.

Joshua and I were sitting on the couch when he slipped off my lap and tumbled toward the floor. Just in time, I caught him by the arm and scooped him up. I held him close, apologized and then looked to see if he was okay. He turned his head away. "Joshua, look at Mommy," I commanded. I knew he couldn't understand me, so I put my face near his. He turned away. I brought my face around, trying to make eye contact, but he turned away again. My son was avoiding me! As a baby!

Amazed, I said my special prayer again, "Lord, I ask that my child be wise. . . ." This time, though, I said it with an inkling of what it means to turn away from the One who loves you.

Jesus, guide me in knowing how to prepare my son's heart to receive You.
—RHONDA J. SMITH

Day Twenty-One

"You make known to me the path of life; in your presence there is
fullness of joy; at your right hand are pleasures forevermore."
—PSALM 16:11 (ESV)

It was October: sunny and cool—perfect walking weather. We didn't have anything planned, so I lugged out the stroller and took Geneva out to enjoy the beautiful fall colors. Off we went, down the steps of our apartment building, through the parking lot, past the playground and out into the neighborhood. I chose a direction where I knew the sidewalks would be lined with elms and maples, great trees that boast of their glory in autumn.

About a block down, I stopped in disappointment. Many leaves had already fallen, and most hadn't turned even a bit yellow! I saw a few reds and fiery oranges, but the foliage seemed lacking, or at least lackluster. Grumpy, I resumed walking. I get cranky when things (or people) fail to meet my expectations.

As I crunched the stroller over dull, dry leaves, I thought about the things in this world that I look to for joy: crisp, sunny days; a new apartment with space *and* a dishwasher; my friends and family. These are temporal things, earthly gifts God has given for my enjoyment. But oh how easily I look to the objects, rather than the Source, for fulfillment! I expect them to supply for me what only the Lord can provide. It's no wonder I end up disappointed.

God, Help me fix my eyes on You, for in You I will never be disappointed.
—LISA LADWIG

Day Twenty-Two

For he himself is our peace, who has made the two one and
has destroyed the barrier, the dividing wall of hostility.

—EPHESIANS 2:14

I tiptoed into my mother's bedroom, hoping the flash from the camera wouldn't disturb her nap. She rested peacefully on her back with her arms raised over her head. Lying next to her was five-month-old Anna, in the same position. My mother's Bible was open across her chest.

I studied the two of them awhile, thinking about my relationship with Mom. I must have lain beside her like that more than once, but things changed. My adolescent years were marked by glaring eyes and screaming matches. Too many times I shrank from Mom's embrace. I moved fifteen hundred miles north and started my own family, determined that things would be better.

Now the woman I'd striven against for so long was not just my mother but Anna's grandmother. She, too, was starting over. I'd watched her bathe Anna that morning in the kitchen sink, lovingly massaging suds into Anna's scalp, the way she probably used to do to me. She'd held Anna at the breakfast table so I could eat, while her own food grew cold. She'd rocked Anna, singing worship choruses softly in her ear, and read her storybooks of Bible heroes.

Mom cried when it came time for me to go. I cried too. For the first time, I said, "I don't want to leave." She handed Anna over to me—our bonding glue.

At home I posted a photo on my refrigerator: a woman and her grandchild, lying down in full surrender to a God Who uses tiny vessels to pour new life into relationships.

Dear Lord, thank You that it's not too late to love.

—FAITH BOGDAN

Day Twenty-Three

Blessed is the man who finds wisdom, the man who gains understanding.
—PROVERBS 3:13

I'm fortunate to be able to work from home. A few months after my son was born, I decided to take a gig with a parenting Web site. On my first day of work, I had a conference call with my new managing editor and the VP of the entire company. No problem, right?

Wrong. About five minutes into the call, my son started screaming. I frantically covered the microphone on my phone with my thumb and whisked Joey off of the floor and into my lap. Open mouth, insert breast.

I bought myself fourteen minutes of silence. But it was an hour-long call, and just as the VP started talking, Joey finished up his little snack. Cue more hysterical screaming. Cue more frantic attempts to do something—*anything*—to get him to quiet down.

I finally hung up the phone. Joey was grumpy. My boss was irritated. And I was exhausted. How could I manage being a mom and an employee at the same time? Is it even possible? I knew the answer: not for me. I can't focus on my work with a baby playing in my lap. Likewise, I can't give Joey the attention he deserves when I'm trying to listen to a call and check my e-mail. I have to separate the two.

The next time I received word of a conference call, I doled out the cash for a babysitter. Joey didn't make a peep the entire time.

Lord, balance is so hard to find, yet I have no choice. Show me how.
—ERIN MACPHERSON

Day Twenty-Four

*And it is my prayer that your love may abound more
and more, with knowledge and all discernment.*
—PHILIPPIANS 1:9 (ESV)

When Solomon was first born, the nurses swaddled him in a pastel-striped hospital blanket. "Swaddling resembles the womb," the nurse explained as she placed Solomon diagonally on the blanket and tugged one corner beneath him. Solomon's eyes closed. Within minutes he was asleep.

"Voilá!" the nurse exclaimed. "Works like a charm."

Before we left the hospital, my husband I were trained in swaddling.

"It's like making a burrito," my husband said. Days later when Solomon was fussy and tired, I overheard Tony singing a soon-to-be favorite lullaby, "Don't cry for me, I give you burrito!" sung to the tune of "Don't Cry for Me, Argentina."

Solomon doesn't need to be swaddled every night anymore, though at times we reach for a blanket and wrap him snugly. I think about what the nurse said and how swaddling resembles the womb.

I can see how the new experiences of everyday life can be overwhelming for a baby, how it must be a relief to return to familiar comfort. I suppose it's like prayer for me. When the world gets to be too much, I close my eyes and connect with the cocoon of peace I know.

*Dear God, thank You for the comfort You give
and the peace I know in Your arms.*
—SABRA CIANCANELLI

Day Twenty-Five

But to me it is a very small thing that I may be examined by you . . .
I do not even examine myself . . . the one who examines me is the Lord.
—I CORINTHIANS 4:3–4 (NAS)

The sun was shining brightly through the sanctuary windows, hitting me square in the face. But I didn't mind. Shiloh had just fallen asleep in my arms and that meant that—for once—I could stay and listen to the Sunday morning message.

Yeah! I silently cheered as I laid Shiloh in her car seat, which sat on the floor by my feet. Pastor Al began to share, and his words went straight to my heart. The people surrounding me barely moved as we all listened intently.

Ten minutes into his sermon, Al stopped to take a sip of water. A stillness settled over the entire congregation. You could hear a pin drop. Actually, you could hear a lot of things! It was at this moment that Shiloh, who still lay at my feet sleeping, decided to burp. It was not one of those quiet, barely noticeable ones either. In fact, it was so boisterous, so unmistakable, that several people in front of me turned around and stared, giving me a mischievous grin. "Caught you!" their looks seemed to say. People behind me snickered as I wiggled uncomfortably in my seat, trying to motion that the culprit lay sleeping on the floor.

"I didn't do it!" I wanted to shout, but sheepishly shrugged my shoulders instead. I couldn't change what people thought about me. It reminded me of the sage advice my father once gave me, "Ruthie, those who matter, don't mind—and those who mind, don't matter."

Father, guard me from valuing the opinions of others too highly.
—RUTH BERGEN

Day Twenty-Six

We have this hope as an anchor for the soul, firm and secure. . . .
—HEBREWS 6:19

~~~~~~~~~~~~~~~

I imagine her submerged in the cavernous store, crumpled list in hand, finally finding the gray stroller now propped against my wall—an adult scavenger's game amidst cribs and rattles. Had she woken that morning knowing she'd run the errand? Had she plotted out the quickest subway route? Or had she merely muttered her way through the whole thing, annoyed at the time and expense?

I did not know. I had not seen or heard from Kimberly since the day I'd told her I was expecting. I'd asked her to lunch and we'd settled comfortably into our furious, funny words. Kimberly was one of my dearest friends, and after a long exile in other cities, we were finally both in the right one at the same time. She had spent a difficult childhood shuttling between Atlanta, Georgia, and Cape Town, South Africa, with unhappy adolescent stops on the Upper East Side of New York.

She grinned upon hearing my news, clapping her hands and howling, leaning forward to hear me better. Our spirited talk, occasionally in Spanglish, was of baby-shower ribbon hats and "respectable" godmothering. She threatened future tell-all sessions with my little girl and spoke of spiriting her off to impossible adventures.

I had made Kimberly happy, and that thrilled me, for such a thing for her could prove elusive.

But soon after, the familiar pattern of unanswered calls and e-mails emerged, with little sense of return. I thought of my daughter roving about within me, and yet knew she was fastened tighter to me by the day. And I thought of my itinerant friend, still searching for safe harbor, her love an anchor she could not, or would not, release.

Lord, be the anchor of love for me, my friends and my baby.
—DEBRALEE SANTOS

Day Twenty-Seven

"When there were no oceans, I was given birth. . . ."
—PROVERBS 8:24

~~~~~~~~~~~~~~~

I saw the ocean through the plane window, heart thumping with excitement. I'd miscarried our first child while living in Southern California. Now, thanks to Todd's work trip, we were returning with baby Zachary on what felt like a victory tour.

It was a ninety-minute drive to the newspaper that was once my creative playground. I pointed out places I'd reported a story, gone to the beach or dreamed about having a child. Zach slept, mostly, in a whale-themed outfit that matched from hat to socks.

Work memories washed over me as I fed him in the parking lot. In we went. Being escorted up the elevator that was once mine with the flash of a badge seemed weird.

They cheered. Everyone wanted a look. About two minutes in, Zach started to fuss—a rarity. His volume rose, and a fellow mom offered an office. As visitors dropped in and out, we changed him, both tried to feed and burp him, and eventually started to undo one sweaty whale garment at a time. My former co-worker—a vision of patience, optimism and technique—was the only reason *I* wasn't also in tears.

An hour in, I realized I couldn't stay. My options for calming Zach were exhausted. When I turned around in the elevator, no one was watching. The place we'd stood had been swallowed up by a meeting. I was so glad to have once been in that mix. And now glad to be walking away.

In the lobby, Zach instantly cooed. To this day I surmise my son was responding to my racing heart. Because motherhood is one big ocean of uncertainty, I'll never know. But it felt good to be riding the waves.

Lord, Your divine sequence is not always something
I appreciate, but always something I need.
—SUSAN BESZE WALLACE

Day Twenty-Eight

*Then Jesus said, "Come to me, all of you who are weary
and carry heavy burdens, and I will give you rest."*
—MATTHEW 11:28 (NLT)

~~~~~~~~~

My head was on the pillow for only a few seconds when I heard a murmur from the other room. Yes, the baby was waking up. Again. I'd managed to nurse her, rock her, walk her to sleep, gently lay her in the crib, tiptoe backward out of her room, stumble back to my own bed and fall onto the pillow, in just enough time to have her beckon me back. I wanted to *scream*!

Before Gabi arrived, I never thought much about sleep. Now I obsessed over it. I'd had sleepless nights in my life, from little-girl slumber parties to college all-nighters, but those were always of my choosing—and always followed by a day of naps to catch up. These days the naps were too infrequent and unpredictable.

I went back into the baby's room and scooped her out of the crib. She immediately stopped crying. I dropped into the rocking chair a half-step away. She snuggled in. We both closed our eyes as I began to rock us back and forth, back and forth. I sensed rest was near. As I drifted to sleep, I thanked God for this precious life in my arms and for new ways of experiencing His provision, even in the most basic things. Finally, sleep, precious sleep, for both of us.

Lord, let me find rest in You regardless of the hours of sleep last night.
—ALEXANDRA KUYKENDALL

Day Twenty-Nine

"Can a mother forget the baby at her breast and have no compassion on the child she has borne? . . ."
—ISAIAH 49:15

Knock, knock. I didn't answer. "Julia?" called my boss. "You in there?" The doorknob rattled as Tom wondered out loud why my office was locked. I huddled behind my desk, half-covered, with the breast pump humming. I wasn't about to let him know why I was barricaded in. Twice a day I sneaked into my office and closed the door for fifteen minutes to pump rich milk for my Elizabeth. Tom hadn't noticed that an insulated cooler now monopolized an entire corner of the office fridge.

Being a breast-feeding working mother was awkward. I was keenly aware that my bust size changed by the hour. I hoped no one noticed, hoped nothing leaked. Fitting in a pumping break before my cups overflowed was as challenging as trying to relax after a morning of high-stress meetings. I often called Andrew at home, pleading, "I need you to make Elizabeth cry. My milk won't let down!" He'd hold her close to the phone, where she squalled obligingly. Soon we were back in production.

It was nutty. No, *I* was nutty. But every mom needs her obsession, and breast-feeding was mine. Breast milk was my link between home and office, the bit of myself I could leave behind for my daughter. At the end of the day I elbowed my way into a crowded subway, silently willing Andrew to hold off on giving Elizabeth a bottle until I arrived. I raced home, flew up the stairs, and unlocked the apartment door.

And there in our living room were Andrew and Elizabeth, doing their late-afternoon wait-for-Mommy waltz. "Wa-wa-waltzing with bears!" Andrew crooned, sort-of along with the music but horribly off-key. Elizabeth grinned. They danced to pass the time until I arrived full of love, full of milk, and ready to nurse my baby.

Call me crazy, Lord, but I want to give my child every drop of love You've given me to give.
—JULIA ATTAWAY

Day Thirty

A heart at peace gives life to the body, but envy rots the bones.
—PROVERBS 14:30

~~~~~~~~~~~~~~~

I was never much of a designer clothes kind of girl, but that changed when Samantha came on the scene. I didn't care if *I* had the latest fashion, but I found myself longing to dress Samantha in designer duds. I wanted other moms to glance over and think, *Oh my, what an exceptionally beautiful baby! And she's dressed in such an exceedingly gorgeous outfit! I wish my child looked half as good.*

I was ashamed. Where did those feelings come from? And the envy that seemed to wash over me when I saw other babies decked out and darling? Not pretty at all.

I knew I had to do something. I went to God, laid out my immaturity and asked for His help. He graciously planted an idea in my heart. Every time I envied another baby's duds, or any time I felt the urge to cast my own girl as a mini fashion queen, I tried to catch myself and whisper a prayer of gratitude instead. *Thank You, Lord, for that beautiful baby. Thanks for her mom and dad—bless that family!* Or *Thank You for providing just what Samantha needs and for kindly ignoring her mama's excessive wants; You are good!*

Over the coming months I worried less about fashion and more about the baby underneath.

Forgive me, Lord, for my envious heart. Grow me up in You.
—ELSA KOK COLOPY

Fifth Month

~~~~

Father,

Having a child is teaching me again that I am not fully master of my life. Thank You for combining this uncomfortable lesson with such joy! I don't like seeing my weaknesses and failings. Yet I thank You that they are being brought to light, for now it's clearer what I need to work on to become a better mom, a better person, a better Christian.

Lord, I acknowledge my shortcomings, most especially [FILL IN BLANK], and I ask You for the grace to help me overcome them.

In Christ, amen.

Tips

» You don't have to answer every time the phone rings, and you don't have to reply to e-mails and texts as soon as they come in. Turn off the sound on your electronic devices, and you'll feel less frazzled.

» Libraries and bookstores are great places to meet other moms. Plus you'll get in the habit of reading to your baby.

» You're more likely to take time for yourself if you make it easy! Keep a box handy, where you'll see it, and fill it with things you like to do (scrapbooking, magazines, manicure supplies). Then use it when your baby naps.

To everything there is a season. . . .
—ECCLESIASTES 3:1 (KJV)

I shoved Anna's car seat into the booth of a dimly lit corner of the restaurant and plopped down beside it. Dave and I made menu selections, and soon our plates arrived under a snowfall of grated cheese. For the next three minutes, two lovers and a sleeping baby dined peacefully, serenaded by the sweet strains of Tuscany.

"This is the best night ever!" I declared between bites of garlic bread. Anna awoke with a cry of protest. I shushed her and rocked the car seat. She continued to fuss and I peeled her five-month-old frame from its resting place. I attempted to attach her to my breast, but space was tight. Dave and I exchanged knowing looks: This was our last dinner out. He took Anna for a pacing session in the lobby while I inhaled one more bite of pasta. We scuttled past patrons with staring problems and slammed ourselves into the car.

Anna fell back asleep to the hum of the motor as we rode home in silence. A soft spring rain greeted us in the driveway and we sat motionless in it. Dave playfully fingered my trademark "poochy lip," evidence of things not going my way. I was certain we would never darken the door of a restaurant again, that we were forever banished to our kitchen table and dirty dishes.

"It's just a season," Dave promised.

His words proved true. Eventually Anna was weaned and left with a babysitter.

I still have a recurring poochy lip. Life's wintery times bring it on. But I can always smile when I remember that another spring is coming.

Lord, please help me see life in seasons. Amen.
—FAITH BOGDAN

Day Two

He put a new song in my mouth, a hymn of praise to our God. . . .
—PSALM 40:3

~~~~~~~~~~~~~

On a sunny afternoon in August I rushed to get my notepad, pen and recorder before I forgot the beautiful melody and lyrics floating around in my head. I sat down on the hardwood floor in my bedroom quickly scratching words onto the yellow sheet of paper. It felt so good to write a new song.

"Sweet is your presence," I sang softly into the speaker, peering at the red light shining above the word *record*. The worship song came to me during prayer time while Kedar was down for his nap. I was so spiritually uplifted in that moment. "Sweet—" I was interrupted by the phone ringing.

Oh no! I dashed to pick up the receiver, hoping the noise hadn't disturbed the baby. *Sigh.* It was an automated message from a telemarketer congratulating me on winning a trip to Disney World.

Directly after that, I received another call. This one sounded something like "Ma-ma," and it came from a little one abruptly awakened. I lifted Kedar from his crib, sat down on the sofa and gently swayed from side to side. "Sweet is your presence. . . ," I sang the small portion of the song I remembered, and it ended up being the perfect lullaby to get my baby back to sleep.

God, I thank you for wonderful songs of praise
that uplift Your name—and my spirits.
—DIANNA HOBBS

Day Three

"As the Father has loved me, so have I loved you. Now remain in my love."
—JOHN 15:9

~~~~~~~~~~~~~~~

Solomon's eyes are emerald green with sparkling flecks of amber, and they follow me wherever I go. Yesterday as he was on his belly on his blanket, I took a spot in my reading chair. He looked up from his toy giraffe and couldn't find me. Darting his head from side to side, he let out a defeated whimper and collapsed on the blanket.

"I'm here," I said coming to calm him. He popped his head up, following the sound of my voice. Our eyes met. His face returned to glee.

"Right here," I said picking him up. I whispered in his ear, "I'm here. I'm here, always here."

I held him in my arms and we danced around the room to the pop song on the radio. We walked to the kitchen and I pointed out the window at the robins eating from the feeder.

"See the birds," I said. His eyes followed my finger and then he looked up at me and smiled.

I hold on to these days as Solomon learns I'll always be there for him. I'll be there whether he's in my arms or in school, when I'm out of sight or right beside him and years from now, wherever his path may take him.

Dear God, thank You for this great love, and for knowing
I am Your child and You are here with me.
—SABRA CIANCANELLI

Day Four

"Therefore what God has joined together, let man not separate."
—MARK 10:9

~~~~~~~~~~~~

Alan insisted I take a bubble bath while he took care of the kids. "You need some time for yourself," he told me. Truer words were never spoken. After soaking for a while, I wrapped myself in a soft robe and headed downstairs to join the family.

Alan was stretched the length of the couch, one long leg hanging off the side, and on his chest, curled in a tiny ball of sweetness, was Grace. Both were sound asleep.

I'm not sure what it is about daddies and sleeping babies, but it stirs something deep within me. I stood on the stairs and watched while they breathed in synchronization.

I stared at Alan's dark lashes and thought of vows so long ago shared. *For better or for worse, for richer or for poorer . . .* I never dreamed in eleventh grade trigonometry that the tall, soft-spoken young man who sat beside me would become my love for life. But it was Alan who held my hand and caught my tears. This man shared every laugh and encouraged every dream. It was even this man who suggested I take a plunge in the tub to find myself again.

To love and to cherish, as long as we both shall live . . . . Grace stirred ever so slightly on Alan's chest, and he unconsciously tightened his grasp. *Do you, Carol, take this man?*

Oh, Alan, I still do.

Thank You, God, for the gift of this man who holds my heart.
—CAROL HATCHER

Day Five

*When I applied my mind to know wisdom and to observe
man's labor on earth—his eyes not seeing sleep day or
night—then I saw all that God has done. . . .*
—ECCLESIASTES 8:16–17

So," I passed my friend Mandy a cup of fresh coffee and nodded toward her daughter, asleep in her arms. "How's she sleeping at night?"

Our babies were born only weeks apart, and I expected to hear a tale similar to my own. I nearly spit out my coffee when Mandy responded, "It's going great!"

Fighting jealousy, I set my cup on the table and looked her in the eye. "Okay," I demanded, "Tell me everything!"

Mandy laughed and reached for her bag, ready for my question, "It was easy! Just read this book and follow the steps." She passed me a thin book. I recognized the author but hadn't read any of his titles.

After Mandy and her daughter left, I put Shiloh down for her nap and pored over every page of the book. I read, memorized and mentally underlined every method and suggestion. When Shiloh awoke, she would have a new mama. Finally, our ticket to better sleep!

The next days were frustrating as I tried to implement the author's suggestions. After a couple of weeks, I finally threw in the towel. "This isn't working!" I moaned to Brian after a particularly chaotic day.

The next time I saw Mandy, I returned her book. "She's sleeping better now?" Mandy asked expectantly.

"Nope!" I answered with a laugh. My friend looked confused. "But I learned something that is more important than sleep." I couldn't believe I was saying that—what could be more important to a first-year mother? "What works for one mom may not work for another. No matter what the best-selling authors say."

God, help me to be me, not someone else.
—RUTH BERGEN

Day Six

*The clouds pour down their moisture and
abundant showers fall on mankind. . . .*
—JOB 36:28

~~~~~~~~~~~~~~

The clouds were low in the sky over Denver, promising to cover the sun for the day. Only one word described this weather: perfect! For this Pacific Northwest native, days like this felt like a quick transport home. They were rare in my sunny new home state.

The only thing that would make this day better is a cup of coffee, I thought. I looked at the coffeepot on my kitchen counter with a tinge of displeasure. It had already supplied two cups, but that was part of the ordinary routine. Today called for something a little extraordinary, something fresh-brewed from a coffee shop. I imagined the cool, misty air outside and the warmth of my hand wrapped around a cup, the heavenly aroma and rich taste of java.

Since Derek and I downsized from two incomes to one, trips to the coffee shop have been cut back to match our shrunken budget. Even the smallest purchases add up, so we make each one with calculated forethought. Could I spare a few dollars?

I reached for my purse and counted out the coins. A brisk walk with the stroller would be the perfect preparation for that special cup with my name on it. I could consider the weather a gift that God ordered especially for me, and the coffee a splurge to celebrate the ways God pours out His love.

*Lord, thanks for Your love poured out for me in things
as simple as a tall coffee with cream, no sugar.*
—ALEXANDRA KUYKENDALL

Day Seven

She dresses herself with strength and makes her arms strong.
—PROVERBS 31:17 (ESV)

My aunt made a trip to see her first great-nephew and came bearing a gift bag full of books.

It was a refreshing offering amid the sea of onesies I'd been given. There were board books, a sing-song tome, stories both classic and unique. My aunt raised three sons with loving focus and creativity, and her gift made an impression.

As soon as his little neck was strong enough to stay atop his body without flopping, I began to read to Zach. It felt silly at first. I knew he had no idea what I was talking about. But I spoke as if he did.

I sang from the songbook night after night. I could soon recite "Time for Bed" from memory. I loved bedtime. Sometimes that was because it meant my mothering day would soon end. But usually I felt a delicious closeness in that denim glider with a bath-fresh child in my lap and a book in my hands. A calm fell over both of us that balanced the stresses of fussy times, illness and endless uncertainties of new parenting.

Reading time was one of the few times I knew I was doing this mommy thing right. I'd digested the statistics on how important reading was. But more importantly, I knew Zach felt loved by our ritual.

Some days, I had to dig deep to muster the energy and enthusiasm it took to animate my voice. But the digging always revealed a treasure. Zach's fingers started to point. His voice started to mimic mine. And his passion for books and a little cuddle time has yet to wane.

God, grant me the patience and energy to do the right things right.
—SUSAN BESZE WALLACE

Day Eight

Be at rest once more, O my soul, for the Lord has been good to you.
—PSALM 116:7

~~~~~~~~~~~~~~~~

I laid my head down on the pillow and closed my eyes. It seemed like only seconds later the phone rang. My eyes sprang open; I cleared my throat and answered the phone. "Hello?" I tried to sound chipper.

"Oh, sorry," the caller, an acquaintance, said, "Did I interrupt a nap?"

Busted! A wave of guilt flooded my heart. "A nap? Oh no. Not me. I wasn't napping. I was just, uh. . . ." I glanced toward the bathroom. "I was just scrubbing the toilet. Yeah. Been doing housework all day."

"Oh, good for you."

"Yup, I'm a housework doer. All day, every day."

I got off the phone and glanced at the ceiling. *Lord, what was that about? I totally lied though my teeth! Please forgive me. . . .*

I felt that God whispered grace to my heart, *Elsa, you're finding your value in what you do in a day. Your value is in my love for you. Rest in me.*

I grabbed my concordance and looked up Bible verses that had to do with God's love and his commands to rest. They were everywhere, calling me to work hard and be diligent, but also to rest well. I knew that taking a nap while my baby napped made me a much better wife and mom—and that could only be a good thing.

> *Lord, when I can find a moment for a refreshing rest,*
> *help me to choose gratitude over guilt.*
> —ELSA KOK COLOPY

Day Nine

And God saw that it was good.

—GENESIS 1:12

~~~~~~~~~~~

"This is a green pepper." I held up the vegetable so Elizabeth could see it from the baby backpack. "And this is an eggplant." I glanced over my shoulder to see my five-month-old looking carefully at the produce. Other people were looking, too, but they seemed to think I was a bit nuts. I wondered momentarily if fruits and vegetables were too advanced for a baby, but Elizabeth seemed interested. "No, I don't buy eggplant often. I only know one way to cook it," I commented. Some day in the distant future Elizabeth would chatter with me while we shopped for groceries. For now I held both parts of the conversation.

Down past meats, up through pasta, and into cereal. Navigating the narrow paths of our eight-aisle city supermarket was easier with Elizabeth in the backpack. She liked being up in the crowd, where she could see. Her cheeks were less likely to be the pinching victims of aggressively enthusiastic old ladies. "Pretty soon you'll be able to eat rice cereal," I told my daughter. "I'm not sure if you'll like it or not. Sounds pretty bland to me." I put a box of grown-up cereal in my cart.

While we waited in line at the check-out, I explained to Elizabeth about tabloids. "The aliens and wolf boy are probably fakes. I don't want to think about giving birth to a sixty-five-pound baby, so I'm not going to buy that paper. When you're grown up you can decide if you want to spend money on things like that," I told her. "But you don't have to worry about it for the next eighteen years or so."

Elizabeth adjusted her weight in the backpack, as if she were considering her options. We paid for our groceries and walked home.

Jesus, green peppers and cereal are good. So is life with my baby.

—JULIA ATTAWAY

Day Ten

Jesus answered: "Don't you know me, Philip, even after
I have been among you such a long time?"

—JOHN 14:9

⁓⁓⁓⁓⁓⁓

Bobbi was the third of five children, precocious yet somewhat withdrawn, when she began to hang out at my house. She and I didn't spend much time with each other when she came over; when Bobbi wanted to talk, she usually spoke with Flynn. He was a father figure to this young girl whose dad had died by the time she was born and whose mom had remarried and was now divorced.

Bobbi said our house was comfortable, a haven from mother-daughter conflict. But I wasn't comfortable feeling like an outsider in my own home. I wanted Bobbi to talk to me like she did to my husband, and to see me as another mother. I tried, and waited, but two years passed and we still barely spoke.

Then I needed Bobbi, because I needed a babysitter. I was going to teach an eight-week workshop on fasting in my home, and the time conflicted with Flynn's weekly workout night. I was nervous about having her care for my baby. She was nervous too. We decided she would keep Joshua in my bedroom while I taught in the living room.

At the end of the first session, Bobbi talked to me a bit about the baby. She opened up a bit more as the workshop went on. Then right before the last meeting, she asked about something she'd overheard that I was teaching. From then on, Bobbi began to talk more freely. Building trust took us a while, but today she calls me her godmother, a position I am deeply honored to have.

Give me patience, Lord, with uncomfortable relationships, and help me see
that You have put people in my life so I can share Your love with them.

—RHONDA J. SMITH

Day Eleven

A cord of three strands is not quickly broken.
—ECCLESIASTES 4:12

~~~~~~~~~~~~~~~

The buzzing of an incoming text message pulled me away from a titillating game of peekaboo. The message was from my husband.

"It's date night. Your mom is babysitting. Be ready at six!"

I should've been excited. After all, I'd hardly left the house since Joey was born. My days had been spent breast-feeding, burping and playing make-the-baby-smile. I was house-bored and lonely. Yet the idea of leaving my baby home—even with my mother—was absolutely terrifying.

I immediately called Cameron. "Sorry! Tonight's not going to work. I don't have a bottle pumped and. . ." I quickly racked my brain for more excuses.

But my husband wouldn't take no for an answer.

So I went begrudgingly, silently fuming that my husband had the audacity to pull me away from my still-newborn son.

It wasn't until my Cameron grabbed my hand and whispered "I've missed you!" that I started to thaw. He wasn't trying to pull me away from my son, but to pull me closer to him. He didn't want our relationship to get put on the back burner just because we had a baby.

As the waiter brought our bread, I winked at Cameron. We chatted about his job and the new book I was reading. We giggled. We held hands over the table. For a few hours I was no longer an exhausted, spit-up-covered new mom, but once again a much-in-love wife—with the high heels and not-so-little black dress to prove it.

Lord, help me invest time and energy to build a strong, godly marriage.
—ERIN MACPHERSON

Day Twelve

There is neither Jew nor Greek, slave nor free, male nor female, for you are all one in Christ Jesus.
—GALATIANS 3:28

When I was a child, I always knew we were close to my grandparents' house when we entered the foothills of San Jose. Right before their house comes into sight, the road makes a dramatic dip and a precariously sharp right turn up the hill. Then to the immediate right lies the stately Japanese house built by my grandfather.

Memories swarmed back as I entered the living room, glanced at family photos on the wall and took in the sights, sounds and smells that signified that I was home.

"She looks exactly like Jonathan!" Auntie Susan proclaimed, taking one look at Llewelyn, "Now *how* do you pronounce her name? Is it Lou-Ellen?"

"No, it's Laa-wellen. It's Welsh, a family name from Jonathan's side."

My grandma, called *Bachan* (Japanese for grandma) by her other great-grandchildren, was sitting across the room, waiting for us. I was proud to introduce her to her new great-granddaughter. "Grandma, this is Llewelyn."

"Hi Ra . . . re . . . ren," she said quietly, smiling gently at the baby. She tried saying her name several times, fumbling over all the *L*'s.

"It's okay. You can call her by her Japanese name, Ai," I suggested.

Bachan smiled. At that moment, it didn't matter that my grandma couldn't say Llewelyn's name or that my daughter looked more like my Caucasian husband. She was part of our family and thoroughly welcome in this home.

Jesus, through You we are made one. Thank You for uniting my family in love.
—LIZ BISSELL

Day Thirteen

For God, who said, "Let light shine out of darkness," made
his light shine in our hearts to give us the light of the
knowledge of the glory of God in the face of Christ.
—II CORINTHIANS 4:6

Glasses clinked over the sound of light jazz. A waiter held a silver tray of crab-stuffed mushrooms in front of me. I took one and skulked off to a corner.

This was the first business event I'd attended since I'd left the career world a year earlier. My husband talked to vice presidents and corporate directors about stocks and mergers and IPO's, but I remained quiet. As I listened to their banter, one thought filled my mind: *I have nothing to offer.*

I'd fallen centuries behind on business trends and industry news. The only things I could think of to talk about were when to introduce solids and which baby wipes are best for sensitive skin. Anyone here would be terribly bored conversing with me.

Just as I'd resigned myself to spending the evening as a living statue, it occurred to me that though I might not be able to drop jargon like I once had, I did have something to offer: the love of Jesus. I looked around and no longer saw executives but souls precious to God, in need of a good dose of His limitless love. If I allowed God's love to pour out through me, I'd go from having nothing to offer to having everything to offer.

I walked up to a previously intimidating pinstriped suit and introduced myself. "Hi, I'm Jennifer. Where do you work?" I began. Because the love of God can't shine through if we don't start somewhere.

Lord, may I always focus less on impressing others
than on letting You love them, through me.
—JENNIFER FULWILER

Day Fourteen

Brothers, choose seven men from among you who are known to be full of the Spirit and wisdom. We will turn this responsibility over to them.
—ACTS 6:3

The pastor selected us to welcome the first-time visitors attending our Sunday morning worship service. That meant Kenya and I had to mount the pulpit, read the names out loud (we hoped without butchering any), and try to get through a prepared script while displaying warmth and personality. I had no idea we were the "chosen ones" until after we arrived at church. I'd snagged my stockings on the way to service, and my panty hose had a huge run. Nice.

I also didn't know who was going to hold Kedar while I fulfilled my duties. Because our church doesn't have a nursery, babies stay with their moms until a trusted caretaker is selected. I was in a frenzy until Kenya mentioned Dominique, a teenager I'd grown quite fond of. She was sweet, responsible, committed to God and a lover of children. When I requested her help, she smiled, showing off her silver braces. "Sure, I'll keep Dar-Dar!" she replied eagerly. She'd been gunning for the job since before Kedar left my womb. With slight hesitation, I handed him off, carefully observing his reaction.

"Hi!" Dominique greeted Kedar in a playful voice. I had never seen him grin so widely for anyone but me.

"You've got the job," I said, relieved. I walked away wishing she had an extra pair of panty hose too. But I'll take what I can get.

Precious Lord, grant me wisdom to choose the right people to fill the roles in my child's life that I can't fill on my own.
—DIANNA HOBBS

Day Fifteen

*Be very careful, then, how you live . . . making
the most of every opportunity. . . .*
—EPHESIANS 5:15–16

~~~~~~~~~~~~~~~~

My creative energies screamed for an outlet at the end of a monotonous day. An array of stickers, die-cuts and photos were spread before me. I wound the baby swing tight enough to click-clack Anna to sleep and dove into a coveted evening of scrapbooking.

No sooner was the first picture mounted than Anna made a fuss. I sniffed her diaper and smeared a dab of teething ointment on her gums. A blissful moment of silence returned. I sat down, turning a cautious eye toward my baby. She grimaced and let out a disheartening whimper. I gave the already-in-motion swing a frustrated push and went into a photo-cropping frenzy.

Anna wailed. I slammed the scissors down and shut the photo album. Lifting my daughter from the swing, I dimmed the lights and slow-danced to Kenny G. Within minutes Anna molded to my body; she was asleep.

I kept dancing. In the kitchen window I caught our reflection: a rosy-cheeked baby nestled happily against her mother's shoulder. I gazed at the scene. She was beautiful—round and plump, with creases in her chubby arms and a tiny fist resting in midair. I kissed her salty-sweet-smelling head, closed my eyes, and swayed until only the hum of the dryer was heard.

*Dear Lord, no scrapbook will ever produce as precious a
memory as the ones You give me to hold in my heart.*
—FAITH BOGDAN

Day Sixteen

We all stumble in many ways. . . .
—JAMES 3:2

. . . .

Can you please pick up Shiloh?" I bellowed from the bathroom. She was crying, Brian was eating, and I had to brush my hair before leaving for church. I needed five quiet minutes to pull myself together before we left; was that asking too much? Apparently.

As I washed my hands, I heard a shout from the kitchen. "Are you guys okay?" I yelled.

"We're fine," Brian groaned. "Shiloh just dumped my cereal all over the floor. What do I use to clean it up?"

We are a family of three; why does a simple trip across town have to be so complicated? I was musing over this as I walked through the doors to church and bumped into Carrie. She gave me a smile and a hug, and I watched as she walked into the sanctuary with her four little children following her. Carrie is a single mom, and her ability to be at every church function, on time, fully dressed, with a smile, always astounds me. But more than her appearance is the measure of grace that I sense coming from her.

"How do you do it?" I asked Carrie one day over coffee.

"Do what?" she laughed as she leaned back on my couch.

"Do life! Get to church on time, alone, with four children?"

Carrie thought about it for a moment. "Sometimes I don't do that as well as you think," she admitted. Then she looked me in the eye and added, "But I do what I can, and let the other pieces fall to the ground."

"Let the other pieces fall to the ground," I echoed, in wonder. "You're an inspiration."

Father, may I please have lessons in graciously letting the things I can't do fall to the ground?
—RUTH BERGEN

Day Seventeen

Oh, how I love your law! I meditate on it all day long.
—PSALM 119:97

~~~~~~~~~~~~~~

I can't read the Bible anymore!" I blubbered to my dad over the phone. I was venting my frustrations over losing my morning quiet time since becoming a mom. I missed snuggling in the green easy chair next to the east window, sipping tea, warmed by the sunrise and God's precious Word.

My days now began, typically, at ten o'clock, after a restless night of nursing and changing diapers. Feeding my rumbling stomach in late morning and tending to a baby took priority over nurturing my hungry soul. I felt the imbalance and was miserable. Seeing no solution, I convinced myself that sainthood would have to be put on hold until motherhood was over.

Dad disagreed. "Since when is there a right way to do devotions?" he asked. "Why not listen to the Scriptures on CD while you're doing mindless work?"

I refrained from telling him that all my work was mindless. I ordered the Bible on CD and listened to it while mopping the floor, with Anna strapped to my torso. With a click of the remote, I could hear verses over and over until I'd memorized them. I placed a pocket New Testament in each bathroom to maximize those precious five minutes alone. I discovered a new prayer closet: the shower. I grew spiritually, even without my morning devotions.

Father, forgive me for limiting You to the confines of my own traditions.
—FAITH BOGDAN

Day Eighteen

She is clothed with strength and dignity; she can laugh at the days to come.
—PROVERBS 31:25

~~~~~~~~~~~~~~~~~

We had our first babies five days apart and lived within the long toss of a baseball. We are the same age. And we are both named Susan.

How perfect. Except perfect is something I am not.

I was usually put-together as a new mom, though I learned something new every day of Zach's life. But when I was with Susan, I always ended up feeling like a mess. We'd meet for lunch, and I'd forget a bib. We'd walk the dogs, and my mutt would nearly tip over the strollers while trying to chase a cyclist. My Zach was a cheery baby, but he saved his fits for when we got together with Susan.

Everything about Susan was immaculate, her home stunningly organized, her parties an orchestrated symphony of fun. I'd rather do anything than clean. How does one have a spotless jogging stroller for years, anyway?

Susan and her orderly ways taught me to give myself grace. I chose to take Zach's dirt and drool as hallmarks of a much-loved life. God asked me to live my life, not hers. She was a good mom, and so was I.

God, thank You for moms who do it differently than I do.
I want to learn from them, not be threatened.
—SUSAN BESZE WALLACE

Day Nineteen

Great are the works of the Lord; they are
pondered by all who delight in them.
—PSALM 111:2

~~~~~~~~~~~

Supper was winding up when I heard the familiar sound of baby gas against cloth diaper. I smiled graciously at our guests—two of Andrew's friends—and excused myself. The meal had gone surprisingly well, and I was pleased at my first foray into the world of entertaining with a baby in the house. A quick diaper change, a wash of hands, and dessert would be on the table.

Elizabeth looked content as I reached down to take her out of her chair. I swung her up and around; then I saw the look of horror on Ron's face.

"What's *that?*" he asked. "That, uh, orange stuff on her back."

How do you explain the concept of nuclear poop to a forty-five-year-old bachelor? I held Elizabeth away from Ron at arm's length, as if distance would halt the goo oozing out the neck of her jammies. Smiling valiantly, I mentally readjusted our dessert time. This was far more than a five-wipe diaper.

I gingerly unsnapped Elizabeth's jammies, marveling anew at how physical the beginning of life is. "Being a mom is a funny thing," I told my daughter. "I've spent more time thinking about the workings of the human body in the past six months than in the past two decades." Elizabeth seemed unimpressed. Her body was merely her body to her; she didn't marvel at its workings any more than I marveled at mine. She pooped when she pooped, and burped when she burped, and I daresay the most interesting thing about it was the reaction of the grown-ups. But to me it was downright awesome.

Lord, could You teach me to live in this state of wonder all the time?
—JULIA ATTAWAY

Day Twenty

So we fix our eyes not on what is seen, but on what is unseen. For what is seen is temporary, but what is unseen is eternal.
—II CORINTHIANS 4:18

I picked up the toys, wiped down the high chair, washed the dishes, washed two loads of clothes, and de-cluttered the kitchen counters. I took a shower and got myself ready. I fed the baby and dressed her. I made mental lists of my accomplishments for the day. That helps me feel productive, even when the list includes the simple tasks of showering and eating.

I'd plopped myself down on the couch to snatch just a minute's rest when the realization hit me: Nothing I have completed today will stay that way. Each thing will be undone and I'll have to do it again tomorrow. I have not created a beautiful painting nor chiseled an exquisite sculpture. I haven't sewn the newest fashion or produced anything lasting.

I wanted to throw my hands up and shout, "Does everything I do come undone? Can't I do anything that lasts?" After some reflection, I decided that wasn't the problem. I'm helping to build a human being here, not things. The tools of my trade are my hands and heart. My job is to paint dreams, build confidence and direct a little one's soul. This masterpiece I'm working on is in a different league than creating sculptures and skirts. A better one.

Thank You, Lord, for allowing me the privilege of being a mother.
—CAROL HATCHER

Day Twenty-One

A fool gives full vent to his anger, but a wise man keeps himself under control.
—PROVERBS 29:11

~~~~~~~~~~~~

It was 5:36 and Cameron still wasn't home. I fired off another text message asking where he was and then slammed the phone down. Didn't he know I needed him to watch Joey so I could get supper on the table?

When my husband finally walked in the door at 5:49—nineteen whole minutes late—I was fuming. I thrust the baby into his arms without a word and turned my attention to the kitchen. I flung hamburger into the pan. Cameron had no idea how hard it was to be at home all day with a baby!

By the time the tacos were ready, I was so angry I couldn't eat. I slid Cameron's plate across the table and stormed out of the kitchen.

In the bedroom, when I finished sobbing, I wondered why I'd I lost my cool so quickly. Yes, my husband was late, but that was no reason to ruin the evening. I hadn't even stopped to ask why he'd been delayed. Perhaps the unreasonable person in this little drama wasn't him, but me. My exhaustion from dealing with a fussy four-month-old and the loneliness of long days alone at home had sure seemed enough to justify my anger. But really, it wasn't.

I sulked back into the kitchen, grabbed some cold tacos and sat down by my spouse.

"I'm sorry!" I muttered, and took a bite. That was really all I could say. Fortunately, it's all I needed to.

Lord, help me keep my cool even when I'm exhausted, alone and overwhelmed.
—ERIN MACPHERSON

Day Twenty-Two

And we, who with unveiled faces all reflect the Lord's
glory, are being transformed into his likeness. . . .
—II CORINTHIANS 3:18

No pun intended, but vomit makes me sick.

I don't like the sight of it, don't like the smell of it or even the sound of it.

All my life I did all I could to avoid throw-up. I even tried to avoid my own by squeezing my eyes shut and spraying air freshener midgag.

As a new mom, I was worried how I would handle it when Samantha was sick. I asked God to give me his grace and compassion so I wouldn't run screaming out of the room.

Samantha's first bodily fluid disbursements were simple enough: a little spit-up here and there after she ate. It wasn't easy, but I could handle it.

A few months in, she had her first bad stomach bug—it took me to a whole new level of mommyhood. What amazed me was my newfound ability not only to put up with it but to actually become my girl's personal throw-up catcher. See, Samantha didn't get sick in convenient places. And I, in all my mom glory, learned the two-handed catch, the one-handed scoop, the dash in a flash (to the bathroom), and even the tender "Ah, poor baby" as she doused me with partially digested baby formula.

Some people say love is all about sweet smiles and shared moments of unhindered joy. I say love is sacrificial. It's laying a cool towel on a fevered head, holding a crying baby in exhausted hands and perfecting the two-handed vomit catch—all while making reassuring mommy sounds.

Thank You, God, for making me more than I am.
—ELSA KOK COLOPY

Day Twenty-Three

A Dad's View

Be completely humble and gentle; be patient, bearing with one another in love.
—EPHESIANS 4:2

K ari shut the nursery door behind her after yet another hour of cuddling Hans to sleep. "I can't believe this child. It's so hard to keep him asleep!" she said, more baffled than frustrated.

I froze, as was my custom when Kari said things like that, and pondered my avenue of escape. Through the window? The hedge would break my fall . . . Run right past her? That might be rude, but it'd spare the glass. . .

"Leroy, what are you thinking?" My least favorite question pulled me back to the present, as I regretted not having crashed through the windowpanes.

"Well . . . ," I stammered. "I'm very sorry it's proven so challenging for you." *What am I, for goodness' sake, a guidance counselor?* Not that there's anything wrong with that, but. . .

In return I got The Look, which meant it was time for take two. "Kari," I said, "I'm sorry I don't always know what to say. I wish I could simply wave a wand and make things work like we want them to." I continued, "And I know how much time you spend nursing Hans and getting him to sleep. It's hard, but he needs it—and I appreciate what good care you take of him." *Did that do the trick? I did mean it.*

"I'm sorry, I don't mean to put you on the spot," Kari said. "I don't mean to complain. I just need someone to listen." We slipped downstairs to the kitchen, where I prepared a pot of tea. *Thank You, Lord*, I thought, *for giving me such a patient wife.*

Lord, give us patience with each other as we raise our child.
—LEROY HUIZENGA

Day Twenty-Four

*The Lord is with you when you are with him. If you
seek him, he will be found by you. . . .*
—II CHRONICLES 15:2

M y morning quiet time for Bible-reading, prayer and journaling had always been important to me, but Michelle's erratic sleeping schedule made solitude elusive. I no longer rose with the sun but dragged myself from bed when she cried. Daytime hours were busy with no roomy spaces of quiet, and I soon felt the lack.

My spiritual life became erratic. The Lord seemed distant. Frustrated, I searched for space to continue my long, focused quiet times and was struck by the obvious: This was the mothering season of my life, and I would need to adjust. The main thing wasn't the length and silence of my devotional time— it was to simply meet God.

I remembered Susannah Wesley, who, with nineteen children, threw an apron over her head to find solitude. And Catherine of Siena, who, when quiet solitude was impossible would "make a little cell in her heart" to meet the Lord. And Brother Lawrence, who turned everything he did into prayer and an offering to God.

So I began to cultivate a mobile prayer life and discovered something else: The mundane nature of housework is its gift. Much of the work can be done almost automatically, and while my hands were busy, my heart could fly heavenward. Suddenly I found endless opportunities for prayer: while nursing Michelle, washing dishes, folding laundry, taking a walk. I breathed requests for strength or guidance. I thanked God for gifts of beauty and sweetness. I lifted loved ones up in intercession. The nitty-gritty life provided a grand opportunity to pray without ceasing, as I learned to quiet my heart and seek God in the midst of things.

*Thank You, God, for offering me an inner solitude that
is not dependent on outer circumstances.*
—SUSAN LABOUNTY

Day Twenty-Five

*Defend the cause of the weak and fatherless; maintain
the rights of the poor and oppressed.*
—PSALM 82:3

W hy haven't you brought me any milk this week?" barked the voice on our answering machine. I rolled my eyes at the familiar request from our friend Tom.

"Why can't he ask more nicely?" I complained to Brian when he got home.

"God doesn't ask us to change our tone, Ruth," Brian said—and reminded me that Tom was in our lives for a reason.

Later that week Brian suggested we should bring Tom some groceries. I tried to find a valid excuse not to go. To tell the truth, Tom made me a bit nervous. He was unpredictable. He was large. He had problems. If Brian wanted to spend time with him, fine, but bring our baby daughter along? That was hard.

As we pulled up in front of Tom's apartment, I wondered what kind of mood Tom would be in. Happy? Grumpy? What if he asked to hold Shiloh? What kind of excuse could I give?

Brian marched up the sidewalk, holding the groceries in one arm and Shiloh in the other. I dragged my heels behind them. No answer. "I guess he's not home!" I said, trying to hide my relief.

"Let's check the garden," came Brian's reply.

Sure enough, Tom sat there, alone, staring into space. When he saw us, his expression changed immediately. He greeted us like long-lost friends, and begged us to sit down. *Oh good,* I thought. *He's happy today.*

We sat for a few minutes until Shiloh started to fuss. "She's tired . . . ," I explained. "I think we'd better go." Tom moved closer and began to tickle Shiloh's feet.

"What's wrong?" he asked her, with a gentleness I'd failed to see before. A smile emerged on Shiloh's face, which quickly broke into a full-out grin. There was no denying their connection, nor my converted heart.

*Jesus, give me the courage and insight to cherish every
human being as much as I cherish You.*
—RUTH BERGEN

Day Twenty-Six

He prays to God and finds favor with him, he sees God's face and shouts for joy; he is restored by God to his righteous state.

—JOB 33:26

I'd cleaned all morning, and now a dozen guests were in my little apartment. Tyler was hungry and crying, which paradoxically made me breathe a sigh of relief. I now had a perfect excuse to disappear and relax.

"Sorry guys," I said. "Please help yourselves; I have to feed the baby now."

I went to the bedroom and closed the door. Once I was comfortable with pillows on my back and lap, I cradled Tyler to my body and began to breastfeed. I leaned back and took a long breath. As the milk flowed from my body, so did my stress. I absolutely love this time. It is a relief to my breasts, to my body that is barely rested and to my mind that can barely catch up to itself. But most of all, this is my time with Tyler—just the two of us. When I feed him I can hold him close, caress his hair and just gaze at his beautiful little face. Everything else has to wait.

Time alone with Tyler is rare. He has to share every moment with big brother Brandon, who demands way too much attention. I treasure our feeding time and am annoyed to no end when it is interrupted—by Brandon (elbow deep in a jar of peanut butter), the doorbell or my husband shouting for a towel from the shower.

But for now, the guests kept Brandon busy. The house was clean. Food was ready. I could relax and spend a while treasuring Tyler, my baby boy.

Lord, help me relish my time with You as much as these sweet moments with my child.

—KAREN VALENTIN

Day Twenty-Seven

~~~~~~~~~~~~~~

Not long before Gabi was born, Derek and I decided to accept a job offer, and we sold our house and packed up in just four weeks. We moved from the Pacific Northwest, where my parents live, to Colorado. The suddenness of the move—combined with the baby's imminent arrival and the increased miles between us—strained my relationship with my mom.

But my mother came to Colorado for Gabriella's birth. The fact that she lived so far away made those days together even sweeter as we shared Gabi's first days of life and my first moments of motherhood. Still, we often struggled to find the best ways to show our love for each other.

A few months later, Gabi and I did the traveling, heading to my parents' house for a makeshift Christmas celebration. Gift-giving time arrived, and the baby and I sat on the carpet next to the tree. I tore the paper off a box and lifted the lid to find a photo book. It was remarkable. My mom had carefully compiled a scrapbook of the story of her granddaughter's birth. She'd selected special paper to correspond with each photo and lovingly thought through this one-of-a-kind gift.

At that moment I had a choice: I could accept the gift at face value, or I could recognize that it represented far more than a photo album. I chose to receive it as a declaration of love.

Jesus, help me open my heart to the love of those who love me.
—ALEXANDRA KUYKENDALL

Day Twenty-Eight

"There is therefore now no condemnation for those who are in Christ Jesus."
—ROMANS 8:1 (ESV)

~~~~~~~~~~~

*H*i, this is Lisa Ladwig. Can we reschedule our physical therapy appointment? Geneva is fussy, and I think she's teething."

She wasn't hungry. She wasn't tired. But Geneva sure was screaming. I couldn't figure out what was wrong. So I did what I always did when I didn't know why Geneva was upset: I chalked it up to not-yet-emerging teeth. I gave her Tylenol, cold teething rings, a gum massage. I rocked her, I bounced her, I walked laps through the living room, dining room and kitchen.

It didn't matter, because Geneva would not settle down. Finally, just so I had something different to do, I went to change her diaper. Oh my! Blistering up at me was the worst diaper rash I'd ever seen. It hurt just to look at it. I felt awful—and foolish. Didn't I know the mental checklist for moms: hungry? tired? *diaper?* Here I'd been entrusted to care for this beautiful baby, and I'd given her Tylenol for a dirty diaper.

I gently wiped up my little girl and applied huge blobs of cream to her behind, wavering on the edge of condemning myself as a complete mom-failure. I let out a sigh, and laughed at myself, instead. Foolish? *Oh yes!* Condemned? *No.*

Thank You, Lord, that even in my failures, I am righteous before You.
—LISA LADWIG

Day Twenty-Nine

I know, my God, that you test the heart and are pleased with integrity. . . .
—I CHRONICLES 29:17

~~~~~~~~~~

It was 11:00 PM, and Andrew and I were having our daily debriefing. I filled him in on events at the office.

"You remember Pete? While I was out on maternity, he made his move. He's being put over the other VPs, and he wants to shift everyone's jobs around."

"What do you think will happen?" asked Andrew.

"He'll get rid of everyone who doesn't think like he does." I replied, "Then he's going to implement his philosophy of 'change for the sake of change.' "

"Do you think like he does?"

"No."

We sat in silence for a bit. Andrew asked, "So what's next?"

"Everyone has to go in for interviews, to see if we fit in the new regime."

"What will you say?" my stay-at-home husband wanted to know.

I shot him a look over the rim of my glasses. "We'd better pray about that," I said drily. "And we'd better pray about how I say it too!"

Being the breadwinner in the family cast my job situation in a different light—one I didn't like. My family *needed* my salary and health benefits. Was what Pete was doing wrong, or was it simply not my way of doing things? Was there a way to be honest without being laid off? How much of my opinion could I conceal and maintain my integrity? These questions were a long way from comfy.

Prayers went up, and the morning came for my interview with Pete. "What are you going to do?" Andrew asked as I kissed Elizabeth good-bye. I knew both of them were counting on me.

"The right thing," I replied. Ten days later, I was out of work.

Jesus, hard decisions call for deep faith. I need You.
—JULIA ATTAWAY

Day Thirty

Don't withhold yourselves from each other. . . .
—I CORINTHIANS 7:5 (GOD'S WORD)

I entered the master bedroom robed in bleach-stained terry cloth and perfumed with *eau de spit-up.* My aching feet thanked me profusely as I collapsed onto the bed and shut my eyes. Sleep was not far away.

Neither was he. I had caught Dave's distinctive grin as he lay there on his side—watching, waiting, hoping. . . .

I never signed up for aerobics at midnight! I groaned inwardly. A minute later Dave turned away with a sigh and I nestled my pillow gratefully. I felt myself falling into a blissful slumber, deeper with each breath.

My conscience held me back from the edge of consciousness. The man beside me seemed miles away, yet I could feel the ache in his chest. He was a man in need, my man in need. Once again, I'd let him down.

It's a small price to pay for love, a voice whispered.

There's always tomorrow! another argued. *I have nothing left to give today.* Nothing left but a worn mass of stretch marks. Somehow, he still found a home there, but I had locked the door.

In the darkness, I willed my body toward Dave.

The next morning I lumbered into the kitchen, where Dave was heartily scrambling breakfast for two. My bones felt heavy with fatigue, but I felt an invisible skip in my step. The chasm between Dave and me was gone. Love—an act of sheer willpower—had opened the door to a free-flowing love, the kind that put a distinctive grin on my face.

Dear Father, help me to say yes *more often, remembering that*
I am the only one certified to satisfy my husband.
May I count it a privilege. Amen.

—FAITH BOGDAN

Sixth Month

~~~~~~~~

Jesus,

Somewhere in this mix of being a mother, a wife and fulfilling my own needs, there must be a balance. Help me find it. Guide my heart so I know the difference between healthy sacrifices that keep self-centeredness at bay and self-sacrifices that deplete me. Show me how to put You at the center of my busy day and in the core of my distracted heart.

Amen.

Tips

» Playing peekaboo? Do your sit-ups next to your baby. She'll think it's funny that you appear and disappear.

» If you're feeling lonely, tell someone: your husband, your mom, a friend, an older woman at church. Loneliness only grows deeper when you keep it to yourself.

» If you cater only to your baby's needs, your baby will never learn you have needs too. Finding a balance will help you both.

Day One

"It is more blessed to give than to receive."
—ACTS 20:35

~~~~~~~~~~~~

As Solomon napped, I went through his overstuffed dresser, packing up the four-to-six-month clothes and filling the drawers with freshly laundered six-to-nine-month outfits. I remembered back to my baby shower, when I thought the six-to-nine-month clothing would take forever to fit.

Time is flying by, I thought. Some of the outfits he'd only worn once or twice.

Stuck way in the back of the drawer I noticed a tiny sleeper and a newborn outfit, both still with tags. Somehow they'd never been worn, never even been prewashed with my special infant detergent.

I'd meant to go through Solomon's dresser every few weeks, to shift things around and make sure he'd worn all the precious outfits given to us by family and friends. We'd missed these entirely.

Disappointed and slightly guilt-ridden, I set the outfits next to the outgrown ones and took a break to get a drink. Then I remembered seeing a flyer at the grocery store for a women's shelter that needed donations of new and slightly used baby clothing. I could drop off the unworn outfits at the shelter the next time I went to town. Perhaps these presents for Solomon were a different kind of gift: an opportunity to help someone in need.

Dear God, give me a heart that gives freely to others.
—SABRA CIANCANELLI

Day Two

"Rise up, you women who are at ease, hear my voice; you complacent daughters, give ear to my speech. In a year and some days you will be troubled, you complacent women. . . ."
—ISAIAH 32:9–10 (NKJV)

When I first came home from the hospital, having Kedar right by our bedside in his bassinet was a great convenience. With frequent feedings, diaper changes and midnight cradling sessions, quick and easy access was a must. Without it, my debilitating pelvic pain would have been too much to handle.

After a while, however, proximity grew to be an inconvenience. Kedar was no longer sleeping in a bassinet next to our bed; he graduated to bunking with us each night. We were squished, uncomfortable, and longing for just-us time. So Kenya and I sat down to talk it over, and we agreed we needed a new plan. The baby had to take his rightful place in his own room, surrounded by Winnie the Pooh and all his friends from The Hundred Acre Wood.

Kedar was already taking afternoon naps in his room, so we had a good start. The following evening we forged ahead. Kedar cried relentlessly—and I almost did too. But after several visits to the baby's room and a few long stretches of listening to him scream, we heard silence. Kedar had finally drifted off to sleep. That night we slept better than we had in a long time. And our queen-sized bed felt much roomier than it had too.

God, help me recognize when complacency becomes an inconvenience, and give me the strength to make the changes that need to be made.
—DIANNA HOBBS

Day Three

. . . That we may live peaceful and quiet lives in all godliness and holiness.
—I TIMOTHY 2:2

The baby cried most of the morning. When she finally fell asleep for her morning nap, I immediately picked up the phone and gabbed with a friend. Then I went online and dashed out a bunch of e-mails while listening to music. Lucy fussed for the rest of the afternoon. As soon as she went to sleep that night, I turned on the television.

I went to bed feeling drained, as though my soul was a wilting flower. I wished I could at least feel stronger spiritually, if not physically. I opened a book and came across this quote from Mother Teresa: "The fruit of silence is prayer, the fruit of prayer is faith, the fruit of faith is love, the fruit of love is service, the fruit of service is peace."

The fruit of silence is prayer. That line hit me right between the eyes. I recalled that in the times in my life when I'd carved out regular time for silence, my prayer life naturally flourished. But ever since I'd become a mother, I'd given up on the concept. I no longer had room for hours of quiet time each day, so I didn't attempt to get any at all. Yet according to Mother Teresa, it all starts with silence.

The next night, instead of flipping on the television as soon as Lucy went to bed, I went into my closet, sat down on the floor, closed my eyes, and spent fifteen minutes focusing solely on God. Sure enough, the silence was like fresh water for my wilting soul, and my prayer life instantly bloomed.

Lord, teach me the value of silence. Even when I have a baby.
—JENNIFER FULWILER

Day Four

The former regulation is set aside because it was weak and
useless (for the law made nothing perfect), and a better
hope is introduced, by which we draw near to God.
—HEBREWS 7:18–19

I met Sabrina as I pushed Lisbet's stroller through the park. We began chatting, and I found out that Sabrina was completely dedicated to motherhood. She wanted to have six children and homeschool them all. Her vision intimidated me: I was more concerned about doing the right thing at the moment, with one child.

Sabrina invited me and a few other moms over for pizza. Not long into the visit, Lisbet began fussing. I opened my big bag and took out a bottle. Sabrina stopped, looked us over and said, "If you don't mind me asking, why aren't you nursing Lisbet?"

I was startled by her directness and felt all eyes on me. "Lisbet is adopted," I answered calmly. Inside, though, I felt "outed." I wasn't sure I wanted to share the fact that Lisbet wasn't my biological child with every person I came across. But it seemed easier than talking to people I didn't know about my struggles with breast-feeding.

I'd tried to nurse. I'd wanted to do everything I could to bond with my daughter. I'd used a supplemental nursing system, a tiny tube that brings formula from a bottle to your nipple. The baby's sucking action is supposed to trick the mother's body into creating a milk supply. After months of trying, I just had droplets of milk.

"You have a wonderful way with your baby," commented Laura, another mom, rescuing me from the awkward conversation. "I've been watching how comfortable you are holding her, and how calm she is with you."

I smiled at Laura's thoughtfulness, and because her words brought home a truth: Bonding was about building a relationship, not just about mother's milk. It was about time together, eye contact, singing, holding. I'd done that and would continue to do it.

Father, I want to bond ever closer to You.
—LENORE LELAH PERSON

Day Five

Then maidens will dance and be glad. . . .
—JEREMIAH 31:13

~~~~~~~~~~~~~~

Sam was in her Jump-Up and I'd just finished the breakfast dishes. I was feeling fat. It didn't help that I'd cooked up a nice breakfast of French toast and bacon—totally delicious, sinfully decadent. I flipped through the TV channels and landed on a super-svelte young mom exercising with her baby. "You don't need to go to the gym!" She smiled at me through the screen. "Just grab your baby and exercise as you play!"

I looked at Samantha. Samantha looked at me.

"Come on ladies, join me!"

Why not? I pulled Samantha out of the Jump-Up and watched the woman on TV. She was holding her baby high above her head. "Together now," she said. "Up and down, up and down!"

I lowered Samantha to my nose, made a goofy face and lifted her back up. She laughed. I laughed. I lowered her again, kissed the tip of her nose and raised her back up. "Up and down," I mimicked in a silly voice. "Up and down, Samantha, up and down!"

We did it ten times. Then I sat on the ground, held her close and did ten half-crunches.

Pretty soon I tuned out the woman on the TV, turned on some music and did my own pretend aerobics class. We did a country jig, a baby waltz, and topped it off with the electric slide.

Thirty minutes later I was breathing heavily and feeling svelte. Sam was smiling and clapping her hands.

Maybe this exercise thing wasn't so tough after all.

*Lord, help me stay active in fun ways, setting an
example of healthy living for my baby.*
—ELSA KOK COLOPY

Day Six

"Man looks at the outward appearance, but the Lord looks at the heart."
—I SAMUEL 16:7

~~~~~~~~~~~~~~~

Robin just called," I reported to Andrew on my second-to-last day of work. "She has a freelance project for me, a big one. I can start the day after tomorrow."

It was fantastic news, bordering on the miraculous. I hadn't even figured out how long my severance payments would last, and now—plop in my lap—was income. I'd worked with Robin, a VP in a different department, on projects in the past. She was competent and businesslike, brassy and brash, funny and fashionable. I liked her. She had a one-year-old son and understood the mommy thing. Sort of.

You see, Robin was a bit neurotic. She was the type of New Yorker who talked about her therapist like he was a member of her immediate family. Robin was passionate about her son and wanted desperately to be a good mom, but she was absolutely certain she didn't know how. So she coped with parenting the way she coped with business: She hired experts. She had a nanny for during the day. She had a night nanny. There was a weekend nanny, too, who helped when Robin freaked out because she didn't know how to interact with her child.

I've read articles about women whose PDAs (personal digital assistants) dictate when mom and child can get together. Robin could have been featured in one. But it would have been a mistake to look at her so narrowly. She was a human being, a mom with a story of the heart behind her parenting decisions. I didn't agree with her choices and wouldn't have taken her path. But I was glad I knew her well enough to appreciate her full character instead of condemning the caricature of a power mom with too many nannies.

Lord, we're all human. Help me find the heart in other moms instead of assuming they don't know, don't understand or don't care about their children.
—JULIA ATTAWAY

Day Seven

"Do not be quickly provoked in your spirit, for anger resides in the lap of fools."
—ECCLESIASTES 7:9

~~~~~~~~~~

I'm going for a run," Derek called out as he walked through the kitchen. I looked up from the dishes in time to see him unravel the cord to his headphones as he headed toward the back door.

I was instantly angry. Why did he think it was okay to just leave? *He assumes I'm always on baby duty! There was no arranging, no negotiating. But I can't up and leave whenever I want! When I need to go out, I leave during nap time, to make it easy on him.*

I knew I could fester in this state indefinitely if I let myself. Once introduced, nasty thoughts can perpetuate themselves from here to Kansas. I was sure my husband loved me, and I loved him, so why this instant resentment on my part?

I examined my feelings as I scrubbed dishes, hoping to discover what was really going on. *Was it that I wanted to go on a run too?* No, definitely not (though it would probably be good for me). *Was it that I needed a break? To do something just for me? Hmm* . . . maybe, but there wasn't anything I was burning to do. *Was it that he didn't ask?* Yes! I felt the anger poke its head up again, as if to confirm this was what I'd been digging for. The culprit was Derek's (apparent) assumption that I was on baby duty 24-7, while he was free to come and go.

Now that I knew what made me so mad, I could address it when Derek came home. I wasn't sure how to choose my words for an honest and productive conversation when the anger was still so present. I prayed:

Jesus, guide my words. Help me to show love as we work this out.
—ALEXANDRA KUYKENDALL

Day Eight

*My frame was not hidden from you when I was made in
the secret place. When I was woven together in the depths
of the earth, your eyes saw my unformed body. . . .*
—PSALM 139:15–16

Henry was outside with his siblings, enduring the traditional Easter photo shoot. Maggie, age six, had him propped into a sitting position. Steven, three, was on the other side. Because Henry was an October baby, this was his first experience of the outdoors other than in a baby carrier. The grass, the sun, the colors—everything was fascinating to him. Between just-missed-the-smile clicks and urging Henry to look at me, I had an attack of thankfulness. Seeing my son out in the world made me infinitely glad he was in it.

You see, Henry almost didn't make it. When I was nine weeks pregnant, I had some spotting. I'd already had two miscarriages, so I was vigilant: I went to the doctor, had blood drawn and a quick ultrasound. The doctor looked— and saw nothing. No baby. I'd been through this before and knew that the usual procedure was to go immediately for a D&C.

But this time the doctor wanted me to wait a few days. He insisted we hold off on the D&C to see if things progressed naturally. I went back home. Nothing happened. Five days later I returned and had another blood test. My hCG levels—and the doctor's eyebrows—went up. Another ultrasound, and this time Henry was there, measuring right on schedule. I don't know where he'd been hiding, but I thank God all the time that my son who was lost was found again and is here with us today.

Heavenly Father, I praise You for miracles both seen and unseen.
—CHRISTY STURM

Day Nine

Let us not give up meeting together, as some are in the habit
of doing, but let us encourage one another. . . .
—HEBREWS 10:25

~~~~~~~~~~~~~~

"Let's go! It's almost ten o'clock," Dave called from the doorway.

"I can tell time!" I snapped, feverishly buttering my toast. "Your pointing it out has never helped us leave sooner and it's not going to help today."

I ate breakfast and smeared on mascara as we bounced over potholes in our dirt road. We drove through town in silence, arriving at church in time for the last song. Anna wiggled and fussed, and I carted her off to the nursery. *What a waste of cosmetics,* I thought. Here I was again, all dressed up and alone on a Sunday. When was the last time I'd heard a sermon? I watched Anna scoot around and wished I was at home.

That afternoon, I phoned my friend Diane. "What's the point in going to church?"

"Well, there *is* a point. But your MOPS [Mothers of Preschoolers] meetings may have to be your spiritual nourishment for a while," she said.

Diane was right. I still went to church, but MOPS became my lifeline. We showed up in sweats and sat around nursing our babies and each other's souls with empathetic words and listening ears. Speakers instructed us in everything from colic to marriage. We made casseroles for each other, crafted together, and in later years carpooled to pumpkin farms and apple orchards. We had playdates and game nights. We prayed for one another and left those Tuesday meetings ready to be moms again. God was in the eyes of my MOPS friends, and for a time I heard Him better there than over the crackling sound system in the nursery at church.

Lord, I'm willing to find You wherever You may be found.
Show me how to draw nearer to You today.
—FAITH BOGDAN

Editor's note: To find a MOPS group near you, visit www.MOPS.org.

Day Ten

I opened the package and removed the brand-new bouncy seat. I'd spent all day researching and finding this springy chair that clipped to the door jamb. Everything I read said it would help improve balance and motor skills.

Finding the perfect spot, I fastened the seat to the kitchen doorway, making sure it was secure. As I lowered Solomon in, his green eyes widened with fear. His mouth curled.

"You're okay," I said. "You're okay."

He moved his toe. The chair bounced. He screamed.

"You're okay," I said. I bent down and picked him up, rubbing his back. "We'll try this again tomorrow," I said.

Whenever we walked near the chair the next day, Solomon's whole body tensed and his grip tightened on my shirt.

"It's all right," I said.

I tried again the next day, and the one after that, without success. Defeated, I put the bouncy seat back in the box and brought it back to the store. We stood on the long line at the customer service desk. *What a waste of time*, I thought. Solomon fussed in his stroller and I picked him up as we moved forward.

"Reason for returning?" the woman behind the counter asked.

"He hated it," I said.

She looked up at us. Solomon smiled.

"Guess he just likes being in your arms," she said.

Day Eleven

You will not fear the terror of night, nor the arrow that flies by day.
—PSALM 91:5

~~~~~~~~~~~~~~~

We had dreamt about this trip for months. We packed up our blue Honda Civic (complete with rooftop carrier), pointed our car west, and planned to drive until we hit the mountains. I was certain Shiloh would love sleeping in a tent.

It took nineteen hours of solid driving to get there. When we arrived at the campground we were exhausted—and a tad cramped from sitting so long in the car. Brian immediately set up the tent, while Shiloh and I made friends with a chipmunk and counted the minutes till we could sleep. Tomorrow would be a new day; tonight we all needed rest.

Our sleeping bags were warm and the air cool as we lay listening to the quiet fireside chatter of a neighboring campsite and the chirping from a nearby bird's nest. Cocooned in the dark night, we drifted off before long.

POW! BAM! ZZZZAP!

I sat up straight. Had that noise been real, or a dream? What time was it? Where were we? Disoriented, I slowly lay back down as Brian unzipped the tent door to investigate.

"Ruth!" He jumped as another crackling noise sounded overhead, "Someone is shooting fireworks in the campground *horizontally*!" Not the best news to hear, especially when you're sleeping in a canvas tent.

Soon after, the park rangers arrived and the fireworks came to an end, though my heart continued to thump wildly. I pulled Shiloh close to me. I guess she *did* like the tent—she was sound asleep; the fireworks had not stolen her rest. No fear, no trauma, no racing pulse to indicate that she felt unsafe. I looked at my serene daughter and thought, *I need more of that kind of peace in my life.*

Please, Lord, teach me not to fear.
—RUTH BERGEN

Day Twelve

"How long before your words will end? Think it through, and then we'll talk."
—JOB 18:2 (GOD'S WORD)

~~~~~~~~~~~~~~~

O pen wide for Mommy," I coaxed in a high-pitched voice as I fed Kedar his first spoonful of sweet peas. Armed with plenty of paper towels, I waited for my little guy to gag and spit the green stuff back at me. I'd been warned by my experienced mom-friends that all babies hate peas. It was a universal law that I was powerless to change. I had accepted it; no biggie. But to my amazement, there was no gagging. No spitting. Just a big open-mouthed grin, and a baby giving off major signs that he was eager for more.

"Good boy!" I exclaimed, half in shock. I'd tasted the peas and they nearly made me hurl, so I was thrilled Kedar responded so well. "*Mmm*, yummy!" I said, giving him another spoonful and then another, and—"Wait a minute. What's that?" I squinted and zoomed in on his chin. I saw a few red bumps. Then a few more. And in minutes, he was covered. I made a mad dash for the telephone to dial our pediatrician and greeted her with, "I need to bring Kedar in! I fed him peas and he has hives everywhere!"

Dr. Clapp responded, without alarm, "Well, how is his breathing? How is he responding?"

"I don't know. He's covered in hives!" I blurted.

"Okay. I need you to calm down and tell me how he's *doing*, so I can tell *you* what to do." I took a deep breath and described a perfectly happy baby with no symptoms other than the hives. That day, Dr. Clapp introduced me to her good friend "Dr. Benadryl." We've been good friends ever since.

Lord, help me gain an understanding of the situation before I speak and react.
—DIANNA HOBBS

Day Thirteen

A woman is bound to her husband as long as he lives. . . .
—I CORINTHIANS 7:39

Friends warned that the world as we knew it would end when we had a baby. We didn't subscribe. After our trials becoming parents, we never wanted to, or felt that we needed to, leave Zach. He accompanied us to a Colorado Rockies game when he was three months old. Adorable in pinstripes, he slept half the game.

When Zach was six months, Todd had a conference in a mountain resort town. Most of his co-workers looked at this as an opportunity for couple time. We too . . . sort of. We worked on the assumption that the couple "us" now included Zach. I was still nursing, and the conference was casual, so I attended cocktail hour with the baby (and baby food) in tow. We went for Mexican food with everyone and ordered a high chair. And I wince to admit that we took Zach to the movies. We jiggled him up and down the side aisle for about half the show.

In the jiggling, something jarred loose in my head. Our friends had been great about having a baby along. But many of them left kids behind— purposely. Going to the mountains as a family: excellent idea. Bringing baby everywhere at a conference: reconsider. I had forgotten the twosome at the root of our threesome and wasn't being considerate of others. Sons are a heritage from the Lord (Psalm 127:3), but I was Todd's wife before I was Zach's mother. Sometimes "us" needs to be just me and my husband, to make the bigger "us" better.

My love for each member of my family needs to be shown one-on-one sometimes, Lord. Help me fill all my roles.
—SUSAN BESZE WALLACE

Day Fourteen

If one person falls, the other can reach out and help.
But someone who falls alone is in real trouble.
—ECCLESIASTES 4:10 (NLT)

Weary after our stressful weekend in the tent, we decided to treat ourselves to a hotel as we drove home. A real bed! The luxury of a shower! And no worry of horizontal firecrackers zooming overhead.

We picked the first hotel we found, checking in with record speed and racing to our room on the fourth floor. Bursting through the door, I collapsed on the bed with Shiloh beside me.

"Man, Shiloh! Did we ever pack a lot of stuff!" I informed her. "And most of it is for you!" I tickled the bottom of her foot, and she laughed.

"Look Ruth, we can see the mountains!" Brian called from the window. I left Shiloh to rest on the bed with a noisy toy and peeked over Brian's shoulder. Suddenly, there was a loud thud, and a moment later, screams.

We turned and raced toward the bed, stumbling over one another as each of us tried to get to Shiloh first. She lay on the floor beside the bed, crying. Brian and I began talking at the same time.

"How did that happen?"

"Did she do it by herself?"

"Should we go to the hospital?"

Shiloh's cries stopped, but my worrying continued. "She's going to be fine," Brian assured me as I wiped tears from my face. "Look," he said, motioning. "She doesn't even have a bump!"

We sat on the bed for a long time taking turns holding our daughter. The fact that Shiloh was doing new things didn't surprise us. We were just a little shocked that she was growing up so soon.

I'm thankful, Lord, for the many times You have caught me when I've fallen.
—RUTH BERGEN

Day Fifteen

*And my God will meet all your needs according
to his glorious riches in Christ Jesus.*
—PHILIPPIANS 4:19

"*Hmm*. It says here that this month Elizabeth ought to be able to rake a raisin," I said to Andrew.

"Rake a raisin? Why would anyone give a six-month-old a raisin?" he replied.

"Dunno. She's also supposed to be rolling over both ways by now." We rolled our eyes at each other. Elizabeth categorically refused to lie on her stomach; this milestone was leagues away. Our pediatrician told us to keep trying to put her on her belly, but he didn't seem too worried about her lack of progress.

"Does it say anything about wanting to walk?" my husband inquired. He'd spent half an hour hunched over that evening, as Elizabeth gripped his fingers and tried to go for a stroll. She had incredibly strong legs, and this was her latest obsession. It was killing our backs.

"Naw. I think this book must be written about a different species," I said. "Or else someone gave Elizabeth the wrong life-instruction manual." Our daughter sat up early and made razzing noises late, babbled only under very specific circumstances, and entirely forgot she was supposed to take naps. We'd come to regard the baby book as a source of humor rather than guidance.

Andrew slid over and looked at the list of developmental milestones. "What do they mean, 'Pays attention to small objects? Stares at a marble?'" We started listing small objects—pennies, earrings, nail clippings—and imagining why a baby would pay attention to them. We grew sillier and sillier until we finally ran out of bizarre ideas.

After a pause my husband leaned over and kissed my forehead. "I love you, you know."

I knew. Yes, I knew.

Father, I'm so glad You gave me the husband and baby that You did.
—JULIA ATTAWAY

Day Sixteen

I consider that our present sufferings are not worth
comparing with the glory that will be revealed in us.
—ROMANS 8:18

The doctor looks at the computer screen after my boys have their exams. "They're due for some shots today," she tells me casually. I look at Brandon and Tyler and feel a tug in my stomach.

Aw, my babies! I say to myself as we wait for the nurse. The poor little stinkers have no idea what's coming as they bounce on Daddy's lap. Tyler flashes his dimples and two little rabbit teeth as I hold my breath and then *wham*! Right in the thigh! There's a moment just before the pain hits when he's still all smiles.

From each of my boys in his turn, I get the same look of shock: *Why did you let her do that to me?* Then comes the bloodcurdling scream that hurts my ears and cuts at my heart. I endure it twice, each time anxiously waiting to snatch my baby into my arms, while the nurse takes too long to put on the bandage. As if they will understand the logic of what I'm saying, I whisper in their ears as they wail, "Mommy let the lady give you an ouchy because the medicine will keep you from getting sick. She didn't do it to be mean."

A few moments pass and they're distracted by something else: a new book for each. They fumble at the pages, the tears still wet on their faces, and I breathe a sigh of relief. I look at my babies, whom I love beyond words and wonder how many times God goes through the same thing. The author of love must know the deep pain of watching His children suffer, for reasons only He can understand.

Lord, guide me through the suffering to the land You have prepared for me.
—KAREN VALENTIN

Day Seventeen
A Dad's View

Like arrows in the hands of a warrior are sons born in one's youth.
—PSALM 127:4

⁓⁓⁓⁓⁓⁓⁓⁓

Can I confess something?" my friend asked. Both relatively new fathers, our family lives had conspired with our professional lives to keep us busy, and thus apart. We managed to find time to catch up over coffee on a Saturday morning.

"Sure," I said, curiosity aroused. "What's up?"

"I'm not sure what to do with my boy," he said, sipping his coffee, pausing. "I mean, I love him, but he doesn't do much."

"Right, but that's babies—crying, cooing, crawling, crapping—" (Men can be somewhat indelicate without the womenfolk around.) "So what's really eating you?"

My friend hesitated before saying, "Well, I know he's mine, and I love him and all, but I don't feel a deep connection. Someday I'll teach him how to play sports, but for now. . ." His voice trailed off.

I stirred my coffee and asked, "Well, what do you do with him?"

"Kristi does most of the work, I guess," he observed, while the waitress reloaded our caffeine. My friend commutes to work early and comes home late.

"Look, it's gonna take energy you don't always have, but you've got to nurture the conditions that make a connection possible," I said. "Take over the baby duties at night, as much as you can. Grab your son, set him on your lap, and eat dinner with one hand. Or take the baby while Kristi finishes dinner. Change diapers. Read to him. Do bath time. And play: Tickle him, nuzzle him, do his tummy time. Make faces. Sing. Be silly. The connection will come . . . but you gotta make time for it."

My friend sipped his coffee, reflecting, smiling slightly as he thought about his boy.

Lord, I pray for all fathers, that You may deepen
their connections to their children.

—LEROY HUIZENGA

Day Eighteen

May the favor of the Lord our God rest upon us; establish the work
of our hands for us—yes, establish the work of our hands.
—PSALM 90:17

I tried to be firm, without offense. "No, I'm sorry, we really cannot make it at 2:00 PM. I cannot—"

No sooner had I begun to explain than I was placed, abruptly, back on hold. The receptionist was in no mood to listen to why I had to reschedule Anjelica's check-up for the second time this week.

I was back at the office full-time, taking calls and holding meetings, filling in the lined pages of my agenda, and finally gathering momentum, but it seemed I always needed to be elsewhere.

I needed to bring Anjelica in for her medical appointments and to take her to the park or the sitter. I needed to leave work a little early to make it to the drugstore for a new teething ring. (Wait, and wipes—did we need wipes?) And I had been hoping to come in just a little later next Thursday so I could take her to that trial mommy-and-baby music class.

I was exhausted from remembering to remember where to be, when, and how to get there. I was numb from remembering what I was supposed to do. The line crackled back to life in my ear.

"I know, I know; you're busy. So 1:00 PM is fine, but come early. . . ."

I *was* busy. I was in the trade of hard work, but not of the kind I'd limited myself to before, appraised by revenue or line items. No, I was now in the real business of child rearing, as gauged by the inch, by the laugh, by the smile. I was measuring success by the standard of Anjelica's promise and grace. I was investing in and for the long term. Yes, I was busy.

Father, keep me busy with Your work as I do my own.
—DEBRALEE SANTOS

Day Nineteen

They said, "If you will be a servant to this people, be considerate of their
needs and respond with compassion, work things out with them. . . ."
—II CHRONICLES 10:7 (MSG)

I was a military brat and moved a lot, so I didn't know my grandparents well. My husband is in the military, too, and though we live a distance from family, I was determined to give my daughters what I'd missed out on.

My parents are only six hours away, and we drove to see them several times. They made the trip to see us as well. We had a wonderful time watching those family bonds grow.

But Jim's parents live all the way across the country. He's an only child, and our twins were their first grandbabies. So when we made the big trip to see Grandma and Grandpa Lyons, I fully expected Jim's folks to be overjoyed. I envisioned them gorging themselves on holding and feeding and snuggling the babies, soaking in all kinds of grandparently warmth.

They did take great pleasure in showing the twins off to their friends. But they didn't seem to want to be involved in hands-on baby care. They weren't eager to hold the girls much and weren't interested in feeding them. "Why did we bother?" I asked Jim, crankily. "All that time and money, not to mention a *long* trip, and your parents don't seem that interested!"

Jim countered, patiently, "Donna, my parents are in their seventies. Maybe getting back into baby mode after all these years is difficult for them."

He had a point. I'd expected Jim's parents to behave as I would under the circumstances. If they were going to form strong bonds with their grandchildren, they'd need to do it their own way.

Father, help me understand other people as they are,
instead of projecting my desires upon them.
—DONNA MAY LYONS

Day Twenty

My heritage is beautiful. . . .
—PSALM 16:6 (NAS)

~~~~~~~~~~~~~~

ive generations of women were present at my great-grandmother's one hundredth birthday celebration. The youngest was six-month-old Anna, bouncing on my knee with her arms spread wide and ready for take-off. It was her last visit with "Mama Earl."

I looked around and thought about the heritage these women represented. Mama Earl once walked the creaky floors of the old house on Chestnut Street in Greensboro, North Carolina, calling on Sweet Jesus for wayward family members. From her rocking chair, she taught my mother (her granddaughter) about God and heaven.

My grandmother, "Mamaw," was a busy mother of four who took in her mentally challenged Aunt Nora and later her terminally ill Uncle Carver. Then she cared for her own Papa Earl until he died. She ran a day care and remembers those children fondly and tearfully, as if they were her own.

Taking the torch of selfless service and a love for God's Word, my mother read to us kids from a set of Bible story volumes purchased for ninety dollars—a lot of money for a poor family in the seventies. She filled the seats of our dinner table with the castaways of society. She pushed us in a makeshift wooden cart to the shady playground in Greensboro's upscale Irving Park, where we enjoyed the ultimate treat: a twenty-five-cent snow cone.

I wonder what memories will come to mind as Anna and her children someday look back on these lightning-fast years under my roof. Will I be the mother, and grandmother, that prayed? Served? Played? What will my descendants know of God, heaven, prayer and love?

Father, help me take the torch.
—FAITH BOGDAN

Day Twenty-One

Let the wise listen and add to their learning,
and let the discerning get guidance.
—PROVERBS 1:5

~~~~~~~~~~

I had no idea that so much drool existed. Anywhere. Ever.

Samantha was teething and I couldn't wipe away the drool fast enough. Most of the time it was okay. I just came to expect the large wet spot that seemed to adorn every outfit. Then my mother-in-law came to visit.

"Her outfit is all wet," she said.

"I know," I said. "It's a way of life these days."

"She'll catch a cold like that. With her chest constantly wet, she's going to get sick—you can count on it."

"She's been fine so far."

"Just wait and see. You better get her a bib." Her tone felt harsh to my sensitive ears. It seemed like time shifted into slow motion. I knew I could reply in one of two ways. I could tell my mother-in-law exactly where she could put that bib, or I could take a deep breath and look beyond the critical tone to the actual advice.

She just wants to help, I reminded myself.

"That's not a bad idea," I managed to say.

I went to Samantha's room and grabbed a bib from the drawer. As I tied it around Samantha's neck, a large droplet of drool escaped and landed on the bib.

"See?" said my mother-in-law. She was beaming from ear to ear.

I couldn't help but smile at her delight. "Yup, you were right. . . ."

Father, help me see the good intentions behind the advice of my loved ones.
—ELSA KOK COLOPY

Day Twenty-Two

This will bring health to your body and nourishment to your bones.
—PROVERBS 3:8

I looked at the sweet potato sitting on my kitchen counter and then over at Gabi perched in her high chair. She looked back at me with expectation. *She thinks I can do this*, I thought, a little unsure of the task at hand. I was about to make Gabi's first solid food. She'd tried rice cereal and wasn't a big fan. She was ready for flavor and texture in her life, and this sweet potato (along with my help) was going to make it happen.

I gathered the tools: the food processor, the baby food cookbook (yes, they do exist) and an ice cube tray so I could freeze the leftovers into perfect baby-size portions. I put the sweet potato in the already-warm oven and looked over again at Gabi. She seemed totally confident in my abilities. We played while the potato baked; then I scooped out the pulp, added a little water, pureed it, and we were done.

As Gabi watched me stumble through this simple recipe, I thought of all the meals I would make for her in her lifetime. She certainly wouldn't see me master many other domestic duties; I can't sew, and anyone who knows me can tell you I'm not a good housekeeper. But cooking is different. Maybe it's because I like the end result: food! But more likely it's the feeling that I've partnered with the Creator to nourish those around me.

Watching Gabi lick her first few tastes off the spoon, I felt satisfied. A new recipe attempted. A new use for the dusty food processor revealed. A new mothering responsibility tackled. A new partnership with the Creator.

Lord, help me to nourish my child, both body and soul,
with the healthy ingredients You provide.
—ALEXANDRA KUYKENDALL

Day Twenty-Three

He who loves a pure heart and whose speech is
gracious will have the king for his friend.
—PROVERBS 22:11

The phone rang at 8:59 PM, just as I was changing into my PJs to enjoy a comfy evening on the couch. It was my friend Hildi.

"Hey! There's a jazz band playing down at *219 West*. Want to head downtown?"

"Um," I stumbled, glancing down at my ratty pajama pants and fuzzy slippers. It was enticing. I missed Hildi. We had been friends since college, but ever since Joey was born, we'd hardly talked. How nice it would be to head downtown, listen to some music and catch up!

But there was no way. Joey would certainly be up before 7:00 AM and staying up late would mean I'd be bleary-eyed and cranky the next day. I had to say no. Again.

Hildi understood, but as we hung up, I felt discouraged. How could I stay connected with my dear (but childless) friend when our lives seemed light-years apart? Hildi worked all day, stayed up late, went to jazz concerts and happy hours and art galleries.

I, on the other hand, hung with my son all day, fell asleep early and listened to Wee Sing Silly Songs.

We lived worlds apart.

The next day, I called Hildi and made a coffee date for Saturday. We headed downtown with Joey in his stroller and talked and talked. Yes, we lived in different worlds, but we shared a common bond: love. And that was enough.

Lord, I feel like a completely different person than I was a year ago, yet
I still love my friends from the past. Help us find common ground.
—ERIN MACPHERSON

Day Twenty-Four

*Train up a child in the way he should go: and when
he is old, he will not depart from it.*
—PROVERBS 22:6 (KJV)

Solomon is mobile! During tummy time on his fuzzy blue blanket, he squirms forward by pulling up his knees and stretching forward like an inch worm. I wouldn't exactly call it crawling, but he is moving forward and definitely getting somewhere.

I place his favorite toy, an extra-large striped caterpillar with plastic bobble eyes, slightly on the edge of the blanket so he has to work toward it.

"You can do it, Solomon!" I say.

Solomon's eyes fix on the toy. He reaches, sees it is just out of reach and squirms and squirms until the toy is right at his fingertips. He squeals with delight as he touches the caterpillar's bobble eyes.

"You did it!" I cheer. Solomon rests his head on the caterpillar and smiles.

Placing objects just out of reach is a little difficult for me. My maternal urge is to give Solomon everything he wants, to please him and make it easy for him. But I know he needs to reach for the things he wants so he can experience the thrill of accomplishment, of grasping his goal with his own hands.

*Dear Lord, parenting is filled with lessons. Guide me as
I learn when to give and when to hold back.*
—SABRA CIANCANELLI

Day Twenty-Five

Be self-controlled and alert. Your enemy the devil prowls around like a roaring lion looking for someone to devour.
—I PETER 5:8

Sauté the onions and garlic until soft. Add plain tomato sauce, basil, oregano, parsley, garlic powder and a pinch of sugar. I was using the recipe handed down to me from my Italian grandmother. I rolled the meatballs one by one and dropped them into the simmering pot. They needed to cook quite a while, and with the baby napping, it seemed an ideal time to sit in the recliner and read a book. As the comforting aroma of an Italian dinner filled the house, I did what any mom does when she puts her feet up: I fell asleep. I awoke, not to the sound of the baby crying, but to the smell of meatballs burning.

That was my wake-up call to pay attention to my weaknesses and limitations—and to build in safeguards. I'm susceptible to catnaps these days, so if the stove is on, the timer should be too. If I plan to be pleasant to my husband Bob in the evening, I'd better remember to eat lunch during the day. My spiritual life needs safeguards too. I know I am prone to temptation—such as skimping on prayer time because I'm tired—so I need to build in ways to keep myself on track. For me, setting the timer for prayer is just as important as remembering it for meatballs.

Please, Lord, show me how to keep the habit of connecting with You.
—LISA LADWIG

Day Twenty-Six

Remember the wonders he has done, his miracles,
and the judgments he pronounced.
—I CHRONICLES 16:12

~~~~~~~~~~

Elizabeth and I headed out to run an errand. We passed a group of people chatting on the shady stoop of a brownstone. My eye latched on to the baby on one woman's lap; he looked to be about Elizabeth's age. But the mom was occupied; I kept going.

On the way home I retraced my steps. The mom with the baby was still on the stoop, but now she was alone.

"How old is he?" I paused to ask, smiling.

"Well, it's hard to say," she replied. "If you count from when he was due, he's three months. If you count from when he was born, he's six."

I did the math in my head. "Wow—so now he's been alive for as long as he was in your belly!"

"He was born at twenty-four weeks gestation," she said, nodding. "Tommy, my miracle boy."

"He looks great," I replied and then introduced myself and Elizabeth. I took my daughter out of her stroller and sat down on the stoop. The babies happily stuffed twigs in their mouths, drooled, and spit up a bit while Annette and I talked. I marveled at the idea of a baby born so small he could fit in his mother's hand. Annette told me of months of living by a bassinet in the ICU, of tying balloons to Tommy's legs to encourage him to move, of three hours a day spent arguing with insurance companies. If Tommy was a miracle baby, Annette seemed like a miracle mama. She was resourceful and resilient, and utterly un-self-pitying. I was in awe.

"Do you live near here?" Annette asked. My apartment was a block away. "Stop by," she said. "Or give me your phone number so we can get together. Being a mom can get lonely."

Lord, thank You for the miracles of tiny babies who survive,
for modern medicine and for incredibly strong mamas.
—JULIA ATTAWAY

Day Twenty-Seven

The Father loves the Son and has placed everything in his hands.
—JOHN 3:35

~~~~~~~~~~~~~~~~

S oon after Joshua was born, my dad began to buy him all sorts of stuff. He bought clothes and practical things, but also whatever else moved him: a pail and shovel, a snack tray, a stuffed bunny rabbit and a personalized Christmas stocking. Among the "Whatcha buy this for? He's only a baby!" items was a cookbook complete with hand-shaped cookie cutters.

Of course, I never said what I thought, because I got a kick out of seeing my dad drop by with his schoolboy smile, the one he'd surely used bringing backyard gifts to his favorite teacher. I don't remember if my dad ever told Joshua he loved him, but I'm sure Joshua will know it. Those gifts that weren't right for a baby are Joshua's legacy now that my father has died. When Joshua is old enough to cuddle the bunny and collect sand with his pail and shovel, those gifts will prompt discussions about who they came from. They will be a tie to the grandfather Joshua doesn't recall but who was generous to my son.

And some day, when Joshua is old enough, we will bake cookies together and cut them out with those handprint cutters, and I will tell him how Grandfather Anderson held him in his own hands and loved him.

Jesus, imprint my hands with love, generosity and thoughtfulness.
—RHONDA J. SMITH

Day Twenty-Eight

But godliness with contentment is great gain.
—I TIMOTHY 6:6

~~~~~~~~~~~~~~

I was going to give the announcements at my MOPS meeting, which meant I had to be on time and somewhat presentable at 9:00 AM. A tough job with a baby to take care of, but I had a plan.

On Thursday night, I mapped out Friday morning on paper. I scheduled my routine down to the minute—figuring out exactly how long it would take to shower, get ready, feed myself, feed Joey and get out the door.

The day started without a hitch. I straightened my hair and put on mascara while Joey slept. I wolfed down a bowl of corn flakes as my son played happily on his tummy-time mat. At the last minute, I fed him, dressed him, and slipped into my gray slacks and purple silk blouse.

I picked up Joey to put him in his car seat, and he immediately spit up— no, make that projectile vomited—down the back of my silk shirt and into my freshly straight-ironed hair.

I looked at the clock. If I was going to give the announcements at the meeting, I didn't have time to shower or change. I grabbed a baby wipe, mopped myself up the best I could and hopped in the car. I wasn't exactly presentable, but I *was* going to arrive on time. One out of two isn't half bad.

Father, remind me that even semisuccess is still success.
—ERIN MACPHERSON

Day Twenty-Nine

*"For God did not give us a spirit of timidity, but a
spirit of power, of love and of self-discipline."*
—II TIMOTHY 1:7

The aroma of Thai food was already in my barely parked car. I checked my lipstick and laughed at the dried milk on my sleeve. Thankfully I didn't have to impress these friends, and certainly not on my first night back.

My book club was an awesome group. From married moms to single professionals, they were smart, funny gals whose taste in books was as vast as a Las Vegas buffet. No limits.

From the Oprah recommendations to the regional biographies, most of the books were ones I'd have never chosen myself. These reads were milemarkers in my life. One I read in Hawaii. One I read during pregnancy bed rest. I loved finishing a book almost as much as I relished the debates over characters.

Book club was one thing I was sure wouldn't change after motherhood. That first night back, I found a comforting piece of my former self after the disorienting all-nighters and constant guessing. I enjoyed myself, worried about what food I should order for nursing and called home twice.

My identity as a mother grew daily throughout Zach's first year. It affected how late I wanted to be out, and the books I preferred, and the things I wanted to talk about. I fought it. Even faked it. Some books I didn't finish. I was embarrassed. I feared becoming mental mush.

But book club taught me to say no. The first time I missed a meeting, the relief was amazing. I didn't want homework. I wanted my home to work. For that month, that meant giving up the book club. Turns out there *are* limits. And that's okay in my book!

*Help me live authentically before my friends, God, and
embrace the changing interests and activities in my life.*
—SUSAN BESZE WALLACE

Day Thirty

"God did this so that they would seek him and perhaps reach out for him and find him, though he is not far from any one of us."

—ACTS 17:27

T he table groaned from the weight of beautifully arranged colorful pastas, salads and meats. There were hamburgers and hot dogs, corn and coleslaw—a perfect late summer's repast. As always at my mother-in-law's, there was no appetite that could not be satisfied, no whim or fancy that would not be contented. She'd prepared an enormous feast for us, her family of happy dozens gathered in her home. Barefoot grandchildren darted under the sprinklers, and chattering adults passed each other condiments.

Anjelica was the youngest of us all, curled onto my chest while I talked with my in-laws and swayed to keep her asleep.

Now my sister-in-law reached out arms for my daughter, insisting I sit and eat. I was grateful for the offer, glad to think I might stretch my aching arms and enjoy dinner in full.

But I surprised myself with hesitation, demurring, "Oh no, don't worry. I'm not even hungry. But thank you."

I had no doubt she would handle Anjelica expertly. A medical professional, a devoted mother of two adolescent girls who were the epitome of coltish grace, she could do no wrong. But I worried that having her care for Anjelica while I ate seemed selfish.

"Oh no, please. I'd love to. You have to eat."

No sooner had she stretched her arms out to embrace my soundly slumbering Anjelica than her husband swooped in behind her, waiting for his chance. "*Oooh*, I got next," called another sister-in-law from the next room.

So I sat at the table eating beside Patrick, in a home that held a circle of arms waiting to relieve my own. Family held our lovely girl in loving turn, and there was nothing selfish about letting Anjelica be part of it.

Lord, for all that is beautiful in my family, I thank You.
—DEBRALEE SANTOS

Seventh Month

~~~~~

Father,

I ask You to put new friends in my path, women with open hearts and lively faith—and babies. Send me companionship for this journey of motherhood. Give me the courage to endure loneliness, form new connections and sustain old relationships that suddenly don't seem to fit as well. Give me a heart for being a good friend to others.

In Jesus' name, amen.

Tips

» Begin a habit of blessing your child whenever you leave home, whether you're going out for work or pleasure.

» Having a rough day? Give yourself a pep talk by telling your baby, "Do you see how amazing your mommy is? Look how hard she's working! She's cleaning up this BIG mess *so* cheerfully. . . ."

» Enroll in a Mommy and Me class—music, yoga, reading out loud—so that for an hour a week someone else is in charge of what you do with your baby. A side benefit: You'll meet other moms.

Day One

When Ruth came to her mother-in-law, Naomi
asked, "How did it go, my daughter?"
—RUTH 3:16

~~~~~~~~~~~~~~

G randma's here," I shouted, as she walked through the door holding a box of diapers in one arm and a bag of new children's clothes in the other. Tyler happily crawled over to her feet.

"Grandma, I want to go bye-bye," Brandon said, because he knows that with Grandma, he always goes somewhere fun. I had time to take a shower and get ready for a date with my husband. I could relax, knowing my boys are not just in good hands—they're with someone who loves them like I do.

I dearly wish my mother lived close enough to do this, but she'd have to fly in from Florida. The Grandma here is my mother-in-law. The term *mother-in-law* drives me insane: it's ugly and carries the weight of every negative image out there. I need a new word. Because I absolutely love and appreciate my husband's mom.

With my own family far away, she's the only family I've been able to count on in a moment's notice. She's here when my kids are sick; she's a shoulder to cry on when I'm feeling overwhelmed. She helps me figure out how to communicate better with her son. My little family is constantly in her prayers, and she encourages me and always tells me I'm a good mother.

"Stop bothering my mom!" my husband once joked as I called to borrow her car.

"Excuse me," I said, in fake annoyance. "She's not just *your* mother any more. Your family is *my* family now." Gary rolled his eyes with a smile, but it's absolutely true. She is family, and nothing less. Now if only I can find a better word to express who she is to me, and the blessing she's become in my life.

Lord, teach me to love all my relatives—including the
ones I don't like—as fully as the ones I adore.
—KAREN VALENTIN

Day Two

*I wisdom dwell with prudence, and find out
knowledge of witty inventions.*
—PROVERBS 8:12 (KJV)

~~~~~~~~~~~~

Our old green-and-yellow Victorian home was cold. The leaky window frames rattled whenever the wind blew forcefully, bringing in a bitter chill from the outdoors.

"It's freezing in here," I said, as Kenya and I huddled together on the sofa under a thick blue comforter. We'd cranked the heat up to nearly eighty-five degrees. But once the draft made its way inside, it immediately snuffed out most of the warmth.

"Maybe the furnace blew out again," Kenya suggested, heading into the basement. That happened a lot in below-zero temps. While he checked the pilot light, I went to sneak a peek at Kedar. I'd dressed him in layers and covered his body in thick blankets, but I wanted to be absolutely sure that Mama's baby was nice and comfy.

I tiptoed into his room and gazed at him by the soft glow of the nightlight. Kedar was sprawled out on his back with no covers on. Hoping he wasn't too cold, I reached down to touch his face. To my surprise, he was moist with sweat.

I'd forgotten that Kenya and I had put up plastic sheeting on Kedar's window as insulation. Apparently it worked, for the room was actually warm! I decided to let Kenya worry about the pilot in the basement—I was going to get busy using Kedar's room as a pilot case for how to warm up the rest of the house!

*Father, there's more than one way to solve a problem;
keep my mind open to creative solutions.*
—DIANNA HOBBS

Day Three

He heals the brokenhearted and
binds up their wounds.
—PSALM 147:3

⌇⌇⌇⌇⌇⌇⌇⌇⌇⌇⌇

I walked into the kitchen and sighed, the morning rolling off my shoulders. The sink overflowed with bowls and bottles. I scooted the high chair out of the way, only to bump into a basket full of clothes to be folded.

My eyes scanned the pantry, searching for something to fill my empty tanks. Cookies sounded delicious, but one glance at my postpregnancy potbelly had me looking for something else.

Then I saw it: the yellow box of whole-wheat goodness. I cautiously handled the package, scanning the side panel for nutrition information. Too tired to do the arithmetic needed to determine how many calories a solitary cracker contained, I tipped the box in search of a broken one. I munched in bliss. Then I tipped and shook again, locating just the right fragment. I ate one broken piece after another until I could eat no more, all the while patting myself on the back because broken pieces don't have calories.

I didn't eat a single *whole* one. Unfortunately, I didn't remember the math of munching and crunching, where the calories of the broken pieces add together to make a whole (or more). No matter how small or broken the pieces, they still have value.

God performs the same miracle with me. When I foolishly tie my worth to such small things as the cleanliness of the kitchen sink and the den floor, God makes me whole again. When every single item on my to-do list is still undone, Christ picks me up, bit by bit, and whispers to my soul, "Even small pieces have value."

Lord, thank You for making me whole again. And help me
remember that broken crackers have calories too.
—CAROL HATCHER

Day Four

"At the time of the banquet he sent his servant to tell those who had been invited, 'Come, for everything is now ready.' But they all alike began to make excuses."
—LUKE 14:17–18

~~~~~~~~~~

The knock at the door made me freeze in my tracks. I looked out the window and panicked; it was my new friend Patsy, the woman who seemed to have it all together. I caught a glimpse of myself in the mirror. Still wearing yesterday's mascara, I looked like a raccoon in a nightgown. Dishes were composting in the sink and a stack of mail on the table was topped off with a nursing pad.

I had forgotten that Patsy was stopping by for Anna's outgrown newborn clothes. There was no time to do anything but grab a plaque I had made for such emergencies and place it somewhere visible:

A Tidy House Is a Sign of Child Neglect.

Then I smoothed my bed-hair and opened the door.

After apologizing a while for everything, I finally offered Patsy a cup of tea and a seat between piles of laundry. We chatted and laughed and enjoyed each other's company. I half expected Patsy to write her name in my coffee-table dust, but she didn't seem to notice it was there.

I took Anna to Patsy's for a play-date the next morning and was pleasantly surprised to find her house looking rather lived-in. What's more, she didn't bother to apologize for the toys strewn all over the floor and the toothpaste in the sink. I felt at home and at ease.

In time, I learned to quit making excuses for my house when company came. The little plaque remained where I'd put it, gathering quite a bit of dust, but the words were still visible.

Father, help me to remember that I am most welcoming when I am real.
—FAITH BOGDAN

Day Five

"How sweet are your words to my taste, sweeter than honey to my mouth!"
—PSALM 119:103

How I loathed her. She was reading *The New Yorker*.

I think I might have had it in for her even if this kind-looking stranger had been reading an Archie comic. She was *reading*, wasn't she? Taunting me with her uninterrupted focus on the words on the page. This innocent woman sitting across from me on the subway was immersed in a world of reverie I hadn't visited, it seemed, in ages. My own newspaper lay folded on my lap, another taunt to my too-weary eyes.

Ah, words! Lots of crisp words, densely packed together in neat columns! How I missed them.

I missed the ones lying at the foot of the rocking chair, collapsed on the kitchen table or upended on the bedside table. I yearned for the words strewn every-which-way in my home, abandoned in haste by Anjelica's sudden cry, or need for a bath or diaper change. Words orphaned by my lack of time or by eyes that could not remain open.

Words adorn every spare inch of our walls, close at hand but these days as far off as can be. French dictionaries line up beside the utterances of Czech poets and Latina union organizers, Boynton board books and political science journals share space with the Gospels.

I am pleased that at seven months, Anjelica extends her hands to snag a book like ripe fruit. I love the evenings, when her sweet face turns to mine as we settle in among the pillows and I dance books in front of her like candy. And I imagine the day when my daughter and I will read together on the subway, our bodies swaying, heads bowed.

Lord, let me pass on a love of words—and Your Word—to my child.
—DEBRALEE SANTOS

Day Six

Whoever has will be given more, and he will have an abundance.
Whoever does not have, even what he has will be taken from him.
—MATTHEW 13:12

I'm watching Henry play with Mardi Gras beads—his favorite thing in the world. He turns them over and over in his hands, looking intently at each bauble, feeling the beads run through his fingers, grabbing them with his toes. Every now and then he lets out a squeal of delight or babbles quietly as if he's telling the beads how much he enjoys them.

Then he moves on to some blocks. He takes one in each hand, struggling because they're a little too big to manipulate easily. His face is open, receptive, concentrating as he figures out how to bang them together.

As I watch my son explore and play, the word *abundance* appears in my mind. I used to think of abundance as an overflow of something, like an abundant harvest. However, as I ruminate on the unexpected word I realize that instead of *having* an abundance of something, Henry *is* abundance. He is abundance in the form of a boy, abundance that helps me appreciate the details of life.

Henry has taught me the wonder of experiencing a cat for the first time. The unbelievable coolness of water. The miracle of reaching a milestone. I hold him close, nibbling on his soft feet that smell of heaven, snarfling his sweet neck to steal his kisses away. I am abundantly thankful.

Father God, I praise You for revealing Yourself in the smallest parts of life.
Thank You for using my child to show me all the brilliant facets of Your love.
—CHRISTY STURM

Day Seven

*You will keep in perfect peace him whose mind
is steadfast, because he trusts in you.*
—ISAIAH 26:3

~~~~~~~~~~~~~~~

I've got to finish this piece by Tuesday," I told Andrew. The look on his face told me something was wrong.

"My deadline's Wednesday," he replied.

Welcome to freelance hell, the place where deadlines coincide. So much for flexibility: There were two adults in the house, and neither of us could take care of the baby. Now what? I looked at Andrew and he looked at me. Neither of us budged.

"We'll have to get a babysitter," he said.

"Uh, yeah. Where?" I asked. We had no family nearby, and with both of us working from home, I'd never contemplated having to find someone I'd trust with my baby.

"Why don't you call Dana? She's well connected," Andrew suggested. Dana was head of community outreach at the mental health clinic where I'd volunteered for years. It turned out her son was newly married, and his wife was out of work. Problem solved.

Newbie that I was, I didn't know how much to pay Maria. I had to look up screening questions to use at our interview. I pulled babysitter checklists off the Internet, which was how I learned I should leave a copy of our insurance card with the sitter. Finally, I packed: bottles of breast milk and formula; two pacifiers, a sunhat, books, a blanket, toys, diapers, a change of clothes. Was that everything? They'd be out of the house for several hours.

Maria arrived, and I showed her how to hold her hand on Elizabeth's cheek to get my sleepless wonder to take a nap. I handed her the overstuffed baby bag and hoped everything would be okay. As my baby headed out the door, I decided vague hope wasn't enough. I kissed Elizabeth good-bye a second time and traced a little cross on her forehead, committing her once again to Christ.

*Jesus, this turning-things-over-to-You business
is hard! Watch over my baby, please.*
—JULIA ATTAWAY

Day Eight

"Watch your life and doctrine closely. Persevere in them, because if you do, you will save both yourself and your hearers."
—I TIMOTHY 4:16

~~~~~~~~~~~~~~

*F*amily dinner. Oh, the joy! Trying to manage to chop and boil and sauté while keeping Joey out of trouble. Trying to scarf down my entire meal in five minutes flat before he gets antsy. Trying to hold an adult conversation when every other word is interrupted by you-know-who.

But I was doing it. Every night. Because that's what the parenting magazines said I should do. And if they said it, I needed to do it, right?

Wrong. One night about a week ago Joey threw an entire bowl of peas across the table, splattering green puree on my nice placemats and my only clean shirt. I was hungry and grumpy, and I was tired of spending my entire dinner making airplane noises. I quit family dinner.

The next night, I tossed a salad while Joey was napping and threw some chicken breasts into the oven while I fed him an early solo dinner. When my husband came home, we bathed Joey, read him stories, said prayers and put him to bed.

Then we went downstairs by ourselves and had family dinner. Just the two of us. No pureed peas in sight. And for once, family dinner *was* joyful.

Lord, help me to know when to persevere—and when to give myself a break.
—ERIN MACPHERSON

Day Nine

You also, like living stones, are being built into a spiritual house to be a holy priesthood, offering spiritual sacrifices acceptable to God through Jesus Christ.
—I PETER 2:5

For months I'd been looking forward to fasting. I'd only been a Christian for about a year, and I was deeply drawn to the ancient practice of forgoing certain foods as a way of detaching oneself from worldly pleasures and focusing on God. I'd planned to eat only bread and water for lunch starting the Wednesday of Holy Week, to prepare for Easter. But when the big day rolled around, I couldn't do it because I was pregnant with our second child. Motherhood had messed up my big plans for spiritual growth.

That night I stood in front of the open freezer, gazing at a gallon of strawberry ice cream, and decided to read instead of eating my nightly bowl—a small fast that I could still undertake. I closed the freezer door and opened my Bible. In the quiet moments that followed, I realized I had missed the point. Limiting worldly pleasures for a time to focus on God may be beneficial, but my daily work was far more valuable to Him than dramatic fasts.

The next day I was on my hands and knees on the kitchen floor, wiping up the pureed pears tossed from Lucy's high chair. With each swipe of the paper towel I could feel with certainty that this was more pleasing to God than a hundred days of eating only bread and water.

Lord, help me to see the value of all the little sacrifices I make as a mother.
—JENNIFER FULWILER

Day Ten

He only is my rock and my salvation, my fortress, I shall not be shaken.
—PSALM 62:6 (ESV)

~~~~~~~~~~~~~~

Solomon and I were visiting my mom, and we sat on an old quilt on the lawn, taking in the beautiful summer day. Solomon crawled to the edge of the blanket, noticed the green grass and came to a halt.

He reached out to touch the green blades and pulled his hand back. He tried again and retreated, crawling backward toward the center of the quilt.

"I guess he hates grass," I said to Mom. "He probably won't be a landscaper."

"Maybe it's just touching it with his hand," Mom said. "See what happens when you stand him up in it."

Picking Solomon up, I braced his bare feet on the grass. Solomon screamed and gripped my arms. He looked at me as if he couldn't believe what I had just done.

"It's just grass, Solomon," I said.

"Poets write about going barefoot, the feel of the grass on their toes," Mom said. "Come on, Solomon, don't you want to feel the grass?"

I held Solomon on my lap, calming him down. He played with his favorite caterpillar toy.

Later, I sat on the edge of the blanket with Solomon on my lap. I touched the grass in front of me. Solomon watched my fingers move back and forth over the tender blades. Slowly, deliberately, he rested his hand on mine.

Dear God, so often I look at new things with fear, things that turn out to be as pleasurable and harmless as the summer grass. Help me remember to place my fear in Your hands.
—SABRA CIANCANELLI

Day Eleven

But from everlasting to everlasting the Lord's love is with those who fear him.
—PSALM 103:17

~~~~~~~~~~~~~~

"What shall we do today?" I asked Llewelyn in a melodic jingle, feeding her a breakfast of applesauce and barley cereal. She gave me a wide grin, accepted another spoonful and immediately spit half of it out. This question had become a daily routine. And, as usual, I was riddled with indecisiveness.

Lord, what should we do today? I prayed.

Silence.

"Why don't we take a walk," I sighed, discouraged. "But first we have to do some laundry."

Some two hours later, Llewelyn and I were finally dressed, the diaper bag was packed and the laundry cart was ready. I swung open the door to our apartment, held it open with my leg and maneuvered the stroller out the door. Next, the cart. "Come on, cart!" I begged, turning the wheels and finally pushing it over the lip in the doorway. I pushed the stroller and dragged the cart slowly down the hallway to the elevator. After more maneuvering at the elevator door, I was grateful when someone opened it when we reached the basement. "Thanks," I said, flashing a grateful smile.

Entering the laundry room, my heart sank: Only one washer was available! *Darn! There is no way I am bringing this cart back upstairs,* I sulked. Just then, a mom I'd seen around the building rushed in. "Are you finished with your washers?" I asked, thrilled to meet her *and* do my laundry.

"Yep. Hey, are you new to the building?" she asked.

"No, but I just had Llewelyn six months ago, and I've only been at home since then."

"Ah. I have two kids: Stephen and Kira. We live in apartment 318. Stop by anytime." she said.

Father, remind me that Your silence doesn't mean You aren't listening.

—LIZ BISSELL

Day Twelve

Is anyone happy? Let him sing songs of praise.
—JAMES 5:13

~~~~~~~~~~~~

The worship song came on the radio and I started to sing. Samantha was in her duck-shaped Jump-Up seat, bouncing away. I moved over in front of her and did a little bouncy worship dance along to the music. She laughed and bounced higher.

"Come on Samantha, sing with me!"

I sang; she squealed.

By the end of the song, I was out of breath. I flopped down in front of her. Sam's bright eyes and drooling grin filled me with love like I'd never known. I fast-forwarded in my brain to the years to come.

"Samantha," I said, pretending she could understand, "I can't wait to worship with you all your life. I want to sing with you when you're five, dance with you when you're ten, pray with you when you're twenty. I want to worship with you when you're all grown up and have your own kids and we're both dancing in front of *your* baby's Jump-Up seat!"

Samantha squealed and smiled again.

I turned the music on, and together we danced another little ditty.

Lord, I long to teach my child how to worship You!
May we grow together in our praise.
—ELSA KOK COLOPY

Day Thirteen

Keep your tongue from evil and your lips from speaking lies.
—PSALM 34:13

⸻⸻⸻

I tried to keep an open mind. Just because it was *usually* hard to get Zach to sleep in strange places didn't mean I couldn't. I'd keep to our routine. A bath, a book, a song. I left the room with confidence, trying to instill some in him.

But soon, be it at a friend's house for a nap or on a holiday stay with far-away family, Zach would protest. Frustration would mount. Exhaustion would kill my kindnesses. After several revisits and soft songs, I would often say things, or act in ways, that later made me shudder.

Once my husband Todd and I were in a hotel room, the portable crib at the foot of our bed. Zach would not sleep. I huffed and puffed, and got up *again*. Todd made a half-hearted attempt to sit up and then said something like "What do you think is wrong?"

I unloaded.

"If I knew I would fix it!" He mumbled a sleepy something, obviously not fully awake. But my exhaustion led to a river of words and tears. I couldn't find my mute button. I don't remember how it ended. But the hangover of regret was crippling the next day. *Who was that woman?*

Someone once offered that "What's said in the night, stays in the night." To an extent, that's true. Couples argue, babies wail. But sleep deprivation, though a wicked parenting reality, is no excuse for being mean. We're on the same team—even the baby.

That night solidified to me that words are like toothpaste: once out, can't put 'em back. I resolved to try harder to keep my cap on.

Lord, be my light, even in the dark.
—SUSAN BESZE WALLACE

Day Fourteen

I do not consider myself yet to have taken hold of it. But one thing I do: Forgetting what is behind and straining toward what is ahead.
—PHILIPPIANS 3:13

The snow had been gone for weeks, and the time arrived that I had been avoiding. I needed to dig out my summer clothes. The ones I hadn't worn since I became pregnant.

Dusting off the box in the basement, I lugged it upstairs and dropped it on the kitchen floor. I opened it and began to dig through the bright-colored clothing.

"Will any of this fit me this year?" I wondered as I held up a yellow T-shirt. Though the size said medium, it looked small. A sudden surge of confidence hit me. Grabbing a pair of pants, I ran to my room before I could change my mind.

As I pulled the pants onto my hips, I sucked in my belly. I still had several inches of abdomen to cover before the top button would close. I jumped up and down and eventually lay down on the bed in an effort to shimmy in. As the button finally slipped into place, I cheered at my victory. *My pants fit!*

Now, how would I get off this bed?

My midsection would not bend, and I was concerned that the pants might split if I tried to sit up. Rolling to the side, I slid off the end of the mattress and then turned around and faced the mirror.

Not bad, I thought as I observed my image. An undeniable bulge hung over the sides of my pants, but I was encouraged. I was wearing nonmaternity pants for the first time in a year, and that was reason to celebrate!

Lord, I may not be where I want to be, but I'm not where I used to be either. Help me look forward with determination.
—RUTH BERGEN

Day Fifteen
A Dad's View

"See that you do not despise one of these little ones. For I tell you that in heaven their angels always see the face of my Father who is in heaven."
—MATTHEW 18:10 (ESV)

T he sun burst bright through the expansive windows on a lovely winter day, the snow radiating bright light that complemented the warmth of a wonderful afternoon of heady theological conversation over piping coffee and crisp cookies.

Hans was wonderfully cooperative, content to be bounced gently on my knee. At a certain point he grew restless and I set him down to play and crawl at my feet, as a couple of other parents around the circle had done with their children.

Hans seized on some blocks at his feet, seemingly content to play with them. I became engrossed in our host's engaging discourse on an important but abstruse Trinitarian topic when. . .

CRASH!

Startled, I twisted, gawking, toward the noise. There, next to my son's little fingers and blond head was a rather large flowerpot, fractured in pieces, its contents spilled across the hardwood floor. *Unlike my son's fragile skull and brains*, I thought, growing faint at the thought of what could have happened.

I had let my attention drift for a moment, and in that moment my little turkey had crawled over, grabbed the base of the wire stand, yanked and had a close call. As I scooped him up, I cursed my own idiocy—rightly or wrongly— and thanked God my boy was all right.

Lord, nothing is certain in this world. Send Your angels to stand watch over my child when from fatigue or distraction I let my guard down.
—LEROY HUIZENGA

Day Sixteen

Remember ye not the former things, neither consider the things of old.
—ISAIAH 43:18 (KJV)

While I was out on maternity leave, I'd planned ministry meetings and a workshop, made calls, counseled people, and cared for my baby and my hubby. I did it all well in the beginning but not so well toward the end. And I definitely did *not* balance it all when I returned to work. Everything became crowded, pushed down or pushed together—and even pushed aside. Plans changed and people had to deal with delays, including late dinners.

"Why do you keep trying to do all this, honey?" Flynn finally asked.

All I could say was, "It's got to get done."

"Who says?"

I knew the answer: I do. *I* put the pressure on me. I wanted my old life back. I wanted to continue being an academician and a minister—and I wanted to do everything well. I didn't want to give anything up. I didn't want motherhood to be about having limits. Flynn's gentle question helped me remember that others only expected me to do it all because *I* expected that I should do it all.

But I did have limits—and they were showing. And now I had a baby, a built-in excuse to say no. No, I couldn't do everything I used to. No, I couldn't do it all. I decided to give myself a break and say it. *No.*

Lord, show me my limits and help me stay inside them.
—RHONDA J. SMITH

Day Seventeen

For the Lord takes delight in his people. . . .
—PSALM 149:4

~~~~~~~~~~~~~

I stepped back into the living room after quickly grabbing something from the kitchen. My eyes went to the spot where Gabriella had been only seconds earlier. Since Gabi started crawling I worry whenever I take my eyes off her that she'll get into trouble. But this time I found her perched, sitting, where I'd left her.

She looked up at me and grinned. Not a polite, isn't-it-pleasant-outside kind of grin, but a full-hearted one of pure joy. It said, "I think you, Mom, are the most incredible person in the world." That surprised me. It's not that I hadn't seen Gabi smile before. I spend all day, every day with her, and we share lots of smiles and laughs. But in that moment, standing in the doorway, I realized that my daughter, my delight, was delighting in *me!*

Not used to that kind of welcome, I wondered if her excitement was a fluke. I decided to repeat my entrance to test it. I stepped into the kitchen, out of sight for a second, and then back into the doorway. Gabi's face was serious, eyes searching for the missing mommy. Her little blue eyes lit up when she saw me. And there was that joyful smile again! I repeated my full-body peekaboo game a few more times. Each time I reappeared, my daughter was excited and pleased by my existence and presence. How amazing! She loves me for no other reason than I exist and I am hers.

Lord, You delight in me each time I enter Your presence.
Help me know Your delight in me today.
—ALEXANDRA KUYKENDALL

Day Eighteen

Praise the Lord from the earth, you great
sea creatures and all ocean depths.
—PSALM 148:7

~~~~~~~~~~~~~

One day while out and about with Elizabeth, we popped into a pet shop to avoid a rain shower. The reptiles left her cold, and the hamsters made her sneeze. But the fish—oh, the fish! They swam and swam for her: bright colors and pretty shapes, close enough that she could see them and track them as they swirled through the tank. I think we stayed for almost an hour.

Feeling indulgent, one weekend Andrew and I decided to go out to the Coney Island Aquarium. We rested Elizabeth on the handrail in front of a large tropical fish tank, where she sat in a state of rapture. Bigger kids came by, barely glancing at the angelfish; preschoolers exclaimed about finding Nemo; the occasional dad spouted false facts instead of scanning the educational displays. My baby was content to sit and watch. "Fish!" we said, pointing. Elizabeth glanced at us with her solemn brown eyes, and turned back to stare at the tank.

We moved on to other exhibits. The bristly walrus was a failure (too far away to see), and the penguins were camouflaged against the rocks. But the sea lion show was a success, with its large, noisy, suddenly-appearing animals. The barking even elicited a rare grin.

We stopped once more to gaze at the fish before heading to the gift shop for a picture book. Then we left the aquarium and went out to the boardwalk. Salty air blew in from the Atlantic. Millions of fish were out there, hidden under the waves, but Elizabeth couldn't see them and decided to take a nap. Andrew and I pushed the stroller along the boardwalk, marveling at seeing God's creation all over again, through a child's eyes.

Wow, Lord, You sure made some amazing things.
Thanks for the variety, and the wonder.
—JULIA ATTAWAY

Day Nineteen

"A new command I give you: Love one another. As I
have loved you, so you must love one another."
—JOHN 13:34

I was a zealous new Christian when Lucy was born, eager to spread my faith. When a group of moms who weren't believers invited me to their playgroup, I jumped at the opportunity. As I pushed the stroller along the sidewalk toward the house where the group was meeting, I thought of how much I would bless them with the peace and love of Jesus. Maybe after being overwhelmed with my warmth and kindness they'd even become curious about my newfound religion!

When I arrived, I stood in the entry hall, where two women continued their conversation without even looking at me. I sat down in the playroom with Lucy, and everyone else gathered next to the toy boxes and plastic slide. They talked about plans for a family barbecue that weekend—but nobody invited me. I withdrew to help my daughter play with blocks. Instead of seeing a passionate Christian on fire for God, my friends saw a pouting grump nursing the wounds to her ego.

Weeks later I heard that the two women who'd ignored me were discussing a family tragedy one of them had just experienced. Another of the not-friendly ones had been battling chronic pain. Someone asked me if everything was okay; why hadn't I made it to the barbecue? They thought they'd invited me. I felt awful. Instead of filling them with Christian love, I'd been looking to them to fill me up. I'd gotten it all backward.

At the next playgroup, there were inside jokes I didn't get, and one of the women wasn't receptive to my efforts at small talk. But this time they received genuine love and warmth from me, anyway. I'm learning.

Lord, let me derive my strength to love from You, not other people.
—JENNIFER FULWILER

Day Twenty

*"And the peace of God, which surpasses all understanding,
will guard your hearts and your minds in Christ Jesus."*
—PHILIPPIANS 4:7 (ESV)

Anna rode happily atop a shopping cart, bumping along the cobblestone floor of the produce section of the grocery store. She waved a chubby hand to everyone who walked by. I was enjoying a day out with my seven-month-old, who was growing quickly—cutting more teeth and even feeding herself. Life was getting easier! Before I knew it, I'd have a *child*, not a baby. I'd finally be past the wearisome trials of the season.

We strolled to the meat department, where I grabbed a package of hamburger. Suddenly I felt sick; nausea overtook me, like an old high-school stalker. Could it be? I turned down aisle seven and placed a pregnancy test kit into the cart—just like the one I'd purchased a year ago. Back at home, I found myself staring at a faint pink line on a pee stick. "Not again!" I wailed. Anna was not yet sleeping through the night. I was still breast-feeding. I already *had* a baby!

I called a friend, who was neither sympathetic nor encouraging. "Weren't you using birth control?" Feeling alone and helpless, I went up to my room and lay on the floor, hugging a box of tissues, crying off and on. I wasn't ready for another child. I was perplexed. Had God done this, or had we?

My mind drifted back to the first positive pregnancy test, taken the year before. I had been just as remorseful. Yet here I was, in love with that baby. Lying there alone beneath clouds of confusion, a small part of me knew that somehow everything was going to be okay.

Father, all I need to understand is that You love me.
—FAITH BOGDAN

Day Twenty-One

We ought therefore to show hospitality to such men
so that we may work together for the truth.

—III JOHN 1:8

I'm so glad he's home, I thought as Mike pulled into the driveway after work. Michelle had been fussy and feverish with yet another ear infection, so we'd spent most of our day lounging around on the living room floor.

I popped to my feet in surprise when two young men followed Mike into the house. "This is Chris, and this is David. They're new to England, so I invited them to eat with us tonight. Sorry I didn't call first, but I knew you wouldn't mind."

I glanced at toys scattered everywhere, used diapers taped into little balls, bits of food detritus on the floor and unfolded laundry piled on the couch. Michelle was still in her pajamas, and I looked a mess.

I smiled through my panic and said, "Welcome to our tidy home!" Chris and Dave laughed. While Mike went to change clothes, I made small-talk, though my friendly chatter belied my inner struggle to come up with a dinner plan.

The fridge and pantry were bare, so when Michelle—in her usual bubbly way—began to entertain our guests, I ran upstairs to brainstorm with Mike. We decided the guys would go pick up Chinese food while I pulled things together at home.

As I tidied the house, I knew I needed to clean up my heart as well. I was worried about the impression we were making instead of being focused on providing a warm, caring welcome. I prayed for a heart and a home full of God's love.

The guys came back, and I relaxed and truly enjoyed the evening. And when Chris and David left, I told them to stop by *any* time—and I meant it.

Lord, help me not to wait for perfect days to share
Your love and hospitality with others.

—SUSAN LABOUNTY

Day Twenty-Two

"The Lord himself goes before you and will be with you; he will never leave you nor forsake you. Do not be afraid; do not be discouraged."
—DEUTERONOMY 31:8

Soft downy hair tickles my arm, and I watch as Grace wiggles, wavering between squeezing out a few more moments of playtime and succumbing to the heaviness falling on her lids. Her eyes blink slowly, and she smiles from behind her pink pacifier. The blink gets longer. I know what's coming, and I wait for it.

Seconds later, as Grace's eyes close, her little arm rises until tiny fingers rest on my face. Then she glides her hand across my cheek. It's a familiar movement. When my tiny daughter can't see me anymore, she reaches out to touch me and make sure I'm there.

I understand that need. I need to know God is nearby. I want to *see* Him, preferably in tangible ways that include positive responses to prayers for bigger paychecks and more patience. When I get silence or "No" for an answer, I fight it the way my little girl battles sleep. I act as if I am losing the One who's promised He will never leave or forsake me. Fortunately, He's patient. He holds me in His embrace, smiling and waiting, until I touch upon the memory that I am to walk by faith and not by sight.

Lord, help me to press deeper into You and walk in trust.
—CAROL HATCHER

Day Twenty-Three

Therefore, if what I eat causes my brother to fall into sin, I will never eat meat again, so that I will not cause him to fall.
—I CORINTHIANS 8:13

Tyler looked at the slice of Valentine's Day cake for a moment and then dove in head first. My father was mortified.

"Why don't you feed it to him?" Papi pleaded.

"This is more fun," I said.

Papi mumbled something to my mother, shaking his head; then he scurried for a small towel from the kitchen.

"Here," he said, tucking part of it in Tyler's shirt. "So he doesn't dirty his shirt."

"It's already dirty." I laughed. "It was dirty five minutes after I put it on."

Tyler took a pause from massaging cake into his hair and ripped the towel off his chest. It landed on the floor. My father used it to clean bits of white frosting and yellow cake from the kitchen tiles. I wanted to tell him it made more sense to wait until Tyler was done, but I bit my tongue.

I love messy eating. I completely enjoy the look on my son's face as he tries to figure out his food. I relish watching him explore the way it feels as well as the way it tastes. I think it satisfies and inspires curiosity and sparks creativity. And to be quite honest, it's just plain cute. I have tons of pictures of my boys in the aftermath of feast/art projects.

Granted, these kinds of feedings don't happen every day. Clean-up can be immense, so if I'm tired or busy, I spoon-feed Tyler. It's not as much fun, but sometimes it's necessary to be a little neater—like on visits to my parents' house. As I watched my father clean the crevices of the high chair with a cotton swab hours after Tyler was finished, I thought, *Maybe I'll leave our little exercises in sensory development to our place.*

Lord, remind me gently that being a parent doesn't exempt me from honoring my own.
—KAREN VALENTIN

Day Twenty-Four

But be sure to fear the Lord and serve him faithfully with all your heart; consider what great things he has done for you.
—I SAMUEL 12:24

~~~~~~~~~~~~~~~~

It's been quiet in Elizabeth's room for a few minutes. Not silent—I can hear her making noises—so I don't feel obliged to supervise every second. But my curiosity is stronger than my desire to avoid hovering, and I poke my head in the door. And laugh. Elizabeth is sitting in front of her dresser, where she's somehow pulled the bottom drawer open. She is gleefully taking out clothes and piling them on the floor.

"Hey, Boo, are you getting dressed?" I ask. She smiles, happy that I've discovered her busy-ness. And I'm thrilled that Elizabeth is discovering how to entertain herself. I love this age, when I can exchange a bit of mess for a few moments of free time.

In the eternal early months of motherhood I smiled wanly when people cautioned that my baby would be grown before I knew it. Elizabeth's first smile was my first clue that survival was possible, maybe even enjoyable. Life grew brighter as colic faded, but it wasn't until the day my daughter sat up on her own that I felt we'd entered the parental Promised Land. The idea that I could *put my child down* was so awesome, so overwhelming, that I found myself singing hymns of praise to the One who came up with such an amazing idea.

I danced over this bit of independence, both Elizabeth's and mine. It was a cha-cha I couldn't have done six months earlier. For now I *savor* two minutes of being able to pop into another room. I relish discovering that my daughter has her own interests. And I pick up my daughter because I *can*, and because I want to, and I appreciate the rich freedom of doing something so simple, by choice.

Lord, I choose to serve You, because I can.
—JULIA ATTAWAY

Day Twenty-Five

"If you, even you, had only known on this day what would bring you peace—but now it is hidden from your eyes."

—LUKE 19:42

~~~~~~~~~~

*I*t felt odd being out all by my lonesome. But this was my big, exciting "Pamper Me Day" suggested by a few well-meaning family members. It consisted of the basics: Go out for the afternoon. Get a manicure. Take myself to lunch. Do a bit of shopping. Yada, yada, yada. All while Kedar hung out with his dad.

So there I was, drifting around the mall, doing my very best not to prove Kenya right. "Try not to call home every five minutes, okay?" he'd teased before I left.

"Ha, ha. Very funny," I responded sarcastically, before kissing him good-bye. But after only an hour, I developed a serious case of mommy-misses-daddy-and-the-baby-itis. My little excursion was turning out to be a real drag.

I wasn't surprised. Even before venturing into motherhood, I was the quintessential homebody. The simple life—spending time with those I love—has always brought me the most enjoyment. So I picked up my cell phone and dialed home.

"Hi Babe," I said, swallowing my pride. "I miss you guys."

I braced for Kenya's "Told ya so!" But instead he replied, "Aw, we miss you too! I was hoping you would call." For the next half hour I sat at a table in the food court, talking and laughing with my best friend in the whole world. It was the most fun—and the best pampering—I'd had all day.

God, help me follow the path that brings me peace and contentment, even when it differs from the route others might choose.

—DIANNA HOBBS

Day Twenty-Six

Therefore, I urge you, brothers, in view of God's mercy, to offer your bodies as living sacrifices, holy and pleasing to God—this is your spiritual act of worship.
—ROMANS 12:1

I held Lucy in one arm while I struggled to sweep up the mess under her high chair with the other. Not particularly appreciative of my multitasking, the baby began to squirm and pull at my clothes. I felt a tug around my neck, and then—*snap*! A thin cold line slivered down my chest, and I looked down to see my golden cross necklace, a treasured gift, in a pile on the floor.

"Why can't I ever keep nice jewelry?" I muttered, grabbing the broken chain and slamming it onto the counter. This was the third necklace casualty from a baby tug in the same number of few months.

I fixated on the necklace as I trudged through my day. I loved my golden cross! How incredibly annoying that it was broken!

I was stopped in my tracks when the thought popped to mind: *But why did you love it?*

The necklace had been a favorite because it was a shining representation of my faith, a proud statement that I am a follower of Jesus Christ. I looked again at the crumpled heap on the counter, topped with a shining cross. My jewelry was ruined because I'd welcomed the gift of a new soul into my life, with all the messiness and sacrifice that involves. The damage was a byproduct of being a parent, of doing the work the Lord had given me. I laughed at myself: In a sense, the broken necklace was a truer symbol of my devotion to Christ than a perfectly unblemished one around my neck.

*Lord, teach me to accept with grace and gratitude the
messiness that comes with welcoming new life.*
—JENNIFER FULWILER

Day Twenty-Seven

When times are good, be happy; but when times are bad,
consider: God has made the one as well as the other.

—ECCLESIASTES 7:14

There I was, wedged between two ginormous guys in one minuscule middle seat, with a screaming seven-month-old on my lap. What had I gotten myself into?

When my husband suggested that I take a trip to Oregon to visit his parents, I jumped at the chance. Why not? I love my in-laws. And they were desperate for some Joey time. And to be completely honest, my stay-at-home-all-day-doing-nothing routine was getting a bit old. I could handle a little four-hour plane ride.

Or so I thought.

Turns out airplane seats are a teensy bit smaller than I remembered. Oh, and no one told me that the only way to calm a baby whose ears are throbbing from the air pressure is to breastfeed. Yep. Just what I wanted: to bare my breast right in front of the two weight-lifting hunks next to me. Uh-huh.

How was I going to survive?

Amazingly, I did. I didn't die, and neither did my son. We stepped off that plane into loving arms, arms that had counted down the days, hours and minutes until our arrival. Arms that made every minute of the nightmarish trip worthwhile.

Lord, sometimes life feels inconvenient—especially when a baby is involved.
But sometimes the most inconvenient journeys end up at the best places.

—ERIN MACPHERSON

Day Twenty-Eight

Indeed, the very hairs of your head are all numbered. Do not fear; you are more valuable than many sparrows.
—LUKE 12:7 (NAS)

My prepregnancy jeans taunted me from the bottom of my dresser drawer. As I reached for a pair of pajama bottoms, the staple of my work-from-home wardrobe, I groaned thinking about a deadline that had been pushed up for one of my freelance jobs.

"My pants still don't fit," I complained to my sister Maria. "I'm tired most of the time. The house is a mess. I have deadlines for work and I don't even have time to take a shower."

"What do you expect?" Maria said. "You're a new mom. You're working when the baby sleeps. Of course you're tired. Cut yourself some slack."

"Slack," I repeated the word to myself. *Slack is exactly what I need, but I also need to go grocery shopping, and the dishwasher has to be loaded.*

Solomon fussed in his playpen and I reached down to pick him up. He had spit up a little on the playpen mattress. *Add laundry to the list*, I thought.

The sunlight streamed in through the window, painting the couch in warm, welcoming light. *Slack*, I whispered, sitting in the patch of sun. Solomon and I cuddled, soaking up the peace and quiet. He nuzzled in my arms and looked up at me, cutting me all the slack I needed.

Dear God, help me be half as patient with myself as You are with me.
—SABRA CIANCANELLI

Day Twenty-Nine

Let us not give up meeting together, as some are in the habit
of doing, but let us encourage one another. . . .
—HEBREWS 10:25

Like a flock of birds they gathered, popping out of their nests in the parking lot at 10:00 AM. Trunks opened, strollers unfolded. Babies were nestled into comfy positions, and the older ones given tidbits of food and drink for the journey.

Zach and I took the trip often that first year, into a retail resort awash in Colorado sunshine, ski-lodge décor and stores as far as the eye could see. I knew where the high-end department store lounge was, perfect for private nursing. I knew what day the children's toy store put out its newest bargains. I knew what time to nab a table by the soaring stone fireplace before the lunch crowds descended.

I did not always know, however, why I was there. Most of us made a purchase or two, to feign purpose. But the only thing I *needed* was a place to be. Zach was my world, but I wasn't always sure what to do with him.

So we strolled. Mommies circled each other for companionship, but seemed content with knowing smiles and few words. I imagined their stories: Up all night? New in town? No friends? I had many friends at that stage, and still felt isolated.

The mall days were precious ones. I learned how to manage a baby in public. I learned to shop a season ahead. I learned how to have lunch dates that involved no deep conversation, amazing surges of love and pounds of Cheerios. And I learned there is value in being alone, together.

Lord, help me find places to spread my wings and
my understanding of my new life.
—SUSAN BESZE WALLACE

Day Thirty

In my distress I called to the Lord; I called out to my God. From
his temple he heard my voice; my cry came to his ears.

—II SAMUEL 22:7

~~~~~~~~~~~~~~

Aches, fever, bleary-headedness: It was as bad as the flu, with the addition of an about-to-erupt volcano in my left breast. My GYN said to continue breast-feeding despite the mastitis, though the pressure of Elizabeth's mouth as she nursed made me gasp.

As I left the doctor's office, she cautioned, "Make sure you take *every pill* in this prescription. Don't miss a single dose, or you may get a recurrence." I nodded, gray-faced. Remembering four pills a day was as ridiculous an idea as thinking I might someday feel better.

Once I was home again, I faced the grim facts. Andrew had just started a new job and couldn't take time off. My family lived far away. My brain was too foggy to think of anyone to call for help. I took two pain pills and the first dose of the antibiotic. *It's you and me, God,* I offered, *and I'm a wreck.*

I put Elizabeth down, dragged out a pile of toys, and curled up with a pillow on the floor. Before I passed out, I scanned the area for chokeable items. For once I was grateful that my baby couldn't crawl. *I can't do more, God. Take care of her.*

I woke to baby-whacks on my head, with no idea how long I'd slept. The achiness had subsided a bit. Elizabeth wanted to nurse. We lay together on the floor, and my usually nap-averse baby miraculously drifted off next to me. I don't remember closing my eyes, but when I awoke again the sun was setting. I remembered it was time for my next dose of medicine. Andrew arrived, and I abdicated all parenting responsibility. Before I tumbled into bed, I wrote a single word on a scrap of paper: *Coverage!* God had filled in for me in a pinch, but I knew it was my job to think ahead to who could help me if I were ever in a similar situation again.

Lord, motherhood is packed with situations I never imagined.
Help me think through what to do if I ever need help.

—JULIA ATTAWAY

Eighth Month

～～～

Father,

I bring before You my spouse, the man to whom You have joined me. I ask You to give him ever-deeper faith, and to make him a living example of Your fatherly love. Keep our marriage strong, Lord. Help us be patient with each other's weaknesses, to support each other wholeheartedly, and to hold our tongues when needed. Make and keep this marriage strong.

In Christ, amen.

Tips

» If you don't pray daily for your child, who will? See page 401 for tips and suggestions.

» Good moms have the good sense to take breaks. Be a mom, not a martyr.

» Instead of tackling big cleaning tasks all at once, break them down into one-minute chores. In the bathroom, wipe off the sink in the morning, swish the toilet at noon, and tidy up on an afternoon visit.

Day One

Be completely humble and gentle; be patient,
bearing with one another in love.
—EPHESIANS 4:2

~~~~~~~~~~

I t was our wedding anniversary, and Billy and I left for one of our first dates since Samantha was born. I was so excited. We didn't have a lot of money, so we decided on a simple dinner and then a movie.

Hold my hand, I thought as we walked from the car to the restaurant.

Hold my hand, I thought, as we waited for our food.

I didn't speak the words, I just yearned. *Please hold my hand. Show me you still love me. Show me you want to be close. Reach over and hold my hand.*

The more the evening progressed, the sadder I became. *He doesn't want to hold my hand!* I wondered why the romance seemed to be gone. I started pouting—hoping he would notice and try to rectify the situation.

Finally, after the movie and a quiet ride home, Billy reached over and grabbed my hand. "Are you okay?" he asked.

I stared down at our hands clasped together. "I wanted you to do that all night."

He looked confused. "You seemed a little distant, so I wanted to give you some space. Why didn't you just reach out and grab my hand if you wanted to hold hands?"

I had no idea what to say. *Because you're supposed to read my mind? Because I'm feeling selfish and need you to be all about me right now?*

"I'm sorry," I said, "I'll do that next time."

Father, please help me talk to my husband, to
share my needs and to think about his.
—ELSA KOK COLOPY

Day Two

After Rachel gave birth to Joseph, Jacob said to Laban, "Send me on my way so I can go back to my own homeland."
—GENESIS 30:25

I was digging through a closet in search of a lost pair of shoes when a stack of pictures fell out of an overflowing box. There was a photo of Joe and me, four years younger and countless pounds thinner, grinning on a street corner in Santiago, Chile. I closed my eyes, wandering back through our big trip to South America. I smelled the ocean on a sun-baked beach in Panama; I tasted the local steak at a rural Argentinean restaurant; I heard the friendly voices of the staff at our boutique hotels.

My mental vacation was interrupted by wailing coming from upstairs. Lucy was awake from her nap. I retrieved her, and as I fed my daughter slow spoonfuls of baby food, a sense of dissatisfaction lingered around me. This was a far cry from that four-star hotel outside of Buenos Aires!

I thought again of the picture, but this time I remembered what was going on in that smiling young woman's head at the time. She was restless. She was acutely aware that these glamorous experiences were fleeting, that in the end she'd be left with nothing but memories and a stack of pictures. No matter how much she partied or traveled, it was never enough. She yearned for something deeper, something that would last.

Lucy giggled, looked right at me, and said, *"Mmm-aaah. . ."* That girl on the street corner in Santiago never would have guessed where she'd find all the fulfillment she ever desired. It wouldn't be in some exotic land, but in a simple house in the suburbs.

Jesus, thank You for helping me find my true home.
—JENNIFER FULWILER

Day Three

Great are the works of the Lord; they are
pondered by all who delight in them.
—PSALM 111:2

After living in a furnished flat in England for three months, we finally settled into our home. It was time to get myself back into good physical condition. I decided to do the aerobic workout I'd followed while I was pregnant. It was quick and I knew it by heart, so I turned on some music and started.

I knew active, bubbly Michelle would want to be in the thick of the action. I gave her a little bowl of Cheerios to munch, thinking it would keep her on the sidelines. The cereal disappeared almost instantly, so I tossed the entire box Michelle's way to keep her occupied. She dragged the box around, spreading cereal across the living room. I sweated and bounced and huffed and puffed, little O's crunching underfoot, dodging my grinning, squealing little girl. Michelle clearly thought all this bouncing and waving was for her entertainment.

I decided we'd go for a walk instead. Aimee, my two-year-old, sat in the stroller, and I carried Michelle—bouncing and squealing, as usual—in the backpack. This was much better than the sweaty, messy living room routine.

We walked along, enjoying the beautiful English gardens and the charming streets of town. We wandered into the countryside, and the memory of hopping around on Cheerios gave way to a cleared mind, grateful for beauty and God's many gifts. Now that I was no longer trying to shoo Michelle from beneath my feet, her bubbly bouncing and chattering in the backpack made me smile. And making walking part of our daily routine produced a bonus: My last, stubborn pregnancy pounds melted away.

Thank You, Lord, for physical strength, fresh
air and the beauty of Your creation.
—SUSAN LABOUNTY

Day Four

God is not unjust; he will not forget your work and the love you have shown him as you have helped his people and continue to help them.
—HEBREWS 6:10

Henry's speech therapy isn't being covered," I say to the insurance person on the phone. "I'm calling to find out why, and how to fix it."

"Well," she replies. "His diagnosis code is for Down syndrome, which we classify as a mental illness. Speech therapy isn't covered for mental illnesses."

"Mental illness?" I question, jaw dropping. "Henry gets therapy because he can't eat. He has oral-motor issues that prevent him from getting basic nutrition."

"Be that as it may," the response came, "We still don't cover it. There's really nothing we can do. Sorry."

Sorry. All my frustration and worry about whether Henry will ever eat enough to grow is dismissed with a *sorry*. We struggled for seven months to get food into Henry. We began in month one by feeding him pumped breast milk with a plastic syringe. We survived bad reactions to two different formulas. Then it turned out that Henry's low muscle tone meant he couldn't swallow baby food. He struggled—we struggled—and we had to keep trying. Giving up wasn't an option: it was *eating*, after all.

We prayed and prayed, and then one day, well into month seven of my lessons in perseverance and resourcefulness, I hit upon a solution. Or a solution hit upon me. I discovered that if I sang to Henry, he continued to eat.

So I sang for his supper, and the food went down. I sang for my son, and Henry grew. And gradually I found myself singing a new song, as something inside me called faith grew bigger too.

Lord, You stick with me. Help me stick with the problems I face until, with Your help, I learn to trust You completely.
—CHRISTY STURM

Day Five

*Start children off on the way they should go, and even
when they are old they will not turn from it.*
—PROVERBS 22:6

~~~~~~~~~~~~~

One of Solomon's favorite games is drive-a-baby. Sitting on the couch, with Solomon on my knees facing me, I hold his hands and pretend he is driving an imaginary car.

"RRRR," I say, bouncing my knees and revving the engine.

Solomon smiles.

"Uh-oh," I say. "Solomon! You missed your turn!" I lean to the side and hold him off-kilter.

"Oh no! Big pothole!" I gently bounce him on my knees.

Solomon laughs.

"Another bump!" I say.

He laughs and laughs, exploding in a burst of giggles.

Together we laugh. We bounce from imaginary road to road, avoiding obstacles, swerving to avoid danger. Then as we sit on the couch, he looks at me with surprise and delight, as if he can't believe the good time we've just had.

I know that the real road we're on will be filled with twists and turns, bumps and potholes too. I suppose the key to getting through the challenges is to hold on to each other, keep laughing and have faith.

Dear God, thank You for laughter, for this journey, this life!
—SABRA CIANCANELLI

Day Six

"She sets about her work vigorously; her arms are strong for her tasks."
—PROVERBS 31:17

ere, I'll hold Grace," my friend Amy said, reaching for my baby while I dug for my keys. Amy talked to Grace and scooted her higher on her hip. When I finally produced the keys, Amy followed me to the car with Grace still in her arms.

As I unlocked the door, Amy shifted her load from one hip to the other. "Wow. She's heavy. How do you carry her around all the time?" she asked.

"You get used to it. Babies arrive small and grow with the passing of time." I replied. It's true: You never hear people complain about the weight of a newborn. Mothers tote their offspring from the start and don't typically notice the incremental increase in weight over time. We grow muscles.

Arm strength isn't the only way I've grown as a mother. At first, getting up to feed and change the baby was all I could handle. Soon I added taking a shower to the mix. Before long, I threw in a hot meal or two. Now I'm finding time to do laundry, put on make-up, and even have some devotional time.

I couldn't have started with all those responsibilities, just as I couldn't have carried a twenty-one-pound baby on my hip the day we left the hospital. Thankfully, we moms get better at this mothering business and grow stronger with time.

Lord, thank You for increasing my strength, slowly but surely.
—CAROL HATCHER

Day Seven

"He was lost and is found. . . ."
—LUKE 15:24

~~~~~~~~~~~~

As Shiloh and I began our weekly grocery shopping, I made sure Pink Bear was firmly at her side. Pink Bear is our stuffed friend that Shiloh has taken a great liking to. He never leaves her side. He's practically part of our family tree. Seeing the familiar soft pink fluff peeking from beneath her arms, I breathed a sigh of relief.

After circling the large store several times, I ticked off the last item on my list. "We are finished!" I announced as I looked down at Shiloh, sitting happily in the child's seat. I attempted to turn my overloaded cart towards the cashier. And then I let out a little scream. Pink Bear was gone!

Panic immediately set in. I scanned the cart, confirming his disappearance. My mind went blank as I tried to remember the last time I had seen him. Without a clue where to start looking, I stopped anyone who happened to cross my path, asking passionately if they had seen our pink toy. They hadn't.

I searched for forty-five minutes, finally accepting the grim news that Pink Bear might be gone for good. Discouraged, tired and sweaty, I slowly made my way toward the cashier once again. I feared the moment Shiloh would notice Pink Bear's absence.

Wait. I stopped my cart and squinted my eyes. What was that? At the end of the aisle? Could it be? Yes, it was! I grabbed Pink Bear from the shelf and handed him back to Shiloh. Our prodigal bear had returned, and I was ready to throw a big party!

Father, thank You for little blessings that show great mercy.
—RUTH BERGEN

Day Eight

She is clothed with strength and dignity;
she can laugh at the days to come.
—PROVERBS 31:25

ow that Elizabeth's standing up, she won't sit down in the tub. She climbs out of the bath ring. I can't reach her around the sliding glass shower door. I worry that she'll slip.

I bought some bath puppets and slid them onto Elizabeth's feet. Whenever she stands up, they disappear under water, so for a while she sat down. Then she figured out she could remove them and whack the puppets against the wall, making a delightfully funny splatter of water. That's even more enjoyable (for her) if she's standing, of course.

Last week I gave up, undressed, and climbed into the tub. Elizabeth and I had a great mother-daughter bath, and we giggled a lot. It was easy to get her to sit down. Problem solved.

Sort of. A few days ago I added this gem to my Things You Never Imagined You'd Need to Know pool of parenting knowledge: Some diaper rashes are yeast infections. They're contagious. So thanks to my bath with my Boo, I'm twitchy and itchy and *very* tender. And so, by relation, is Andrew.

Today at Elizabeth's check-up I asked, with keen interest, what to put on her inflamed, baboon-like bottom. The doctor blandly recommended an over-the-counter antifungal cream. Andrew and I exchanged glances of intense relief; there are adult versions of the same stuff. My husband ran to the pharmacy next door while I paid the doctor's bill. For $31.72 worth of cream, lotion, and spray we are now on our way back to health. Relief!

But Elizabeth still won't sit down in the tub.

Lord, make me a resourceful problem-solver.
—JULIA ATTAWAY

Day Nine

*He died for all, that those who live should
no longer live for themselves. . . .*
—II CORINTHIANS 5:15

<hr />

I slammed the snooze button, not wanting to get out of bed to go to MOPS that morning. Anna had wakened and fussed a few times in the night. My tired limbs begged me to sleep in, asking, *What's in it for you? Will today's speaker be interesting? Relevant?* My brain reasoned that twenty minutes wasn't enough time to get me to the meeting in a recognizable state. But my heart said otherwise: maybe I was needed, somehow. I dragged myself and Anna out of bed and went to the meeting.

The presenter that day was a police officer, who spoke on the importance of infant car seat safety. It was a rare disappointment; we were *moms,* for crying out loud—already well-versed on the topic. During the lady's talk, a foul odor filled the room. Every mom holding a baby lifted it and sniffed its rear end in hopes of discovering the culprit stinker. No one 'fessed up, so we sat covering our noses until the speaker ended by apologizing for her police dog's bad case of flatulence.

After the talk, the moms mingled, and that's when I learned that Ruth's husband was out of work. I listened to her for a while and encouraged her as best I knew how. Ruth seemed a bit cheerier when she went out the door. I was very glad I'd come.

Lord, help me remember that living for You is always worthwhile.
—FAITH BOGDAN

Day Ten

*As you do not know the path of the wind, or how the body
is formed in a mother's womb, so you cannot understand
the work of God, the Maker of all things.*

—ECCLESIASTES 11:5

~~~~~~~~~~~~~

Here's one thing I want to ask God when we meet in heaven: Why are babies born without teeth? They arrive with hair, eyelashes, fingernails and toenails—so what's with the teething?

And what's up with having teeth erupt one at a time? Couldn't they all pop in at once, so we could get it over with? I don't understand: We moms have already *done* sleep deprivation. I, at least, could manage without all the crying, fever, diarrhea, sore gums and drooling. Extra laundry, no thanks.

According to what I've read, babies teethe until they're at least a year old. They'll generally have all twenty of their primary teeth (forty in my case, since I have twins) by the time they are three. That's a *lot* of teething.

I trust that God fully grasps and sympathizes with my impatience. I am an exhausted mom, after all. Perhaps someday He'll enlighten me on how teething is part of His divine plan. Until then, I'll start saving my tooth fairy dollars for when those forty teeth all begin coming out.

*Lord, there's a reason You're in charge, not me. Help me be
patient with the parts of parenting I'd rather do without.*

—DONNA MAY LYONS

Day Eleven

~~~~~~~~~~~~~~~

I entered the fast-food restaurant with Llewelyn in tow. I was supposed to meet up with an immigrant woman I'd been told about by a missionary friend. Francisca had moved to New York City and was pregnant and alone.

A short woman with neatly braided black hair entered the restaurant and smiled at me as I waved her over. "Are you Leez?" she asked quietly in heavily accented English.

"Yes, nice to meet you. This is my daughter Llewelyn." Llewelyn was sitting quietly in her stroller. She was an easy and calm baby, so I asked Francisca to watch her while I ordered. As I waited in line, I looked over to see Francisca smiling as Llewelyn grasped her finger with a tiny hand. Even though Francisca said she was not hungry, I wondered when she had eaten last and bought her the healthiest salad on the menu. "Oh, thank you!" she exclaimed with surprise.

We talked for some time about Francisca's pregnancy, her family in Indonesia and her current living situation. It was not good. *Lord give me wisdom,* I prayed, *Help me help her.* Later we watched and marveled at Llewelyn together. Francisca was delighted with how Llewelyn played with her feet while we talked. "Being a mom *is* difficult," I told her. "But your baby will fill your life with joy. I am sure you will be a wonderful mother."

Francisca looked just a little bit less timid. "Thank you," she said with a smile.

*Lord, open my eyes to mothers around me who
need Your love and encouragement.*
—LIZ BISSELL

Day Twelve

He guides the humble in what is right and teaches them his way.
—PSALM 25:9

I wanted Zach and his big, blue eyes to be a little Superman for his first Halloween. But no cheesy store-bought get-up would do. I could do better. The hunt was on.

The royal blue sweatshirt was easy enough to find. The craft store had bright red and yellow felt for the emblem. I could print the big *S* from the Internet, trace and cut. Then I hit a wall.

Royal blue tights. Surely they exist? I searched hard, finally finding some online. Once in my mailbox, they were *not* Superman blue and could have fit a four-year-old. Creating red briefs for an eight-month-old was proving to be a hassle too.

A little obsessive? Nah—I thought I was just particular and . . . motherly. The way I was with hand-me-downs that I was certain weren't what I wanted for my baby. Particular.

One day I grudgingly boxed up some outdated girl clothing a relative had sent when we were still in the gender-guessing stage. No use for these in my world of plaid and denim! But then I saw them: small velveteen bloomers, candy-apple red.

Amid my joyful discovery I had to wince. I'd been so dismissive of these clothes, so twisted up in my desires, that I'd forgotten what the goal was. I was going to repurpose part of a decade-old girl's Christmas outfit for my costume—*his* costume.

When the sweetest Superman ever rang his first doorbell, his mom had already had an important door opened. Anything I do for my child should be about how much I love him. And the devil can truly be in the details.

I can get lost in my projects, God. Help me do everything in love while keeping perspective.
—SUSAN BESZE WALLACE

Day Thirteen

Dear friends, if our hearts do not condemn us,
we have confidence before God.
—I JOHN 3:21

So when are you gonna get back on the praise and worship team?" asked a friend before church one cool Sunday morning.

"Maybe soon. We'll see," I smiled. But I honestly didn't know if I was ready to throw myself back into singing full-time. Whenever I resumed, I wanted to be confident that I could keep up with the rehearsal schedule, be present at each service, and do so without feeling overextended.

When church got underway that morning, I was fully engaged and ready for a spirit-filled worship experience. "The presence of the Lord is here!" belted out the praise leader as he charismatically led one of my favorite songs. I rocked back and forth in my seat, observing other congregants joyfully jumping, dancing and shouting, "Hallelujah!" Kedar's eyes sparkled as he sat in my lap taking in the sights and sounds. But after about fifteen minutes, he lost interest and began to squirm and fuss.

I quickly picked up his diaper bag, tiptoed out of the sanctuary and headed downstairs. About forty-five minutes later, fed and dried, Kedar's happy disposition returned. I'd missed out on a good bit of singing, but that was okay. I looked into my son's smiling face and knew I wasn't ready yet to be on the praise and worship team. I was praising God by doing exactly what I should be doing at that moment: being Mommy.

God, give me the wisdom to know when to take on new responsibilities
and when to be content with the ones I already have.
—DIANNA HOBBS

Day Fourteen

When anxiety was great within me,
your consolation brought joy to my soul.
—PSALM 94:19

~~~~~~~~~~~~~~

I t was our first Fourth of July with Samantha. I dressed her up in a red, white and blue T-shirt, put on her star-studded ball cap and off we went to the fair. People oohed and ahed at my smiling baby and she obliged them with a drooling grin in return.

Everything was perfect—until the fireworks. Oh, Sam loved the bright lights and bursts of color, but the loud booms did nothing for her. After three or four in a row she scrunched up her face and started howling. Nothing would console her. I put my hands over her ears, I tried to distract her by making faces, I gave her a bottle. Now people gave me dirty looks.

Like you can even hear her above the fireworks noise! I thought gruffly in their direction.

We were in the middle of the crowd, so our exit involved climbing over people with my girl in my arms as Billy lifted the stroller over parents, children and small dogs. Finally we reached our car—only to have Sam stop screaming. She pointed back toward the crowd with a longing whimper.

Billy and I climbed onto the hood of the car, where we held Samantha and watched the rest of the show. During one particularly bright burst, Billy leaned over and smooched me.

Sam laughed and tried to get in on the kiss.

No people were around to offer a disapproving glance.

I relished the moment and smooched them both back.

Lord, help me to go with the flow. When things don't turn out
as I hope, help me to find the joy in whatever comes.
—ELSA KOK COLOPY

Day Fifteen

A Dad's View

Is not life more than food? . . .
—MATTHEW 6:25 (ESV)

~~~~~~~~~~~~~

Can we afford it?" Kari asked, as she changed Hans.

I didn't like the question at all. I had always been one to spend money freely on little things like ordering pizza or grabbing a coffee or going out to eat with friends. Before Hans came, we were classic DINKS—Dual Income, No Kids—and that meant we could eat out whenever we wanted, without thinking about it.

"Yeah, I think we can," I said, without really knowing. Actually, I knew: It wasn't going to break us, but we probably shouldn't spend the money. No one gets rich teaching college, and since Kari stopped working to stay home with Hans, we were living on one income.

"You sure?" she asked, hesitant.

I was sure I hated these discussions. My body and voice tensed: "Yes, we can," I said deliberately, in an attempt to conceal my rising impatience. I wanted my chicken burrito and my chile relleno from my favorite restaurant, and that was that. "Look, we've had a long day, and I don't feel like cooking or cleaning up."

"You're *sure* we can afford it?" Kari asked, one last time.

My wife is wiser than I, and we'd had discussions about how having children would involve serious sacrifice. What she was telling me was that now was the time to sacrifice, not just talk about it.

Wincing, I let go. "Y'know," I admitted, "it's probably best if we make dinner here." I smiled at my wife and son and went to the kitchen to make burritos as best I knew how.

Lord, teach us to enjoy living simply as we sacrifice for our child.
—LEROY HUIZENGA

Day Sixteen

Jesus said, "That's what I mean: Risk your life and get more than you ever dreamed of. Play it safe and end up holding the bag."
—LUKE 19:26 (MSG)

~~~~~~~~~~~~~~

hy am I doing this? I wondered as I unpacked our towels in the recreation center locker room. I knew the answer: I was lonely. The mommy-and-baby swimming class sounded like a great idea when some women from my hospital new-mom class suggested it, but now it sounded awkward and freezing.

I walked out to the pool to join the other mothers and babies. I was early, wanting to grab every second of socializing possible. We'd moved to Denver only months earlier, and I'd left many trusted girlfriends behind. Now my heart ached to know and be known.

I hesitated before approaching the group of moms and started an inner pep talk for myself. *Be bold!* I said silently. *You have a lot to offer!* My insecurity countered, *Really?* It was like being in seventh grade all over again.

Walking up to the group I found the conversation was focused on how cute the babies were in their tiny swimming suits. Not exactly the deep exchange I was hoping for, but a safe starting place. Obviously, the moms wanted their babies to be noticed. Even though I thought the towel-wrapped person in my arms was the most precious being on the planet, in that moment *I* wanted to be noticed for me.

I felt the heartache pulling again. I resumed my inner pep talk. *You have to be here for anything to happen. You're not going to make friends at home, alone.* Then I squeezed Gabi a little tighter and joined the conversation.

Lord, I want to live more fully, even if it means taking risks in my relationships.
—ALEXANDRA KUYKENDALL

Day Seventeen

Listen to my cry for help, my King and my God, for to you I pray.
—PSALM 5:2

Over and over I'd asked the Lord for help. I was drowning, trying to keep up with all the aspects of motherhood.

Then Riley and Carmen, a couple of ten-year-old girls from the neighborhood began stopping by my house after school. Their parents worked long hours and they enjoyed being around baby Lucy—and they even offered to help! It seemed like an answered prayer.

Joe encouraged me to accept their kind offer, so I did. The next day the girls took the dishes from the sink, loaded the dishwasher and ran it. After they left, I opened it to behold dishwasher chaos. Cups were overturned, a plastic plate was on the bottom rack, one of the baby's spoons had fallen onto the hot coil and melted. As a dishwasher perfectionist, I was horrified. Didn't they know there is a right—and a wrong—way to load the dishes?

I announced to Joe I would gently decline the girls' next offer to help. He wisely encouraged me to reconsider. "You're going to reject the help that God sends you because it's not exactly right?" he asked. He pointed out that my perfectionism was interfering with a blessing God was trying to give me. I decided he might be right.

Riley and Carmen showed up a few days later, eager to be of use. For the next several months my young neighbors offered much-needed help, and the only cost was a couple of melted baby spoons.

Lord, teach me to accept imperfect help.
—JENNIFER FULWILER

Day Eighteen

For with you is the fountain of life; in your light we see light.

—PSALM 36:9

~~~~~~~~~~~~~~~~

Gently I brought Solomon over to his crib and put him down for his nap, careful not to wake him. As I walked out the door, he began to cry.

"Oh, Solomon," I said, picking him up. We sat in the rocking chair and his eyes fixed on the ladybug pattern of the curtains.

"Those are your curtains, Sol," I said. "I made them just for you."

I'd spent hours searching for the fabric when I was eight months pregnant. I bought a sewing machine and eagerly set it up on the dining room table. I ironed the fabric, cut the pattern, pinned the seam, loaded the bobbin, threaded the machine and began.

Reaching over my belly, I slowly pressed the sewing machine pedal. The first few inches went perfectly. Just as I began to think I was a natural sewer, everything took a turn for the worse, the needle broke and the hemline dipped downward.

Four panels and two days later, I threaded the curtains on the rod and positioned them over the nursery windows. I stepped back. The curtains looked fine when they were open, but they were an inch too short on one side when closed. The cute pattern of ladybugs sloped downward. I pulled on the short end hoping it would level, but it was no use. When Tony first saw them, he tilted his head and said, "Well, they certainly are one-of-a-kind."

Now Solomon's eyes kept focus on the patch of sunlight that sneaked in from the bottom of the uneven hem. "Yes, Solomon, Mommy put a lot of love in these curtains."

Slowly he fell asleep.

Dear God, when I'm frustrated and want everything to be just right,
help me remember that my best effort shines with Your perfect love.
—SABRA CIANCANELLI

Day Nineteen

Jesus said, "Let the little children come to me, and do not hinder them, for the kingdom of heaven belongs to such as these."
—MATTHEW 19:14

~~~~~~~~~~~~~

Stacy drove me to the police station, where they were giving away infant car seats. In a few months I'd be needing one for Anna's new sibling.

We sat in the parking lot filling out the necessary paperwork: questions about our children's ages, sizes and weights. I found it difficult to concentrate with Stacy's three kids making wild animal noises and bouncing up and down in the back of her minivan.

Then three-year-old Seldon began to bat his mother with a long, wiener-like balloon, laughing each time he did it. Stacy ignored him and kept writing, her hair transformed into a dandelion gone to seed by the balloon static. Annoyed, I wanted Stacy to make Seldon stop, to turn around and explain how he should be adultlike. I thought she should get him to sit quietly in his seat and not interfere with our important, potentially life-saving paperwork.

Seldon continued his head-bopping game, now standing up and swinging body *and* balloon around for repeated head-on collisions with his mother in the driver's seat. Stacy finally put down her pen and turned to face her son. Far from reprimanding him, she giggled and wagged her head side-to-side, nosing Seldon's face. They kissed like Eskimos alone on the tundra, unaware of time.

I looked down at my papers, feeling very small and frail as a mother. Eventually Stacy and I retrieved our new car seats and Stacy drove me home, where I raced into the house and buried my face in Anna's belly, blowing billows of laughter out of her body and into my well-composed world.

Father, help me practice childlike joy.
—FAITH BOGDAN

Day Twenty

Then God said, "Let us make man in our image, in our likeness, and let them rule . . . over all the earth, and over all the creatures that move along the ground."

—GENESIS 1:26

~~~~~~~~~~

"Did you know that disposable diapers are destroying the environment?" The young college student glanced with disdain at the diaper peeking up behind Samantha's pants. "It takes over eighty thousand pounds of plastic and two hundred thousand trees to make those diapers annually!"

"We don't use very many," I said weakly. "Maybe just a tree or two for our family." He shook his head, unimpressed. "Besides," I said, "we recycle. We do try to do our part."

The young man stalked away, clearly irritated. I tugged down my daughter's shirt to hide the incriminating evidence, and wondered at my environmental sin. *But wait,* I thought, *I do care about the environment. I recycle newspaper, plastic and aluminum. I walk instead of driving. I turn the water off when I brush my teeth. So maybe I use disposable diapers—for now that's a vice I'm willing to live with.*

I physically shook the guilt off my shoulders and, in a miniact of defiance, pulled up my girl's shirt to expose the diaper again. Maybe I would reconsider in a day or two, but for today, I would be content with the good we chose, instead of wallowing in guilt over what we didn't.

*Lord, I want to be a good steward of the environment.
Help me balance my own needs with the earth's.*

—ELSA KOK COLOPY

Day Twenty-One

In that day men will look to their Maker and turn
their eyes to the Holy One of Israel.
—ISAIAH 17:7

~~~~~~~~~~~~

I was distracted. The phone rang, the teakettle whistled, the alarm sounded. All at once. At least it seemed that way. But even if our apartment had been shaken loose from its perch, I should have been paying closer attention to the earthquake by the couch.

In turning away to tend to all the inconsequential rest, I missed Anjelica's first stand-alone moment, the instant when she eased her fingers' grasp on the frame of the couch and stood, without support, on her own two wobbly legs for the first time.

I was only two feet away, but I missed it. I knew because now her two glorious pegs swayed and buckled, and I watched as that tiny tower of strength fell, with a soft *thump*, onto its swaddled rear. Her forehead grazed the sofa's edge on her way down, leaving a blotch that sprang up red and quick.

Anjelica's round face pivoted on to mine from her seat, her eyes scanning my own to determine the nature of this event for her. I recognized this newly established pattern, our own Morse code. When she's taken a hard spill or her forehead has connected with a solid object, be it floor or shoulder, her eyes find mine, and mine hers.

It happened now. And I smiled and clapped my hands once, twice, and dropped to the floor beside her. "Mamita, you did it! You were standing!"

She swatted at her chafed forehead with her hands, uncertain, and then fell forward into my embrace, her forehead coming to rest on my chest. *"¡Qué niña grande!"*

We rocked back and forth gently on the floor. She absolved me of my distraction; I banished her pain. We were interpreters, one for the other, newly skilled in this ever-changing broadcast of life.

Father, let me turn my eyes to You when I am troubled and need help.
—DEBRALEE SANTOS

Day Twenty-Two

Follow my example, as I follow the example of Christ.
—I CORINTHIANS 11:1

~~~~~~~~~~~~~~

I was a rookie. But I had a book. I like clear instructions, so I knew if I followed my book I'd raise my child the best possible way. It wasn't quite the "Epistle from the Apostle Paul to the Parents," but I treated it almost with the authority of the Gospel. I knew someday I could shake my head condescendingly at new mothers and say, "Oh, my dear, things will go so much better for you if you just follow this book!"

But I couldn't say that to my friend Devon. When her baby whimpered, Devon naturally and discreetly nursed her into a peaceful slumber. She didn't look at the clock to see if it was time for a feeding. She didn't time herself to make sure the baby ate a full ten minutes on each side. She didn't second-guess herself. This was her second child, and she was a pro.

Everything she did seemed effortless.

My book approach took a lot of work, and it wasn't always successful. Devon had a toddler and a well-fed, happy baby; I paced her living room trying to calm my Little Miss Fussy. I left Devon's house and put my book on the shelf for a while when I returned home. I wasn't quite the novice I had been before: Now I knew there was more than one way to learn to be a mom.

Lord, help me learn from every resource You put in my path.
—LISA LADWIG

Day Twenty-Three

Children's children are a crown to the aged, and
parents are the pride of their children.
—PROVERBS 17:6

~~~~~~~~~~

The two grandmothers sat in my living room playing with my boys. "Wow, Connie," my mother-in-law said. "Before you know it we'll be going to high school graduations."

My mother, who is twenty years older, laughed and shook her head. "I don't think I'll be around for that," she replied. My heart dropped, and a knot formed in my throat. They continued talking while I went into my bedroom, closed the door and sobbed.

My relationship with my mother has not always been smooth. Before I was married, I lived with my parents longer than I care to admit. When I finally moved out, it was a welcome separation. Eventually my parents moved to Florida, but I didn't fully grasp their absence until Brandon and Tyler were born.

Now I was reminded that not only do they live far away, but soon they won't be here at all. My sons will only experience the tenderness and love of their grandparents for a short time. There may not be any graduations or weddings with them, only faded memories of these moments we're sharing now.

For the rest of my parents' visit I took lots of pictures of them with the boys, snuggled with my mother and took long walks with my dad. I'd never imagined needing and wanting my Mami and Papi as much as I did when I was a child—but as their visit came to an end, that's exactly how I felt.

Lord, help me cherish and appreciate each day
You have given me with my parents.
—KAREN VALENTIN

Day Twenty-Four

*"As a mother comforts her child, so will I comfort you;
and you will be comforted over Jerusalem."*
—ISAIAH 66:13

~~~~~~~~~~~

I ran out of the kitchen when I heard Kedar yelling. His leg was stuck between the rails on his mahogany crib. I snatched off my oven mitt and tried to help, but with only a couple of inches of wiggle room, I didn't know how to angle Kedar's little limb without making matters worse.

Every time Kedar's trembling voice cried "Ma! Ma!" my heart grew more guilt-ridden.

"Aaargh!" I groaned.

Beep! Beep! Beep! answered the smoke alarm, alerting me that the chicken in the broiler was burning. I snatched up my oven mitt, bolted out of Kedar's room and grabbed the pan out of the oven. Shoot! Charred skinless breasts.

Back to Kedar's room I darted, trying to remain calm. Thankfully, before I completely lost my composure, Kedar's leg popped out with a couple of twists. "Oh, baby!" I crooned, holding him close and stroking his back until he finally relaxed.

I traipsed back to the reeking kitchen and plopped into a chair to think about what else to cook for dinner. Moments later Kenya walked in, sniffing the air and fanning away smoke.

"What happened?" he asked. I told him about my frenzy of competing emergencies. "Aw, baby," he replied sympathetically. Then he held me close and stroked my back until I finally relaxed.

*Dear Lord, thank You for the times You pour back
into me the comfort and love I pour out.*
—DIANNA HOBBS

Day Twenty-Five

I'm so sorry, this isn't . . . uh, I mean. . ." I practiced in the mirror. "It's just that . . . I, uh . . . this isn't working out for us." My babysitter was arriving in ten minutes, and I was going to have to tell her that we were letting her go.

I'd hired her to help me with Lucy a few hours a week, but after only a short time it became clear it wasn't a good situation. She sometimes used a clipped tone of voice when interacting with my baby, and I often walked into the living room to see her focusing on text messages while Lucy had crawled off to places unknown. She sometimes canceled at the last minute, leaving me dragging an overtired baby to appointments that I'd planned to attend alone.

As the minutes ticked by leading to her arrival, I paced the house in anxiety. Did this make me a terrible person? Was it an un-Christian thing to do? Would she hate me forever?

Knock-knock-knock. It was time. I silently prayed for the Holy Spirit to guide my words and welcomed her inside. After a moment, I finally said it: "I'm so sorry, but this isn't working out for us." Without going into detail, I simply explained that we wouldn't be needing her services after the end of the month. I braced myself for her response.

Relief. With a sigh, she said that she had just been about to tell me that she'd realized that she wasn't good with babies and didn't feel up to the work. We both laughed with gratitude that the tension that had been building for weeks was finally broken.

Lord, give me the strength to make the best decisions for
my family, even when it makes me uncomfortable.

—JENNIFER FULWILER

Day Twenty-Six

*In the morning, O Lord, you hear my voice; in the morning
I lay my requests before you and wait in expectation.*
—PSALM 5:3

When did I lose it?

Grace lies beside me on the bed and kicks her feet. Her eyes sparkle as I kiss her baby-soft cheeks. I raise my hand high above her body and wiggle my fingers. She giggles.

As my hand lowers, she kicks and tenses her body expectantly. She shrieks with laughter, and I haven't even touched her. My eight-month-old loves to be tickled. Her peals of laughter and excitement can be heard before I even get my tickly fingers on her little body.

Anticipation. A sense of expectancy. When did I lose it?

I used to get out of bed every morning excited. Excited to see what God was going to do that day. Expecting Him. My face, my heart, my attitude showed it.

Lately, I've been so consumed with my daily routine that I've forgotten to wait with expectation. My mind is focused on time and tediousness. Which items on my list are the most urgent? Do I have time to run errands before naptime, dinnertime, bedtime? How few loads of laundry can I do and still get dressed tomorrow? And while I'm busy asking questions, perhaps I should add these: Is God present in all my actions, my words, my heart? Or have I relegated Him to my to-do list?

Today, Lord, help me look forward above all to You.
—CAROL HATCHER

Day Twenty-Seven

Older women likewise are to be reverent in behavior, not slanderers or slaves to much wine. They are to teach what is good, and so train the young women to love their husbands and children.
—TITUS 2:3–4 (ESV)

I spoke with her briefly on one of the first Sundays at our new church. The conversation consisted of the typical introductions, with added comments and questions about Geneva. We concluded with "Have a good week!" as we parted ways. Her name was Beth. I repeated it to myself so I wouldn't forget. Thankfully I remembered, because a few days later Beth called and invited me to come over for tea. *How exciting! How . . . grown up!*

I needed new friends. My days at home with Geneva were lovely but stretched out long and lonely. Beth and I sipped tea and ate oatmeal cookies, and she told me how her children were doing at college and reminisced about when they were young. She made me laugh with stories about when her Joanna was a baby. Her tales of Nathan's struggle to learn to read broadened my perspective. There was life beyond diapers! There really was. Parenting was about more than applying cream to rashes, pureeing foods and baby-proofing electrical outlets. I would get there, Beth assured me. I would get there.

Lord, thank You for the gift of godly older women.
Could You send a few more into my life?
—LISA LADWIG

Day Twenty-Eight

Then Esau looked up and saw the women and children. "Who are these with you?" he asked. Jacob answered, "They are the children God has graciously given your servant."
—GENESIS 33:5

I was having a moment. I couldn't get over how my entire life was now reduced to bodily functions. I was on call for hunger, thirst, pee, poo, drool, slobber and boogers. And it was not going well. I longed for all the things that once occupied my time: college, work, responsibilities, friends and grown-up conversation. I recalled how I once interacted, made a difference, communicated thoughts and ideas.

This new adventure that once seemed so glamorous had come to feel completely uninspired. What was I doing to change the world? How was I making an impact? Of what use was I beyond being a superefficient diaper changer, bottle cleaner and boogie wiper?

My girl yelled from her bedroom and I walked in to get her. I stopped abruptly when I saw her.

"You're standing!"

Samantha gripped the edge of her crib and smiled at me. She slowly wobbled back and forth, teetering. Then she let go and landed squarely on her bottom.

I scooped her up and held her high. "You stood!" Any thought of a grander purpose fell away—at least for the moment.

Lord, You have called me to raise this child; in the midst of small tasks, help me remember this is a unique and wonderful calling.
—ELSA KOK COLOPY

Day Twenty-Nine

"Praise him, all his angels, praise him, all his heavenly hosts."
—PSALM 148:2

~~~~~~~~~~~~~~

When I told my father he'd be a grandfather, my words were awkward and new-sounding, and his surprise and joy were immediate, if muted by his quiet diffidence.

And now my father speaks my daughter's name out loud, sometimes in soft alarm, as she speed-crawls, darts under furniture, and cruises easily from one surface to the next. Her beautiful dark hair is long enough to just rest on her shoulders, and her smiles abound any time he nears.

"Anjelica, Anjelica," he calls as he buries his face in her soft belly and she, giggling, pummels him with curled fists.

It is his mother's name, the name of that redoubtable, beloved ninety-year-old woman, the first Anjelica of my life. She, of impeccable manners, graceful disposition and an unstinting heart, of a land of coconut trees bearing hard fruit and flinty men. It was she who brought my father forth and nurtured his small form, his own tiny flailing fists. It was she who offered me my first taste of sweet, strong café con leche with a buttered piece of hard bread during my first trip alone to Santo Domingo at age twelve. It was she who sat with me on the back patio, the merciless sun at the edge of our feet, reveling for hours in easy talk of family, politics, food.

Anjelica. *Of the angels.* My father's mother, my grandmother. My daughter, his granddaughter. One name, in tribute to so many gifts given, and hoped for.

Lord, may my child live up to her name and live to glorify Yours.
—DEBRALEE SANTOS

Day Thirty

~~~~~~~~~~~~~~~~

I'm coming to accept that my house will always be a mess. Living in a one-bedroom apartment with two boys and a boyish husband equals disarray. This morning, when my two little ones were out with Gary, I stood in the middle of the disaster, not knowing where to start. I wanted to wiggle my nose or clap my hands and watch everything miraculously put itself away. Then I'd be able to do something exotic, perhaps take a nap or eat in peace. But I knew the next few hours would be dedicated to sweeping cereal from the floor, putting toys in bins and a million other tasks.

When the apartment was finally clean, I sat back and took it all in. It was wonderful to see shiny floors instead of clutter, closets closed, sparkling countertops and an empty kitchen sink. But then they came home.

At first I protected my territory like a lioness. I growled at my husband when he tossed his shoes in the middle of the floor. I gave Brandon water instead of sticky juice. I followed Tyler around like a shadow to prevent him from emptying a box of plastic play-food on his head. It didn't take long for the Cheerios to find their way back onto the floor, or for toys to scatter, or for my shiny table to drown under a community of knickknacks that don't belong.

I waved an imaginary white flag and played with my boys in the returning chaos. I'm hoping this battle will be easier in years to come, with a bigger house and well-trained boys. But until then, I'll have to accept a bit of defeat with lots of patience and joy.

Jesus, help me lighten up as I pick up—and pick me up while You're at it!
—KAREN VALENTIN

Ninth Month

~~~~~~~~

Jesus,

Love and worry sometimes go hand-in-hand these days. Show me how to focus on the blessings and rein in the what-ifs. Guard my heart from anxiety; help me remember that I don't need to be the perfect mother any more than I need to be perfect for You to love me. Fix my eyes on the big picture—Your picture—and remind me that my number one goal should be to draw closer to You.

Amen.

Tips

» Make prayer part of your bedtime routine for the baby. She won't understand yet, but regularly hearing *thank you* and *I'm sorry* and *please bless* will plant the seeds of habit.

» Find another mom to be your exercise buddy. Meet for brisk stroller walks and take turns as you each go out for half an hour *alone*.

» Planning out weekly meals takes time, but it goes a long way toward solving the 5:00 PM panic of getting dinner ready. Big slow-cooker meals can be frozen in portions so you don't have to cook every day.

Day One

*Two people are better off than one, for they can
help each other succeed.*
—ECCLESIASTES 4:9 (NLT)

Life in England meant tea shops, historical sites, growing flowers—and Mike routinely flying off to other countries with his squadron for weeks at a time. The separations were difficult at first, but eventually Michelle and Aimee and I worked out a smooth daily routine during Mike's absences.

The house stayed tidy and our meals were simple. We lived slow and easy, at our own pace. When the girls fell asleep at night, I relaxed with a book and a cup of tea. I missed Mike, but I learned to appreciate the retreatlike tranquility.

So I felt a jolt one autumn evening when Mike returned home from a trip overseas. He dropped his bags in the living room, dirty clothes went on the floor, the bathroom became an instant mess, and there was lots of noisy play and hugging between Mike and his girls. Then, "What's to eat?"

After dinner, an exhausted Mike said, "Sorry for the mess. I need to sleep now, but I'll clean in the morning." He went to bed, and I surveyed the scene. Stuff was everywhere. The kitchen was a disaster. Michelle was overwound from excitement and likely wouldn't settle down for hours. It was tempting to view Mike as an intruder, but of course he wasn't. I simply needed to recalibrate to his presence at home.

And anyway, I believed God's Word: "Two are better than one." By myself, life might seem tidier, quieter and more under control, but a relationship is a profound gift. I was learning that an easily upset peace is not peace at all and that a truer, deeper, more resilient tranquility can develop right in the middle of the noisy, messy rub of relationships.

*Lord, may I learn from everything that arises in
each relationship You have given me.*
—SUSAN LABOUNTY

Day Two

*"But I have prayed for you, Simon, that your faith may not fail.
And when you have turned back, strengthen your brothers."*
—LUKE 22:32

A friend and I stood outside our church, bouncing our babies on our hips and talking about how we could help our children stay strong in faith through adulthood. Erica said she would make sure her son received a solid Christian education. I said that I would talk to Lucy about my experience with doubts and spiritual dryness.

A stately woman with silver hair approached, and we recognized our mutual friend Susan. She has six adult children who are all strong believers, so we eagerly invited her to join our conversation.

"How much time do you spend praying for your children?" Susan asked.

Erica and I sheepishly acknowledged: very little. "Deep faith comes from God," Susan reminded us. "You're talking about it as if it's all up to you. Parents influence their children's faith for better or worse, but in the end it's God's work."

That night I paused during my evening prayers and spent a few minutes praying for Lucy. I asked God to help her grow in wisdom and stature. I pleaded with Him to give her strong faith all her life. I begged for the grace to see what to nurture in her and the wisdom to know how to nurture it. And finally, I committed Lucy once again to Him, knowing that He was in charge, not me.

*Lord, may I never think that my children need my
words more than they need my prayers.*
—JENNIFER FULWILER

Day Three

Then, because so many people were coming and going that they did not even have a chance to eat, he said to them, "Come with me by yourselves to a quiet place and get some rest."

—MARK 6:31

*I*t was after midnight, but I couldn't sleep. Jonathan lay next to me, his breathing heavy, while thoughts swirled in my mind. I finally got up and moved across the room to sit by the window. The street lamp below cast a faint glow. I lit a candle so as not to wake Jonathan, and opened up my journal.

As an introvert, one of my most difficult challenges of motherhood was the lack of alone time. It wasn't just physical space, though that was an issue: We had given our bedroom to Llewelyn and were sleeping in the living room, crawling all over each other. Once the baby was in bed, there was simply nowhere to escape—except the bathroom. Some evenings I wanted to pull my hair out!

I was desperately lonely for friends and at the same time rarely had any solitude. So here I was, sitting in the dark while my husband slept nearby. *Lord, sorry for not prioritizing my time with you every day. This must be part of the reason I have been a little unhappy lately, a little sad about my life even though Llewelyn is a joy to me.*

In the dark, watching the flickering candle, alone, I experienced a deep stillness. I could feel God's presence, and knew that even though I'd failed to meet with Him regularly, He was delighted to be with me now.

Help me, Jesus, to find the quiet places in my day and within my heart where I can rest, at peace, in Your presence.

—LIZ BISSELL

Day Four

~~~~~~~~~~~~~

*T*yler screams to be picked up as I finish cooking the pasta Brandon requested. "I'll be right with you Tyler," I call, as I mix in the sauce and
serve it in a bowl.

"No want pasta!" Brandon shouts. "Peanut butter jelly!" I breathe in
deeply, breathe out slowly. Then I pick up Tyler, who has not stopped crying.
In a second he changes his mind, too, and squirms to get down.

I'm having a change of heart as well. The two little boys I found so adorable an hour ago aren't so adorable anymore. *I don't want to be a mother
today!* I scream in my mind. Happily, my cousin is visiting and sees the look
on my face. She offers me some time alone to take a breath, a shower, a nap—
whatever it takes to change my attitude. As much as I hate to admit it, my
emotions can go up and down as quickly as Tyler wants to be lifted in my arms
one moment and then put back down and left alone the next. I turn to the One
Whose love does not waver, and pray:

*Thank You, Lord, that You are constant, and constantly
loving. Teach me to find an even keel.*
—KAREN VALENTIN

Day Five

"May it be to me as you have said."
—LUKE 1:38

~~~~~~~~~~~~~~

I couldn't believe I was doing it again.

I'd been obsessed with the calendar and potential pregnancy for years. But this time a nine-month-old slept down the hall.

Zach was my answer to prayer, my miracle. God knew my prayer well: "Just one. Please. Just one." And it happened. So why was I thinking about having number two when I was still getting to know number one?

The guilt of wanting—while having—was eating at me. I loved being a mom. I meant what I told God. It had been so difficult to get and stay pregnant that one child was fine if that was the plan. I just favored my own plan.

While writing at my computer in November, my fingers walked astray to search the potential due date of a potential pregnancy. The wondering and what-ifs were as normal to me as breathing. When it hit me what I was doing, *again*, I put my head in my hands and squeezed off tears. "Focus, Susan, focus," I said, half plea, half command.

I returned to my article, which involved Christmas and Mary's getting the incomprehensible news from an angel that she would bear the Savior. Though I'd heard the story dozens of times, it was as if I'd never digested it before.

"I am the Lord's servant," Mary answered the angel. "May it be to me as you have said." She let go. Gave her life to God. *Trusted*. In that moment, I realized that after years of yearning, only one thing would offer freedom: Letting it be His plan.

Mary's words became a mantra I used in ultrasounds, appointments, C-sections and premature births through the completion of my family.

Lord, I'm Yours. I'm never too old to learn; please keep teaching me.
—SUSAN BESZE WALLACE

Day Six

*"Above all, love each other deeply, because love
covers over a multitude of sins."*
—I PETER 4:8

---

*B*eing a new mom often seems akin to holding a sign that says "Attack me,
if you please." I don't know about you, but people seem to offer their comments as though I'm some clinical experiment incapable of feeling. Once when
this happened to me, I attacked back—and the situation wasn't pretty.

Bobbi, my teenage goddaughter and number one babysitter, had taken
Joshua to the church nursery to change his diaper. While there, Joshua reached
to hug Bobbi and held her tight. Marsha, a member of our church, noticed it
and commented, "He must not get many hugs from his mother."

When Bobbi reported this to me, I decided to let Marsha's comment go.
But I clung to it. It stung. Marsha had been to my house for Bible study, we
were in a small prayer group, and we had a rapport. *Why would she say that?*
And the comment hit a personal sore spot, because I'd always been afraid I
wouldn't be affectionate enough with Joshua.

The more it festered, the angrier I became. I finally called Marsha to
confront her. After dogging me for listening to a teenager, Marsha told me
exactly what she disliked about me and my family and how we made her feel
inadequate. I got off the phone, regretting having made the call. "But honey,
if you hadn't called, you might not know how she really felt about you," Flynn
counseled. "Now you can pray specifically for her needs."

So I did. Compassion came. I wrote Marsha a poem and gave it to her. She
cried and gave me a monogrammed shirt. We loved one another. Our fellowship was restored.

Thank You, Lord, for showing me how to love others when I'm feeling hurt.
—RHONDA J. SMITH

Day Seven

[Love] always protects, always trusts, always hopes, always perseveres.
—I CORINTHIANS 13:7

~~~~~~~~~~~~~~

It was our first spring trip to the park, and my friend Annette and I were way more excited than our kids were. "I'm glad we're both in-the-sandbox kinds of moms," Annette grinned as we settled in to play. We'd brought spoons and shovels and happily showed Tommy and Elizabeth how to scoop the bright, clean sand and pour it out on their bare legs. Elizabeth, ever the independent one, wanted to hold the spoon herself. I handed it to her before turning to say something to Annette.

"Whoa!" Annette blurted, pointing. Elizabeth had a spoonful of sand headed straight for her mouth. I gently tipped the spoon so the sand fell back into the box. "No, honey. We don't eat sand. Not in your mouth." I turned back to Annette, grinned, and rolled my eyes. Annette gave a pointed glance back at Elizabeth. The spoon was full again and on its way. I repeated my earlier message and dumped the would-be meal.

The third time, I tried the old switcheroo: I removed the spoon and showed Elizabeth how to use her hands. Two minutes later a chubby fist full of grit was headed north. I pried Elizabeth's fingers open and repeated, "No, honey. No putting sand in your mouth." Patience is one of the hallmarks of a good mother, and I wanted to be a good mom.

For the next five minutes there were no more incidents. Pleased with my parenting success, I mentally patted myself on the back. Then my determined daughter, obedient to my command not to bring sand up to her face, did a most amazing thing. She flung open her arms. She opened her mouth. And she dove, face first, into the sandbox.

Father, help me persevere, both in patience and in faith.
—JULIA ATTAWAY

Day Eight

Do not be like them, for your Father knows what you need before you ask him.
—MATTHEW 6:8

~~~~~~~~~~~~~

*B*espectacled, serious men and women milled about in New York City black, clutching books and waving to each other in the university auditorium. The literary event was Patrick's and my first outing in the nearly ten months since Anjelica was born. It was the perfect evening, the kind we had three or four times a month prior to parenthood. Now readings and outings required too much effort and negotiation to seem worthwhile. But I had pushed for this night for Patrick, a reassuring reminder of our shared love of words.

I looked back and spotted my husband, programs in hand, making his way down the far aisle. But then the lights dimmed suddenly, and everyone scrambled to sit. Moments later, the moderator appeared onstage, inviting the author to join him. Light applause, and a hush.

I knew Patrick would not be able to find me in the cavernous dark; moreover, I knew he would not try. He was far too polite and mindful of others to fumble in the darkness and disturb them. No, he would have found a spot in the back and settled in, resigned to our spending the next hour—of our only evening in ages—apart.

I craned my neck to look back, hoping, stupidly, to spot him. I love this reserve about him, his unstinting thoughtfulness. It is not his nature to plough through the unforgiving crowd. But we had expended so great an effort this evening to be together, in the world, that to find ourselves apart seemed an awful parody.

I slid down into my seat, feeling like a petulant child. *How romantic.*

Then, with a wordless sigh, Patrick slid in beside me and leaned to kiss my temple as he whispered, "Did I miss much?"

*Lord, sometimes You make me gasp in wonder
at how perfectly You understand me.*
—DEBRALEE SANTOS

Day Nine

*Charm is deceptive, and beauty is fleeting; but a
woman who fears the Lord is to be praised.*
—PROVERBS 31:30

I stepped back from the mirror and sucked in my stomach, turning sideways to catch my best angle. *Ick.*

Nothing seemed to be in the right place anymore. My breasts were saggy, my hips wide. That whole "nine months on, nine months off" thing was clearly not working for me. At a time in my not-so-distant past I'd worn skinny jeans and figure-hugging sweaters. Now a frumpy mom was staring back at me, a mom who couldn't quite get rid of the last ten pounds of baby weight.

Just then my husband Cameron came up behind me. He wrapped his arms around my waist and kissed my neck. "You're beautiful, you know." And he meant it.

I glanced back at the mirror, trying to see myself from his perspective— and more importantly, from God's. Nine months of pregnancy had certainly taken a toll on my body. But when I looked beyond my new-mom skin, I saw that nine months of motherhood had brought about some beautiful changes. Weeks of pacing the floor on sleepless nights had stripped off layers of selfishness. My son's constant cries had erased my tendency toward laziness. And lonely days at home with no adult conversation had taught me the value of turning to God.

No, I wasn't the same woman I was before I had my son. But I *was* beautiful—extra ten pounds and all.

Lord, thank You for loving me for who I am becoming on the inside.
—ERIN MACPHERSON

Day Ten

So there is a special rest still waiting for the people of God.
—HEBREWS 4:9 (NLT)

~~~~~~~~~~~~~~~~~

What do you do for fun?" I asked the young mom I'd just met. "Do you have any hobbies?"

"No, I don't have time for that sort of thing," she replied.

There was an awkward silence. I wondered if she envisioned Anna scavenging under the table while I gallivanted around pursuing my interests. Her husband's smile and helping hands suggested he'd be more than willing to allow her a day at the spa.

That evening I packed up my scrapbooking supplies, kissed Dave and Anna good-bye and headed toward freedom. I hadn't been out of the house for so long that driving felt strange. Everything around me was bursting with color: the fiery pink sunset, the blazing autumn leaves. I put the windows down and let the wind rip through my hair, like a leaf blower blasting away the stresses of a week saturated in baby care and housecleaning.

I spent the evening at Tammy's house, decorating photo album pages with colorful borders and delicate prints. My body relaxed as I realized I was going to start and finish a project in one sitting, with no curious fingers there to unravel it. There were four of us—all moms with the same stories of cabin fever and endless chores. We vented, raved over photos and ate lots of chocolate. We joked and laughed until we cried, doubling over in stomach pain. Near midnight, we all went home. Dave took one look at me and smiled, knowing he had a new wife and Anna had a new mother.

Father, help me remember that to take care of my
family, I need to take care of myself.
—FAITH BOGDAN

Day Eleven

*They raise their voices, they shout for joy; from the
west they acclaim the Lord's majesty.*

—ISAIAH 24:14

~~~~~~~~~~~

I'd seen a million storms before, but this was the first good one with my
baby girl. I held Samantha in my arms as we looked from a safe distance
out our kitchen window. The sky was dark and the lightning flashed across the
sky.

Each time the thunder cracked, Samantha opened her eyes wide and
clapped her hands over her ears. But the lightning—oh, how she loved the
lightning! She'd spy the zigzag in the distance and squeal with delight. Over
and over, she crowed for the light and covered her ears when the thunder
rolled.

When she saw me laughing at her antics, her actions became more pronounced. I began to mimic her with one of my hands as the other held her
close. Cover, squeal, cover, squeal. She began to laugh her deep baby belly
laugh.

As the laughter rolled with the thunder, I thought to myself, *This is what
it's all about. This moment. This second right here. Discovering the world
with my daughter, enjoying and delighting in her awe.*

*Lord, I'm sure I've missed many other moments, but
thank You for giving me this one to treasure.*

—ELSA KOK COLOPY

Day Twelve

Carry each other's burdens, and in this way you will fulfill the law of Christ.
—GALATIANS 6:2

~~~~~~~~~~~~~

At first glance, Maria and I weren't likely friends. From life experiences to languages spoken at home, our personal resumés screamed our differences. But standing in her front yard on the day we met, I recognized the lonely, overwhelmed look in her eyes. I'd seen it before, in the mirror. I wrote down my phone number and told her to call if she ever wanted to walk to the park with the kids.

My days moved forward, filled with friends whose lives looked like copies of my own. I didn't think much about Maria until she called a month later. As we took stroller walks around the neighborhood, I learned more about her life. The details offered me some perspective. When my stress level rose, I reminded myself of Maria's circumstances, and my heart shifted toward gratitude.

One day I sat at Maria's kitchen table as our children played next to us. Maria listened to my rusty Spanish while our babies did fine with their universal language of peekaboo. Maria's eyes grew big as I shared some of my personal struggles. "I thought *I* was the only one with problems!" she said. To me, my stress was obvious; to Maria, my life was a pretty package, wrapped in a perfect family. Her surprise surprised me. Our lives were so different, and yet we shared this: the need to hear someone else's worries to gain perspective on our own.

Dear God, help me be vulnerable so others can see You at work.
—ALEXANDRA KUYKENDALL

Day Thirteen

Of these you may eat any kind of locust, katydid, cricket or grasshopper.
—LEVITICUS 11:22

~~~~~~~~~~~~~

*Y*esterday I found one of my twins crawling around the living room floor with two antennae sticking out of her mouth. When I finally managed to pry Ashleigh's mouth open to remove the grasshopper, all I found were the remnants of a leg. The rest of the poor fellow undoubtedly ended up in her tummy. My daughter didn't seem to mind her snack, but I was horrified and immediately called Poison Control. The woman said that as long as my daughter wasn't choking, I shouldn't worry. She added that grasshoppers are high in nutrients, and I should keep an eye out for the remains in Ashleigh's diaper in a day or two.

Once I got over this incredible news, I looked down at Ashleigh and realized she would survive. I picked her up for a big kiss. The moment was spoiled a little by the poignant smell of insect on her typically sweet breath, and I took a moment to thank God again that she hadn't choked. I reminded myself that this was probably not the only emergency I would encounter in the lives of my children. I counted my blessings: I'd managed to remain calm (well, mostly), the Poison Control people are just a phone call away, and Amanda hasn't shown any inclination to eat things with six legs.

Lord, who knew there were so many things to be thankful for?
—DONNA MAY LYONS

Day Fourteen

*B*ills are late, I'm putting way too much on my credit card, the overcrowded apartment is a wreck and my writing deadline is about to slap me in the face. I want to head for bed, not because I'm sleepy, but to disappear.

I sigh, frustrated. Tyler crawls over and pulls on my leg to get me to pick him up. I sit down on the floor instead, burying my fingertips into his curly hair. He smiles. His dimples, two tiny teeth and huge brown eyes penetrate my frazzled heart. "I'm sorry, baby boy," I say with a knot in my throat. I feel like a failure. So many bills, not enough money. I want to give them more.

My father's words echo in my ear. "I'm sorry I couldn't give you more. I wanted to give you so much." If he could, he would have bought me a house, provided money so I could see the world, and given me savings to keep me secure for the rest of my life. Now I understand the regret in his words, but I also recall my response.

"Papi," I said, hugging him tight and kissing his cheeks. "You've given me more than you will ever know. The love you and Mami have given me makes me rich in ways that money could never satisfy. You've given me everything I need, and I love you so much."

Tyler touches my face and wakes me from my reverie. Brandon sneaks up from behind and throws his arms around me. Tyler cracks up and dives into my open arms. I hug him close and press my cheek to Brandon's head, which rests on my shoulder. "It's enough," I tell myself, knowing it was always enough for me. My love is more than enough.

Jesus, Your love is always enough, even in the hard times.
—KAREN VALENTIN

Day Fifteen

"David and the whole house of Israel were celebrating with all their might before the Lord, with songs and with harps, lyres, tambourines, sistrums and cymbals."

—II SAMUEL 6:5

~~~~~~~~~~~~~~

C'mon, Henry, you can do it!" These six words have been a mantra for us. I used them with my first two, writing down when they smiled or rolled over or lifted their heads, when they sat or stood or cruised or walked. But Henry's twenty-first chromosome threw a wrench in the milestone timetable. We knew he'd be late, but kept reminding ourselves "Henry will do it when he's ready." Even so, Henry's schedule never lined up with mine.

When Henry scootched forward about three feet on his belly, I almost didn't believe it. I moved him back and watched. He did it again. I continued moving him and watching him, and then I sobbed like Sobby McWeeperton during The Grand Festival of Sobbing and Weeping. Except I was crying with joy. Henry was moving!

It's amazing how big a deal the simplest milestones are in a child whose development is different. And the *big* milestones? They're earth-shattering.

I called my husband Steve to tell him the news. Steve said, "What kind of cake should I get?"

I replied, "What?"

"To celebrate. We're having a cake."

Because with some things it's just necessary to sing and dance—and eat cake—before the Lord.

Father God, keep me focused on who my child is instead of on what he can do.

—CHRISTY STURM

Day Sixteen
A Dad's View

So then, there remains a Sabbath rest for the people of God, for whoever
has entered God's rest has also rested from his works as God did from his.
—HEBREWS 4:9–10 (ESV)

I'm pooped," my wife Kari said. "It's endless: changing, nursing, getting him to sleep and scrambling to keep up with the housework before he wakes up again."

A responsible, hardworking person, my wife appreciates a tidy home. And babies are neither tidy nor leave time for making life tidy. I stood there, not knowing whether to speak, hug or retreat, while the dishes sat strewn across table and counter, festering.

Not ten seconds later, a tiny, sustained cry came from the nursery. My wife closed her eyes, tensed and waited. Another cry. "I am so, so tired," she said. "But there's so much to do."

"I can take the baby," I offered.

"No," she said. "He wants me. Doesn't need to eat, probably just wants to pretend to nurse for comfort. I'll try to get him down and take care of the kitchen a little later."

I looked in on them an hour later. The baby was asleep on Kari's chest, and she herself was asleep, a slight smile on her face, her hands resting on Hans, both of them sleeping deeply. I loaded the dishwasher, wiped down the counters, and then crawled into bed next to them and fell asleep.

Lord, teach me how to support my spouse when we're both exhausted.
—LEROY HUIZENGA

Day Seventeen

But when you ask him, be sure that your faith is in God alone.
Do not waver, for a person with divided loyalty is as unsettled
as a wave of the sea that is blown and tossed by the wind.
—JAMES 1:6 (NLT)

~~~~~~~~~

I't's rickets," Dr. Leslie Clapp said with an intense look. And that wasn't good. "Kedar is a beautiful boy, but his growth is way under the curve for babies his age," she explained. I peered into the light-brown eyes of the woman who had also been my pediatrician. I knew this was serious. Dr. Clapp was missing that happy grin that always lit up her mocha-colored cheeks. And when she sat me down to talk about specialists, physical therapists and additional testing, my jaws tightened.

I knew all about this disease, which is caused by vitamin D and calcium deficiency. It could lead to softening of the bones that might result in deformities and fractures. Already the effects were showing on Kedar. His short, severely bowed legs left him hobbling when he attempted to walk—a manifestation of his condition.

And his thyroid disorder prevented him from absorbing calcium. So my breast milk, foods and juice enriched with vitamin D and calcium, and all the vitamins Kedar was taking did him no good. He had to graduate to a strong steroid medication that wasn't guaranteed to work either.

"I know you're a woman of great faith," Dr. Clapp said before I left her office. "So make sure you pray." That was the best and most effective prescription of all, and the one I believe led to his full recovery.

Dear Lord, when everything else fails, my trust and hope
remain steadfast that You will answer my prayers.
—DIANNA HOBBS

Day Eighteen

The goal of this command is love, which comes from a pure
heart and a good conscience and a sincere faith.
—I TIMOTHY 1:5

~~~~~~~~~~~~~~

I think we should stay home tonight," I said to Joe when he called from work to check in.

"Whatever you think is best," he said, though I could hear the disappointment in his voice.

My mother-in-law was visiting and had offered to be our free babysitter while we went out to dinner, but I'd said no. I'd tried to go to the grocery store alone that morning, and Lucy threw a screaming fit when I left. She eventually calmed down, but my mother-in-law reported that it took about fifteen minutes.

I put the phone back on the cradle and walked downstairs to the living room, where I saw Lucy and her grandmother on the floor together. My mother-in-law was playfully encouraging her to walk, but Lucy giggled and fell into her lap instead. I stood at the foot of the stairs for a moment, watching the tender scene.

Thinking again of the disappointment I'd heard in Joe's voice, I turned and ran back upstairs to grab the phone. "Can you make reservations for seven o'clock?" I said as soon as he answered.

Sure enough, Lucy screamed like it was the end of the world when Joe and I tried to leave that night, almost pulling a button off my blouse as she clung to me. But when we called to check in an hour later, I heard her squealing with delight. My mother-in-law sounded overjoyed as she reported the fun they were having. I looked across the restaurant table at Joe and held up my glass in a toast to this desperately needed evening out that was good for us—and for Lucy.

Lord, help me remember that the goal of love isn't to protect my child
from every stress and bit of harm, but to encourage her to grow.
—JENNIFER FULWILER

Day Nineteen

Two are better than one. . . .
—ECCLESIASTES 4:9

I steered my cart through the crowded produce aisle of our English military base commissary. Traffic jammed, and as I paused, watching for a clear lane, a cheery voice beside me said, "Hi! When is your husband coming home from Spain?"

I turned to the woman who spoke and drew a blank. I had no idea who she was, but she seemed certain she knew me, so I stammered, "Next week." Then I took a wild guess: "When will *your* husband be home?"

"Oh, Dean's coming home next week too." *Whew.*

We chatted lightly until I found an escape route. When my husband called that evening, I asked, "Do you know a guy named Dean?"

"Yeah. He's the pilot I fly with." And he briefed me on Dean and his wife Luanne.

Mike and I had lived in our English neighborhood for six months with baby Michelle and her two-year-old sister Aimee. I loved England and the people I'd met, but I had no close friends. Mike was away from home frequently, and an aching loneliness was my steady companion. I'd been praying God would send me a friend.

The next Sunday at church, I noticed Luanne sitting in the back pew. Smiling, I slid beside her and said hello, and this time I knew who I was talking to. I noticed that, like me, Luanne was expecting a baby. As we talked, we found we had much in common. We continued our conversation after church—and frequently for the rest of the year.

Jesus, when I am lonely, turn my heart to You for help.
—SUSAN LABOUNTY

Day Twenty

*I consider my life worth nothing to me, if only I may
finish the race and complete the task. . . .*
—ACTS 20:24

~~~~~~~~~~~~~~~

I met Em on the street in the middle of winter. Our introductions were short and sweet; it was –35 degrees centigrade outside at the time. But soon we began to spend more time together. She came over to my house and drank copious amounts of coffee while sharing her journey. Em grew up in a broken home that was filled with tensions I'd never imagined, much less seen. She dropped out of school, and shortly after that became pregnant. Em had to grow up fast.

Our unlikely friendship grew. Me with my husband, baby and perfect little world; Em, who struggled to pay her bills each month on social assistance. Our little girls played at our feet as we talked about the trials of life.

"I'm thinking about going back to high school," Em told me one day. "The only thing is," she pointed to her daughter Kate, "I don't know what I'm going to do with her."

Day care was out of the question given the expense, and her family didn't live close by. "I can take her!" I offered. Em agreed to the plan.

Kate and Shiloh became fast friends, playing—and fighting—together on the days that Em had class. At the end of the day, Em came to pick up her daughter, "Those kids are so young!" she'd complain. She felt old, and out of sync. I cheered her on.

As I looked at the faces of the graduates that year, I had no doubt which one was appreciating the moment the most. Em's journey had a few hurdles in it, yet she didn't stop until she completed the task before her. She learned what she needed to learn to graduate, and she taught me something I needed to learn about life in the process.

Lord, keep me from giving up when I feel discouraged.
—RUTH BERGEN

Day Twenty-One

Give thanks to the Lord, for he is good; his love endures forever.
—PSALM 118:1

I'd just left an inspiring MOPS meeting. My Zach stretched out his chubby arms to greet me. We were on our way home on a brilliant fall day in Colorado, the sky so blue it belonged in a Disney movie.

I made a spontaneous detour to a scenic park, wanting to prolong the happy feeling that was embracing me. Golden trees and crisp air lured us down a path that curved its way into a heaping wonderland of fallen foliage.

Something unexplained had moved me to take the camera that morning. I plopped Zach and his denim overalls down in the golden carpet. It was lunchtime, but he seemed content to feel the crackly texture of leaves while I shot frame after frame of his fascination.

By now, the happy feeling had become a euphoria draping itself over my shoulders. I wondered how, if every woman experienced this kind of love for her child, the world could be such a troubled place. I had lost two babies. Is that what was making me feel this so deeply? Would I not appreciate the little things if it weren't for the devastation I'd once felt?

The words *thank you* spontaneously tumbled out of my mouth once, and then again and again. I shed tears thinking of the sleepless nights and the feelings of maternal idiocy. I was thankful for it all: for my sweet boy who was gumming nature, and for the loss too. If one had to make way for the other, I was more than okay with that.

God, I saw Your beauty today in soft cheeks and a season of change. Thank You. Thank You. Thank You.
—SUSAN BESZE WALLACE

Day Twenty-Two

Better a meal of vegetables where there is love. . . .
—PROVERBS 15:17

~~~~~~~~~~~~~

I carefully peeled the last peach and plopped it into the steamer on top of the already-peeled sweet potatoes and steel-cut oats. I glanced at my watch. Joey would wake up from his nap any minute, and I wasn't even halfway finished with this batch of homemade baby food.

Turning the burner up, I willed the water to boil, praying that I'd be able to get one last batch of superhealthy, superorganic baby food made before my son woke up and needed my attention. These days I felt I was spending every free moment I had peeling and pureeing and steaming and freezing. But it was worth it, right?

Of course it was. Joey was my baby and I was going to make sure that every morsel that crossed his little lips was the perfect combination of organic produce, fresh whole grains and grass-fed poultry. All made by my loving hands, of course.

Just then, Joey woke up. My homemade sweet-potato-peach oatmeal was only halfway done. I had a choice: homemade baby food or my baby.

And I chose Joey.

I turned off the stove and retrieved my son, deciding I'd had enough. No more peeling or pureeing. No more steaming and blending and pouring bright-green purees into ice cube trays to freeze. Sure, making my own baby food was noble, but it was sucking up my time and energy. Something had to give. Joey could eat all-organic, superyummy peaches from a jar.

Lord, help me to love fiercely, even if it means
sacrificing some things I'd like to do.
—ERIN MACPHERSON

Day Twenty-Three

Just as each of us has one body with many members, and these members do not all have the same function, so in Christ we who are many form one body.
—ROMANS 12: 4–5

It was our fourth day in a row at the doctor's office. On Saturday they said Grace had a virus and sent us home. On Sunday her temperature hit 104, and we rushed to the urgent care center, where they said she had a kidney infection. Monday she wasn't much better, so we were at the doctor again for an antibiotic shot. Tuesday, we repeated it.

Grace wasn't improving, and our pediatrician searched for answers. She called the lab to get the culture results from a sample of Grace's urine. The lab wouldn't release the results to her because the urgent care center took the specimen. But when we contacted the urgent care center, they said the lab hadn't sent the results yet. How annoying! If everyone does the job they've been given, life is much smoother.

Ah, yes. *If everyone does the job they've been given, life is much smoother.* I have a hard time remembering that, myself. I compare myself to other women and wonder why I don't have a best-selling book or a huge speaking ministry. Why don't I have the talent to decorate my home like a magazine or cook the way *she* does? Perhaps because God hasn't called me to do those jobs. He's called me to be me. I'm not always sure what that means (other than that I'm a mom!), but I do know this: One of my jobs is to praise Him and love Him. And another is to be patient as He helps us find that urine culture.

Father, use me as You see fit, and help me see clearly the job You want me to do.
—CAROL HATCHER

Day Twenty-Four

*Whoever finds his life will lose it, and whoever
loses his life for my sake will find it.*
—MATTHEW 10:39

hunderous applause erupted from the bleachers as my sister performed on the stage of the Chemung County Fairgrounds. Grace was dolled up in a pink dress and ponytails, singing the part of a giddy little girl dreaming about her prince. I sat beaming on the front row, introducing myself to those around me as "Grace's sister."

She was charming and carefree, my Amazing Grace. She was also single and childless. I, on the other hand, was trying to placate baby Anna with bits of cereal to keep her from crawling away. I could scarcely enjoy the show. I wanted to be *in* the show; I had the same loud mouth and dramatic flair as my sister, but motherhood limited me to performing on a laundry-room level.

I enjoyed ten whole minutes of Grace before I caught the unmistakable stench of a dirty diaper. Grabbing daughter and diaper bag I stomped off, wondering if God was aware I'd had this musical on my calendar for two months. I saw another mom on baby duty, and plopped down in the grass beside her. She looked stressed and tired and was wrestling a twoish boy who looked like he'd gone for a spin in a cotton candy machine.

For the next hour, Liz told me about her son's delays and health challenges and the problems that kept her up at night and on the edge of insanity. Sitting there listening to her, stroking the boy's sticky hair, I knew the real reason this date had been on my calendar for two months. It wasn't me. But it *was* grace.

Father, use me to lift someone up today.
—FAITH BOGDAN

Day Twenty-Five

We all stumble in many ways. . . .
—JAMES 3:2

I'm afraid my girl is going to have social issues. She had a playdate and gummed her new friend twice. I tried to correct her: "Sam, friends don't bite friends." She looked at me, cooed and reached over to chew on Kyle again. Kyle is a quiet baby. He rarely coos, barely drools and definitely doesn't bite. His mom, Amy, frowned and pulled him away.

Sam looked at me and then at Kyle and began to scream at the top of her little lungs. I panicked a bit, wondering what Amy must think of my mothering skills. I scooped up Sam and cradled her against my shoulder. "Shh," I whispered. "It's okay."

Kyle watched it unfold with big, blue, unblinking eyes. His mom held out a pacifier to distract him. He ignored it and sunk his sharp new bottom teeth into her hand.

I may have read too much into it, but it seemed Amy packed up soon after—making an excuse about somewhere else she had to be. As she walked down the driveway, I took a deep breath and smiled into Sam's ear. "A bad influence already? Oh, Samantha!"

Sam cooed again and tried to nibble my cheek. I kissed her nose and gave her a teething ring to chew on instead. Some lessons would have to wait.

Father, please help me know what baby behavior is worth
worrying about and what I should set aside.
—ELSA KOK COLOPY

Day Twenty-Six

The Lord upholds all those who fall and lifts up all who are bowed down.
—PSALM 145:14

~~~~~~~~~~~~~~~

Elizabeth was dolled up in her Sunday dress. Brand-new white Mary Janes covered the lace-trimmed anklets on her tiny feet. Those feet were walking now; her fierce determination had finally paid off. She clattered down the wood-floored hallway, her stride purposeful. And then, without warning, her feet slipped. Over backward she went, straight as a board. My stomach lurched at the sound of skull hitting floorboards.

Andrew and I were there even before Elizabeth's howl emerged. "Get some ice!" I yelled, scooping up my screaming child. Andrew returned with a frozen teething ring, and I sent him off to look up the symptoms of concussion. Elizabeth wasn't confused or vomiting. Her pupils were their normal size. Slurred speech and headache? Couldn't tell, at her age. All looked well, so when the sobbing finally subsided we decided to go ahead to church, watching for adverse symptoms like hawks. Apparently she was fine.

After church we took Elizabeth home and into our bedroom. I stood her in the middle of our queen-size bed and gave her a gentle push. She stiffened and fell over backward, completely straight, exactly as she'd done that morning. I'd never seen anything like it. "She needs remedial falling-down lessons!" I joked to Andrew. For the next half hour, we made a game of knocking over our little girl until she finally learned to land on her padding. We pushed, she laughed, and for the time being we closed the door on the school of hard knocks.

Jesus, when life knocks me over, teach me to land on my knees, in prayer.
—JULIA ATTAWAY

Day Twenty-Seven

"Do not remember the former things, nor consider the things of old. Behold, I will do a new thing, Now it shall spring forth; Shall you not know it? . . ."
—ISAIAH 43:18–19

*V*room! *Vroom!"* Grandad Brinson pushed the red car as Kedar lay on his stomach, smacking the floor and kicking his legs wildly. "Go and get it, man!" my dad called, smiling. And away Kedar went, crawling at lightning speed to grab the plastic automobile he adored. Seeing those two together was really nice, now that my parents had relocated back home from Atlanta.

Four years earlier, when Mom, Dad and six of my younger siblings left Buffalo, I cried for days. At the time, my husband Kenya and I attended Dad's church, where I headed up the music department—and several other departments too. Kenya was an assistant pastor. The Sunday afternoon they announced that my whole family was leaving—and the church was closing down—is still vivid in my memory. With anger, shock and disbelief, I wondered, *Why didn't my father tell me?*

"Alright! That's Grandad's boy!" Dad praised Kedar for getting the car, as I observed from the doorway. I love my dad and love seeing him with my son. I was no longer angry or hurt over my family's abrupt departure. In fact, I was thankful. I now possessed something I didn't have before they left: healthy independence and real confidence in my ability to stand on my own two feet as a wife, mom and servant of God. Sometimes the best gifts come only when you let go.

God, teach me to see beyond the past and to enjoy all the new things You have done in my life.
—DIANNA HOBBS

Day Twenty-Eight

Be devoted to one another in brotherly love.
Honor one another above yourselves.
—ROMANS 12:10

~~~~~~~~~~~~~~

Tyler puts everything in his mouth: dirt, leaves, grass, a fistful of stolen pasta from his brother's plate. On his first trip to the lake my son could not resist the temptation of sand. "No, baby," we'd say, doing our best to scoop it out with our fingers. "Yucky."

That sand turned out to be yuckier than we thought, and two days later my baby had a temperature of more than 104 degrees Fahrenheit, with vomiting and open blisters in his throat. "There's nothing we can give him for this," the doctor said, after diagnosing him with Coxsackie virus. "He just has to ride it out for five to seven days." That was too long to bear. My calm little baby who rarely cried for anything was screaming in pain, and I could do nothing to give him relief.

As I watched him suffer, I couldn't imagine the strength it takes to watch a child in pain every day. My friend's daughter Rafaella has a disease that constantly creates open sores in her skin, mouth and even internal organs. While Tyler was sick, Rafaella was miles away, undergoing a stem-cell transplant to tame and hopefully cure her epidermolysis bullosa. Suddenly I connected with their pain and struggle in a very personal way. Rafaella and her family had always been close to my heart and in my prayers, and when Tyler finally cried himself to sleep, I sat down to write them a message. Every emotion I'd felt the past few days I now felt not only for myself and Tyler but for them as well. Perhaps a note of empathy could ease a little bit of pain, somehow.

Jesus, use my love for my child to teach me how to love others more deeply.
—KAREN VALENTIN

Day Twenty-Nine

You gave abundant showers, O God; you refreshed your weary inheritance.
—PSALM 68:9

~~~~~~~~~~~~~~~

I had forgotten what it was like to sleep past 7:00 AM. I couldn't recall the last time I'd gone out in public without a diaper bag and baby spit-up on my shirt. But when I started putting Shiloh's diapers on backward, my husband knew it was time to step in.

Brian decided to send me on a twenty-four hour vacation. Alone. Just me. At a hotel. Did I mention *alone*? I reluctantly agreed to the plan. I craved time to myself, but I wondered if Brian and Shiloh would survive without me. Would he know what to feed her? What would the house look like when I returned?

Rolling his eyes as I shared my thoughts, Brian led me to the car with the small overnight bag he had packed. "We'll be fine!" he assured me. I wasn't so sure.

My fears lessened as we drove down the road, and by the time we reached the hotel, I was positively giddy. Anxious to start my brief holiday of solitude, I gave my husband a quick kiss and jumped out of the car. Waving quickly to Brian as he slowly drove away, I ran off to find my room.

The evening was gloriously spent reading, writing, and then going to bed early. I slept eight hours straight—a miracle that hadn't happened since Shiloh's birth. It was an amazing gift. But after waking the next morning, I couldn't wait for my family to come pick me up. Absence might be known to make the heart fonder, but so does a rather generous helping of sleep.

Lord, let me rejoice in my family today as if I hadn't seen them in weeks.
—RUTH BERGEN

Day Thirty

"I know that you can do all things; no plan of yours can be thwarted."
—JOB 42:2

~~~~~~~~~~~~~~~

Joey still doesn't know how to crawl. He does this weird army-commando thing, inchworming his head forward and then flinging his shoulders behind him—before he flops flat on his face.

I confess: I've been a bit (okay, a lot) worried. Is he always going to lag behind his peers? Will he never play football like his daddy? Is this a sign of future delays?

One day recently at playgroup I was surrounded by crawling babies and their proud mothers. My son lay in the middle of the floor. He tried to move to get a toy, but a seven-month-old whiz kid cruised in and snatched it from him. I watched—and immediately broke down crying.

My friend Trish came to the rescue. "Erin, you *know* God has a perfect plan for Joey," she counseled. "Whether Joey crawls or doesn't, whether he becomes a pro ballplayer or is only the water boy—God's plans won't be thwarted!" She was right: I did know that. I'd forgotten.

So I've stopped obsessing over developmental charts and milestones. I'll cheer when Joey finally gets up on all fours and moves like the other babies, but somehow it isn't as important as it was before. Because if crawling isn't in God's plan, something else—something greater—certainly is.

Lord, thank You for the knowledge that Your plan
for my child will never be thwarted.
—ERIN MACPHERSON

Tenth Month

~~~~~~~~

Father,

I praise You for all the people You have put in my path to help me this year: family, friends, co-workers, acquaintances. I ask Your blessing upon them. Keep me mindful of the needs of others, and show me how—even within the constraints of busy motherhood—I can be Your hands and heart in the world. Nurture in me a desire to encourage new moms, and open my eyes to see their unspoken needs.

For Jesus' sake, amen.

Tips

» Give yourself permission to limit your dinner menu to meals that can be prepared in fifteen minutes. Make an entertainment box of kitchen supplies your baby can play with while you're cooking.

» When you're annoyed with a mom friend, find something good to point out about her baby. It will help you both.

» If your baby gets sick, remember only three things can happen: she can get better, stay the same, or get worse. Usually you only have to worry about one of those trends.

Day One

They will perish, but you remain; they will all wear out like a garment. . . .
—PSALM 102:26

My groceries were bagged and paid for, but we were back in the aisles. The hat was missing again.

It was a frustrating outing. Lines were long. Zach was clawing at the straps restraining him. I was weary. But this wasn't just any hat.

I paid just five dollars for it. It was royal blue fleece with a few bright stripes and two tassels that stuck up like friendly horns. When Zach's blue eyes peeked out from under it, grinning was a reflex. Everywhere we went, people reacted. They winked at him, smiled, turned around for another look. It was part garment, part social experiment. We called it "the happy hat."

We'd lost it lots, but each time, someone behind us would hurry to hand it back. Or it was outside in the snow, just waiting. Once we retraced our steps in an airplane terminal. There it was, no matter what.

This day, we found it in the cereal aisle. Boy and hat were reunited again. I slid it on his noggin and paused to drink in his cuteness. My weariness abated. It wasn't the hat I was afraid to lose, I thought, it was the happy.

I was a lot like that hat. Lost some days, snug and secure on others. But the hat's days were numbered. We'd been lucky so far, but I knew the fit—and the perpetual finding—wouldn't last. I resolved to make sure we had pictures of him in it before it was too late.

The hat could get lost. The happy could not. That was my choice to make every day.

Lord, dress me every day in the joy that comes from knowing how much You love me and my child.
—SUSAN BESZE WALLACE

Day Two

He will call upon me, and I will answer him. . . .
—PSALM 91:15

<hr>

I have a bad habit of leaving the phone lying on the couch. It wasn't a problem until Shiloh grew big enough to reach it. She loves to press the buttons, hold the receiver to her ear and "talk"—just like Mom and Dad.

I was clearing the supper table recently when I noticed Shiloh hard at work with phone in hand, sitting on the couch beside her dad. "Brian!" I screeched to get my tired husband's attention. "The phone!" I yelled, pointing toward Shiloh.

He reached over and took it from the baby. Checking the screen as he ended the call, he laughed. "Ruth!" he held the phone in the air as I walked over to retrieve it, "Shiloh just called 911!"

My mouth dropped, and I shook my head, "It's a good thing you took it away when you did." That girl was getting so fast!

I put the phone back on its receiver and it instantly rang. "Hello?" I answered, leaning against the kitchen counter. It was Jocelyn, my sister-in-law. She began to talk and as she did, I noticed—out of the corner of my eye—car lights coming into our driveway. *Who could that be?* I wondered as I pushed back the curtains over the sink to look.

As I recognized the familiar flash of red and blue lights, my hand covered my mouth in horror. "I gotta go, Jocelyn," I said, interrupting her midsentence, "The police are here!"

Dear Lord, thank You for hearing me—even when I don't think we connect.
—RUTH BERGEN

Day Three

Casting all your anxiety on him because he cares for you.
—I PETER 5:7

~~~~~~~~~~~~~~~~~

As soon as I found out I was pregnant, I worried about losing the baby. When I made it to the pivotal point of three months, I breathed a sigh of relief. At each doctor's appointment with no problems, I relaxed and let myself think that maybe, just maybe, this dream of mine of having a baby was going to be perfectly fine.

After Solomon was born and I held him in my arms, most of my fears subsided. But every now and then a gnawing, terrible worry haunted me. *What if,* I thought, *what if he just stops breathing?*

When Solomon reached the age where such things are rare, I thanked God and expected my fear to go away. It did, mostly, but there were times when I found myself thinking, *What if something else happens to Solomon?*

"I can't bear to think of it," I confessed to my husband one night.

Tony put his hand on mine. "Don't think of it, then," he said.

"But what if . . . what if we ever lost him?"

"Stop spoiling your love with worry," Tony said. "Just love him."

Love him. He was right. I was completely in love, and instead of enjoying it, I was splintering it with worry.

Dear God, help me put my fears aside and love with my whole heart.
—SABRA CIANCANELLI

Day Four

*Besides, they get into the habit of being idle and
going about from house to house. . . .*
—I TIMOTHY 5:13

~~~~~~~~~~~~~~~

I crept downstairs in the murky light of early dawn, walked past the kitchen and slid into my familiar seat at my desk. With a wiggle of the mouse my computer came to life, and I clicked away. Lucy woke up an hour later; as soon as I dressed her and gave her her morning bowl of cereal, I sneaked back over to my computer. It lured me like a magnet.

When Joe walked through the front door that night, he saw a living room floor covered in toys, lunch dishes on the kitchen table, clothes from a laundry basket that Lucy had discovered strewn across the couch—and me staring into my computer monitor with the baby playing with her doll on a mat next to my desk. I looked up, met his gaze and then looked out at the chaos around us. He didn't say anything; he didn't need to. I knew then there was a problem.

It had started out as a good thing: in those early days when I was stuck at home with a newborn, the Internet had given me an opportunity to seek encouragement and connect with like-minded women. But an hour a day had turned into two hours and then to four, and at some point being online had become my default activity, my real life shoved to second place.

I spent an entire week offline to reset my idea of healthy Internet use. On my first day back online after my "fast," I was able to check some favorite sites—and then cheerfully walk away when real life beckoned.

*Lord, help me to know when my use of
a good thing has gone too far.*
—JENNIFER FULWILER

Day Five

A cheerful heart is good medicine, but a crushed spirit dries up the bones.
—PROVERBS 17:22

I'm so, so sorry," I apologized to the friendly stranger with the bright red mark on her alabaster cheek. Kedar had clawed at her face when she squatted down to admire him in his stroller. Talk about being mortified!

But my ten-month-old was growing increasingly mistrustful of strangers. Whenever someone he didn't know tried to get close to him, Kedar cried or lashed out. Unfortunately, when he was in the mood to do the latter, he had an affinity for scratching and hitting. And the random admirer in the mall that day was just his latest unsuspecting victim. Thankfully, the blonde-haired woman was gracious, assuring me it was no big deal. I didn't feel any better about it, though. And I certainly didn't like the unpredictable nature of Kedar's behavior; Kenya and I had been doing our best to teach him right from wrong.

When I shared with Kenya what had happened, he laughed uncontrollably. "I bet you wanted to disappear!" he said, doubled over.

"I can't believe you're laughing!" I replied, miffed, though he *did* add a bit of much-needed levity to the situation.

"Well, hey," he said, composing himself and wiping away tears, "You don't worry about the things you can't control."

Father, help me not to allow small mishaps
I can't control to take over my life.
—DIANNA HOBBS

Day Six

O Lord, you have searched me and known me! You know when I sit
down and when I rise up; you discern my thoughts from afar.
—PSALM 139:1–2 (ESV)

~~~~~~~~~~~

After months of agonizing over my lonely life as a stay-at-home mom, I set out to join a mothers' group. It seemed easy enough, but it meant meeting new people and trying to make new friends. *What if I don't meet anyone I like? What if they don't like me?*

I found a group and somehow mustered the courage to go. But it met at 8:30 in the morning, and I only knew one person. She introduced me to a few moms, who politely said their hellos and quickly moved on to talk with friends. I stood awkwardly, alone, trying to appear preoccupied instead of uncomfortable. The group was reading a parenting book together, something too advanced to help me with Llewellyn.

"It was all right," I told my husband that night. "But I was hoping to make a connection with other moms, and I didn't." The disappointment of the day began to show in my voice as I added, "Plus it was stressful getting out the door first thing in the morning, and you know how nervous I am driving!"

"Liz, it's okay. If it's stressful, don't go." Jonathan reassured me.

"I know, but I feel like I *should*," I confessed.

"Listen, there are other ways of making friends. It's okay."

He was right. God would provide the friends I needed; my job was to keep an open mind, and keep trying.

Lord, You see the secret places I hurt; please heal them.
—LIZ BISSELL

Day Seven

Bear one another's burdens, and so fulfill the law of Christ.
—GALATIANS 6:2 (ESV)

~~~~~~~~~~~~~~~~

Anna's wailing roused me from a restless sleep. "I'm coming, sweetie!" I managed, rolling slowly to the nightstand. I stopped to rest my throbbing head and felt for the thermometer, delivering it with a trembling hand to my ear. Dave was working out of town, unaware that 101 degrees of fieriness bound me helpless to the bed.

Anna gave me no mercy. I crawled on all fours down the hall and into her room, where she greeted me with swollen eyes and crying that had slowed to hiccups. Her nose ran and her diaper sagged.

I summoned enough strength to lift Anna out of the crib before hearing a whooshing noise; everything went momentarily dark. I collapsed to the floor, cradling Anna in my arms. She cried again. "I can't do this!" I moaned. Then a thought occurred to me: *Call Aunt Joy.* I dismissed it as quickly as it came.

I lay on my side, unbuttoning Anna's sleeper. A wave of nausea surged up to my throat. I crawled back down the hall, detoured to the bathroom, and continued to my bedside. I picked up the phone and dialed. Seconds later I choked out three delicate words: "I need help."

That afternoon I awoke to the piney smell of a clean house. I could hear the creak of the rocker beneath Aunt Joy's soft lullabies. Relief washed over me and I closed my eyes, thanking God for rescue—not only from a disastrous day, but from my disastrous pride.

Dear Lord, help me to humble myself enough
to ask for help when I need it.
—FAITH BOGDAN

Day Eight

~~~~~~~

I quickly learned that a trip to the store to buy diapers didn't constitute a full-day's activities, even if I extended the outing by picking up a latte and camping out in the toy section while I drank it. I *had* to get out of the house—I was going insane.

I packed up Joey and walked to the park, looking for a shady spot to park my Cheerio-and-spit-up-covered stroller. Looking around, I saw hoards of happy preschoolers and realized I was out of place. My baby couldn't even walk yet, much less climb the jungle gym and whiz down the slide. I parked under a tree at the edge of the playground, trying not to look too conspicuous.

A cheery, dark-haired mom walked up to me and introduced herself. "I'm Megan! You live around here?" She had three kids: a two-year-old, a four-year-old and a six-year-old. But she hadn't forgotten the early days of motherhood, the long days, the loneliness, the *I-have-to-get-out-of-the-house-this-instant-or-I'm-going-to-lose-it* feeling.

Twenty minutes earlier, I'd been scared to death of park politics, scared that the other moms were looking at me as the crazy-desperate new mom who had the gall to enter a public park with a ten-month-old. Instead, they welcomed me. They understood where I was; they knew that someday I would be the one with screaming preschoolers clinging to my legs, and I would spot the desperate new mom at the edge of the sandbox. And I would walk over to her and feed her lonely soul with adult conversation and welcoming arms.

*Lord, convert every ounce of loneliness I've felt this
year into a willingness to reach out to others.*
—ERIN MACPHERSON

Day Nine

*And when she finds it, she calls her friends and neighbors together
and says, "Rejoice with me; I have found my lost coin."*

—LUKE 15:9

~~~~~~~~~~~~~

When I walked out of the dressing room and looked at myself in the three-way mirror, I was in shock. *I look good*, I thought to myself in disbelief. *Dare I even say sexy?* Between almost back-to-back pregnancies and months of breast-feeding after each birth, my body hadn't felt like my own in quite a while. I was no longer a housing unit for a growing baby. Tyler was completely on formula, so I was no longer the nourishment center either. I could burn my stained breast-feeding bras and maybe buy some cute ones in different colors, perhaps with a little lace. I no longer had to concentrate on eating my veggies or skip the fudge brownie, but as I smiled at my reflection, I thought, *Maybe I'll keep watching what I eat—but this time for me.*

My hair stopped falling out, and I even got my period! I never thought I'd be so happy to have that little irritant back in my life, but it was a sign that things were falling back into place. I stood in front of that mirror for a long time. I twirled around; I put on a pair of heels. I played with my hair—half up, half down, a neat little bun, loose and crazy. The price tag kept tickling my arm as if telling me to make a decision. It was more expensive than I would have liked, but I made my way to the counter with a smile anyway. This was more than just a dress; it was a welcome-back party for the body that finally felt like my own once again.

*Ah, Lord, I haven't lost myself after all!
And You knew it all along. . . .*
—KAREN VALENTIN

Day Ten

Hatred stirs up dissension, but love covers over all wrongs.
—PROVERBS 10:12

~~~~~~~~~~~~~~~~~

Samantha ate an ant. I didn't feed it to her; she grabbed hold of a green bean, raised it to her mouth—and in that moment I noticed the ant. I reached for it, howling, "*Noooo!*" but in it went. I followed after it and pulled out a slimy green bean, but no ant.

"Samantha Kelly," I said. "You just ate an ant."

She smiled and pounded her fist on the high chair.

"That was so completely gross."

She had no clue.

I inspected the rest of her green beans. No more critters.

"She ate an ant?" my husband said later. "Why did you let her do that?"

"I didn't *let* her eat an ant; she just ate it. It was on her green bean."

"You have to watch her, Elsa. You can't let her eat stuff like that!"

"I *was* watching her!"

He glared at me. I glared back at him.

Finally I turned away and mumbled, "You feed her next time if you're so perfect."

He grunted. "Yeah, very mature."

We didn't talk for hours. Finally I grew tired of it. I went to the kitchen, grabbed a few raisins and set them on a plate. I brought them over to him. "Good afternoon, sir." I said. "Our special is ant today. Full of protein. Care for one?"

He laughed and pulled me onto his lap. "I'm sorry, honey. I shouldn't have jumped all over you like that."

"I'm sorry too." I said, popping a raisin into his mouth and then mine.

"She'll be okay."

"Yeah, she will."

Lord, help me find ways to turn tension into laughter.
—ELSA KOK COLOPY

Day Eleven

Therefore, if your whole body is full of light, and no part
of it dark, it will be completely lighted. . . .
—LUKE 11:36

A picture? Of course. What mother doesn't carry around evidence of her adorable child, particularly in the first year?

This mother. I explained sheepishly that I had just sent off a slew of pictures to be printed, but, no, I didn't have any with me. We continued the chatter, my work colleague looking for another easy exchange.

"How old is she now?"

My mind raced. "Ehh . . . ten . . . no . . . yes, ten months."

I groaned inwardly. How to explain that I *am* a good mother, despite all the evidence to the contrary? Of course I know how old Anjelica is. And I do have hundreds of photos stored in my groaning camera to prove my devotion.

But other mothers, it seems, have pictorial evidence on hand and can readily identify their child's age to the hour. They have signed their babies up for yoga and art, delivering them to class personally in ergonomic strollers with a packed organic lunch. Their babies wear the kind of socks a ten-and-a-half-month-old would never consider taking off repeatedly.

But I am Anjelica's mother. And despite the lack of snapshots and, occasionally, baby socks, there is no more perfect combination of grit and grace than my daughter and me. As I field work calls and throw together lunches (hers and mine), as I decide between racing home or pushing through another hour at my desk, as I try to wield laptops and sippy cups without incident, and as I choose whether it's her head or mine that gets brushed in the mornings, there's no part of my life that doesn't scream how deeply I care for this girl. She is imprinted on every inch of my being, a living picture of love. I'm hopeful anyone can see that.

Jesus, I pray that Your imprint shows in me with unmistakable clarity.
—DEBRALEE SANTOS

Day Twelve

My roots will reach to the water, and the dew
will lie all night on my branches.

—JOB 29:19

~~~~~~~~~~~~~

Pushing Shiloh in her stroller through our small-town grocery store, I turned a corner and nearly collided with an old friend. I hadn't seen Stacy in years! We shrieked, hugged and began to reminisce, while Shiloh sat contentedly chewing on some Cheerios.

Gradually the conversation turned to the days when I used to wander the globe. In the years before I married, I traveled a lot, serving a variety of mission organizations.

"You must miss that so much, Ruthie!" Stacy sympathized. I looked at her, thought about it for a moment and then shook my head. "Actually . . . ," I began, knowing my friend would never understand what I was about to say, "I don't miss it at all."

"Really?" came her predictable response. "I'd think swimming in Israel or drinking cappuccino in Italy would be way more interesting than changing diapers." Her tone seemed to say she didn't believe me.

"That was a lot of fun," I said as I remembered the time I covered myself with mud on the beach at the Dead Sea and my first attempt at ordering coffee in Italian. But looking down at Shiloh, who was now throwing her cereal all over the floor, I continued, "But this is better."

I couldn't find words to explain the shift in my priorities that had occurred since Shiloh's birth, or why a trip to the other side of the world paled in comparison to being the first person my daughter saw each morning. In my life before Shiloh I had always looked for excuses to run. To escape. To hide. Travel was an easy mask. But now I had a reason to stay and let my roots go deep. Which is where they can find water and where I can grow.

Father, let my life be a continual journey closer to You.

—RUTH BERGEN

Day Thirteen

He will yet fill your mouth with laughter and
your lips with shouts of joy.
—JOB 8:21

~~~~~~~~

Last night my husband and I checked in on Ashleigh and Amanda before heading off to bed, just as we've done every night since they were born. We enjoy observing them—and praying for them—while they sleep.

We quietly pushed open the door to their room and began walking lightly toward their cribs. As we approached Ashleigh's, she popped up out of her sleep and began pulling herself up to peer over the bumper pad, trying to see what was going on.

Military man that he is, my husband hit the floor. I darted to the corner and hid next to the dresser. Like commandos, we stayed frozen in position as Ashleigh rustled about and Amanda stirred in her crib. Anything to avoid waking the babies!

Amanda never awoke. Ashleigh eventually settled down and drifted back to sleep. Then, using hand signals, my husband and I made our break for the door. I tiptoed quickly toward the hallway. He low-crawled out of the room. And once we were safely out of earshot, we laughed hysterically.

Lord, thanks for the fun—and funny—sides of parenting.
—DONNA MAY LYONS

Day Fourteen

"My lips will shout for joy when I sing praise to you—I, whom you have redeemed."

—PSALM 71:23

I turn on the bathtub tap and wait. One . . . two . . . three . . . four seconds pass, and I hear an ear-piercing squeal, a garbled *"Baaaath!"* and Henry scrambles to get to the tub. I struggle to put him in without dropping him, and allow him to splash the water as hard as he can with both hands. He sparkles and chortles with glee. His face dips down to the water and he comes back up, surprised that he accidentally got a mouthful.

This is joy. Joy in the smallest, most seemingly insignificant moments of the day. When Henry is happy, he lights up. He smiles so infectiously his whole face disappears. His delight is visceral and palpable. Henry's grin is a wonderful boost to my often downtrodden mood.

I see it every day: Fun activities become an unbound exercise in jubilation. Henry's body vibrates, his eyes go wide with excitement and he lets out a totally exuberant, ear-piercing roar. What's supercool is that so many things can elicit this response: music of any kind, something yummy at mealtime, dancing, and most especially the bath. It's amazing to watch, exciting to be part of. And I do hope one day I'll enter into joy that intense and worship God with the same wholehearted purity.

Thank You, Father God, for the exuberance and wonder I experience through my baby. Help me to foster it in myself so I can give it back to You.
—CHRISTY STURM

Day Fifteen

*". . . So that they may encourage the young women
to love their husbands. . . ."*
—TITUS 2:4 (NAS)

~~~~~~~~~~

I thought I'd mail-ordered the perfect husband. On my list was "loving, patient, dark hair." When Dave stood before me that August morning in 1993, wrapped in a tux and tied with a bow, I just knew God had fulfilled my requisition completely.

It didn't take long for me to look for a money-back guarantee. I'd failed to read the fine print on the marriage license: Warning—not all men know where to find the clothes hamper; prolonged blindness may occur, especially while the wife is wearing a new red dress; garage may be used as a collection container.

As I was grumbling about such things, a baby came along and my husband became a father. He brought Anna to me each time she awoke for another swig of milk in the night. He changed soupy, mustardy, up-the-back diapers and then walked the floors with Anna, singing, "You're my little pumpkin, pumpkin pie." He vacuumed, mopped, washed loads of laundry and brought me breakfast in bed. He cooked dinner and massaged my feet.

One day I visited a friend who was feverishly vacuuming cat hair off her stairs. "Mark will be home from work any minute, and he'll have a fit if this isn't cleaned up," she said. She'd scrubbed the tile in her bathroom that morning in anticipation of his homecoming.

I thought about my slightly-less-than-neat, un-color-coded-sock-drawer hubby—my perfectly good, patient and kind servant-of-a-hubby. I decided, right then and there, that I'd keep him.

Father, thank You for every good thing you gave me in a husband.
—FAITH BOGDAN

Day Sixteen

Jehu said, "Come with me and see my zeal for the Lord"....
—II KINGS 10:16

I was learning quickly that if a line was drawn in the sand, Joey was going to barrel right over it.

That's why I was strict with him about the barstool-height dining room chairs. He viewed the dining set as a jungle gym created just for him—and he made his way there whenever he thought I wasn't paying attention. But the stools were high, and the tile floor was hard. I didn't want him to fall.

One day, after gently reminding him 436 times that the dining room was off limits, I ran to the kitchen to grab a cup of coffee. When I returned to the living room, he was nowhere to be found. Surely he hadn't gone into the dining room.... Had he?

He had. Not only had he climbed onto a chair, but he'd even made his way onto the table, where he stood flicking the dangling beads on the chandelier with his unsteady hand.

Why was my son so dead-set on being naughty? Had I done something wrong?

While I was pondering that thought, Joey jumped into my arms, slid down my body and crawled across the floor to his toy chest. He began stacking blocks, creating a fortress that seemed far beyond his years. He was independent. Creative. Strong. Full of personality traits that could be used to honor God and improve the world. Instead of thinking of Joey as naughty, I could view my son as having the seeds of *zeal*. We'd still have to weed out the naughtiness, but we also needed to recognize and nourish his God-given energy and gifts.

Lord, help me nourish my child's inborn traits so they
grow into strengths that will help him serve You.
—ERIN MACPHERSON

Day Seventeen

Blessed are those who find wisdom, those who gain understanding.
—PROVERBS 3:13

~~~~~~~~~~~~~~~

My extended family gets along well, even to the point where we get invited to my sister-in-law's for functions. Still, I was concerned about navigating with a baby at a crowded family dinner at the Moore home. Mrs. Moore keeps her home neat, with ornate trinkets on living room end tables. Babies and breakables are a nerve-wracking combination, but the ladies stayed here until food was served.

Once dinner was ready, Flynn fixed our plates and we headed to the basement, where there was more room. Flynn sat with the men, watching football on the big-screen TV. I sat in a corner with Joshua on my lap behind a folding snack table.

Just as I was into position to feed us both, Joshua began to cry uncontrollably. I held him on my shoulder, jiggled and patted him, but his cries did battle with the blaring ball game. I'd dodged damaging Mrs. Moore's domain but didn't think I could do the same in male territory. I began to walk with Joshua until Flynn came to see if he could help. As I handed over my crying baby, Mr. Moore looked at me and smiled. "Oh, crying doesn't bother me. It's the sound of life. If you don't hear a baby cry, that's when you have to worry."

Lord, I praise You for a different
perspective on a baby's crying.
—RHONDA J. SMITH

Day Eighteen

The name of the Lord is a strong tower;
the righteous run to it and are safe.
—PROVERBS 18:10

⌇⌇⌇⌇⌇⌇⌇⌇⌇⌇

I carried Gabi to the car from the playground, both of us sweating from the summer heat. It was approaching noon and we'd stayed longer than we should have.

As we walked to our parking spot, I remembered that Derek and I had switched cars for the day. Unfamiliar with the locking system on the van, it took me a few attempts to get the door open. When I finally succeeded, a wave of heat pushed itself out. I threw the diaper bag in the back, the keys in the front and buckled my now-screaming daughter into her car seat.

I ran around to the driver's side to get the car going and the AC running as quickly as possible. But when my fingers pulled on the door handle, the door didn't budge. Locked. I heard Gabi crying inside and ran around to try the passenger-side door. Locked too. I frantically tried every door, sweat running down my forehead, the pit in my stomach growing tighter, terrible news stories of kids in hot cars pushing their way to the front of my brain. Every door was locked.

At the closest house, a kind stranger answered my desperate bangs on her door and quickly called 911. When the firefighters arrived, they had the car door open and the baby out within seconds. After a fast check of Gabi from head to toe and a brief lecture about hiding a key somewhere on the car, they handed me my baby and were off. I hugged Gabi tightly, both of us sweating and crying, and prayed:

Lord, thank You, thank You, for every moment
of every day You protect my child.
—ALEXANDRA KUYKENDALL

Day Nineteen

Give me wisdom and knowledge, that I may lead this people,
for who is able to govern this great people of yours?
—II CHRONICLES 1:10

~~~~~~~~~~~~

Elizabeth's fever was 103. Again. I called the pediatrician, packed up my baby, and off we went on the fifty-minute subway ride to the doctor. This was the third or fourth time she'd had a high fever. Each time it was the same routine: listen to chest, palpate tummy, look in ears—all clear.

"There doesn't seem to be anything wrong, Mrs. Attaway," the doctor said, apologetically. "She has a pink throat, but that's about it. Wait a day or two, and we'll see what happens."

By now I was getting used to it. As I wearily recounted the day's events—and expense—to Andrew, he commented, "My mom said I used to get high fevers whenever I had a sore throat as a kid." I blinked in surprise. Could it be that some kids are more fever-prone than others? I was a little irritated that the pediatrician hadn't raised the possibility. Whenever I called with a concern, the receptionist at his upscale office cheerily offered to set up an appointment "if I was worried about the baby." Was I paying for medical care, or paying to have someone coddle me through new-mom worries?

The next time Elizabeth's fever rose, I called the doctor's office, taking a slightly different approach. "At what point do I need to worry about my baby's fever?" I asked. "She has a history of getting high temperatures from nothing more than a pink throat." The receptionist patched me through to the nurse-practitioner, who asked me a series of questions.

"It doesn't sound like anything serious," she concluded. "You can give her some baby Tylenol and wait a day or two. You don't need to come in. But if you're worried, of course you're welcome to set up an appointment."

I decided I wasn't a copayment's worth of worried, and passed.

Jesus, a little wisdom is a good thing. Would You send some more my way?
—JULIA ATTAWAY

Day Twenty
A Dad's View

Husbands, love your wives as Christ loved the Church and gave himself up for her.
—EPHESIANS 5:25 (ESV)

W hat a day!" Kari said as she grabbed the diaper bag, put shoes on our son's feet, and made for the door. "Got a lot to do. Playdate and grocery shopping this morning, and then clean the house this afternoon while he's napping," she sighed.

We had company arriving that evening to stay with us for a couple days. My wife thinks godliness is next to cleanliness, and I could tell from her tone that she was stressed. "Well, have a good morning out, and don't worry about the house—it'll get done," I said.

"Yeah, I know," she said. "It always does. It's just a lot."

The truth is, it was a lot—eighteen hundred square feet of carpet, tile and toilet. Fortunately, I was speaking in double entendres. When I said "It'll get done," I meant it.

Although I had planned to spend the day working—preparing for the next days' classes, writing, proofing, translating—I sprang into action as Kari and Hans pulled out of the driveway. I threw on a T-shirt and sweats, assembled the cleaning supplies and prepared to make war on dirt and disorder. I knew I only had a few hours.

I worked feverishly, putting away toys, emptying the dishwasher, sweeping, mopping, vacuuming. The clock kept ticking, my brow kept sweating, but the dirt and disorder kept receding.

A little after noon I was finished. I put the supplies away, ran upstairs, cleaned up, dressed and returned to my desk to resume work as if nothing had happened.

Some minutes later I heard the door open and my wife and son stumble in. And then—"Oh my goodness! You didn't!"

For once, I did.

Lord, show me how to love my spouse in ways she truly understands.
—LEROY HUIZENGA

Day Twenty-One

All the days of the oppressed are wretched, but the
cheerful heart has a continual feast.
—PROVERBS 15:15

*I*t started when I was getting Samantha dressed. She was on her back, and I made a goofy face as I tugged on her pants. She began to laugh.

Samantha has the best belly laugh, and seeing her pants-less legs jiggling in the air made me laugh too. In the midst of my laughter, I inadvertently snorted. That made Samantha laugh harder, which made me snort more. The cycle was furious and random and fun.

Billy walked in on his girls. "What's going on in here?"

We stopped short and then looked at each other and busted out in unison. Tears rolled down my cheeks and my tummy muscles cramped.

It felt so good to laugh and to see my girl laughing. In the midst of the madness of every day, in the middle of colds, sniffles and sleepless nights, in the heart of financial worries and marital changes, it felt wonderful to cut loose and laugh about nothing.

I snorted again.

It made both Samantha *and* Billy laugh.

With the three of us laughing and snorting in goofy fits, it felt so much like a joyful family. It felt…perfect.

Thank You, Lord. Don't ever let me get
too grown up to not give in to giggles.
—ELSA KOK COLOPY

Day Twenty-Two

*"Therefore, as we have opportunity, let us do good to all,
especially to those who are of the household of faith."*
—GALATIANS 6:10 (NKJV)

The snickerdoodles, peanut butter blossoms, cherry chocolate chip cookies and slices of pumpkin bread were neatly arranged on plates, wrapped in plastic and tagged with a Christmas-themed Bible verse. I slung Geneva on my hip and headed down the hallway to make our first delivery. I was determined to overcome my shyness and to reach out to the neighbors in our apartment building. Surely baked goods and an adorable baby would break the ice.

It did. We chatted with Hannah and her son, with Lynn across the hall, and with the family next door. Then we headed downstairs to apartment twelve, where we met Selena. As she stood in the doorway, she rubbed her belly and smiled at the baby in my arms. "Did you know I'm pregnant?" she asked. We shared the unspoken but understood new-mom connection.

Those simple plates of cookies opened the door to new friendships. The little card with the Bible verse hadn't gone unnoticed either. At first there were neighborly exchanges: "May I use your phone?" and "Do you have any extra quarters for the laundry machine?" Along with that were conversations about churches and the Bible and, with Selena, babies. When I learned that Selena would have to return to work after a short maternity leave, I offered to provide child care. I hadn't given the idea much thought, but suddenly someone in my path had a need, and I had the opportunity to serve. And as a result, I was blessed with a growing friendship and a few hours a week with another adorable baby in my living room.

Lord, help me seize opportunities to show Your love.
—LISA LADWIG

Day Twenty-Three

For where your treasure is, there your heart will be also.
—MATTHEW 6:21

My good friend Mary and I were having lunch. She sat across from me, and I held Solomon on my lap as we ordered.

"And the baby's fine, right?" the waitress asked Mary. "No juice or anything?"

Mary shook her blonde curls to say no.

It wasn't the first time someone else had been mistaken for Solomon's mother. I suppose my strong Italian features are difficult to connect with Solomon's blond hair and green eyes. The other day at the park a woman asked me how long I'd been a nanny.

"I guess the waitress thought I was his mom," Mary said. "Does it bother you?"

"Oh, it's fine," I said. "I'm used to it." From the moment Solomon was born, it was obvious he inherited his father's looks. "Besides, have you ever seen a cuter little guy?" I rubbed Solomon's back and picked up the toy he'd dropped on the floor.

The waitress brought our drinks and set a basket of bread on the table. Solomon reached for the basket and the waitress looked at Mary. "He really is adorable," she said.

We had a great lunch catching up. As we were leaving, Mary nudged me. "Well, I think he looks like you," she said.

I smiled.

"Especially your smiles," she said. "You both have the same smile."

I can't think of a better way to resemble one another, in joy.

*Dear God, thank You that it isn't only our genes
or looks that connect us, but our love.*
—SABRA CIANCANELLI

Day Twenty-Four

And the peace of God, which transcends all understanding,
will guard your hearts and your minds in Christ Jesus.
—PHILIPPIANS 4:7

I received an invitation to speak at a conference in Charlotte, North Carolina. There had been other invites since Kedar was born, but I hadn't felt ready. I sensed a tugging at my heart to move on this one, though. I could feel a desire building to share the message of God's love and grace from behind the podium again.

Public speaking has come naturally for me since I was eleven years old. When I was young I don't think I ever considered continuing along that path. Quite honestly, I didn't even realize I was *on* any particular path. But with much prayer, I finally recognized and accepted—albeit reluctantly—that this was God's will for my life. And over time that reluctance was replaced with a true passion and eagerness to reach others with the message of God's love and grace.

"So are you gonna do it? Are you up to it?" Kenya asked me over dinner one night.

"I'll pray about it a bit more before I give them an answer," I said, contemplatively.

As the weeks passed, my eagerness to accept the invitation only grew. "Okay, I'm ready," I told him. I felt the normal jitters about balancing mother-hood and ministry, but there was peace in my heart. And that made all the difference.

Heavenly Father, I know the only way to find balance is if I'm
centered in You. Remind me to seek Your guidance.
—DIANNA HOBBS

Day Twenty-Five

O n my twenty-sixth birthday I was pregnant and preparing a nursery for our first child. Dave handed me a small, velvet box. Inside was a heart-shaped gold charm with the word "MOM" gleaming across the front.

I looked at Dave, confused. "What's this?" I asked. My mom's birthday was a few days away. *He got my gift mixed up with his mother's!*

He smiled, and that's when it hit me. *I* was "Mom." The charm was for me.

I stared at the three letters; they stared back at me in bold declaration. I formed the word on my lips, whispering it softly at first and then loudly. With a tearful laugh I looked at Dave and confessed, "I'm a mom!"

After Anna's birth I wore the charm faithfully. It was yanked, tugged and drooled on by the baby that entitled me to wear it. Each time I clasped the golden heart around my neck I saw three prestigious letters behind my name: M-O-M. They didn't represent an advanced degree or a six-figure salary but a profession requiring supernatural skill: that of shaping the character of a human being.

Most days the necklace was hidden away, unappreciated, in a dark jewelry box. It wasn't befitting to wear gold over a faded sweatshirt, dangling over the dirty places I scrubbed while on my hands and knees. But on the days I washed my face and went out to smile at the world, I wore my charm as an emblem of someone who happily found her identity in the word *Mom*.

Dear Father, help me to find the satisfaction and fulfillment
You intended when You made me "Mom."
—FAITH BOGDAN

Day Twenty-Six

May integrity and uprightness protect me,
because my hope is in you.
—PSALM 25:21

~~~~~~~~~~~~~~

To PB&J or not to PB&J. That is the question. I had read somewhere that it was a no-no to give babies high-allergen foods such as eggs and nuts, but Joey's pediatrician assured me it was just fine. So I carefully cut up a PB&J on wheat and gave it to him. And he loved it.

But then Joey's Sunday school teacher told me about a study she had read where kids who were exposed to high-allergen foods were more likely to develop life-threatening allergies.

Gulp! I felt stupid and careless, as though I had been caught letting my baby play with a hunk of asbestos or something. I started crying. Had I scarred my child for life?

Back home, I grabbed the jar of peanut butter and hurled it into the trash, not willing to risk a lifetime of allergies for a silly sandwich. But then I remembered I had asked the pediatrician. I *had* done my research. It's not as though I had given my son a cupful of poison.

Why had a friend's well-intentioned advice thrown me into such a spiral of worry and self-disparagement?

I dug the peanut butter out of the trash. People have differing opinions about baby care. Some moms let their babies cry it out. Others choose formula over breast-feeding. And some crazy, over-the-top moms give babies good old-fashioned PB&J before their first birthdays.

And I am one of those moms.

Lord, give me the serenity to heed the advice
that I need to hear, ignore what I should, and rest without
feeling I've failed when I don't know the difference.
—ERIN MACPHERSON

Day Twenty-Seven

*And the Lord said to Moses, "I will do the very thing you have asked,
because I am pleased with you and I know you by name."*
—EXODUS 33:17

race's babbling over the baby monitor drew me out of sleep. I listened, smiled and rolled over. Her constant, incoherent chatter soon lulled me into drowsiness, until two syllables snapped me awake.

"Mama."

Not sure I'd heard correctly, I reached across the pillows to turn up the volume. I listened to Grace rustle around in her crib until she said it again, this time drawing it into a song.

"Mamamamamamamama."

A smiled flooded my face as I headed down the hall to get my baby girl. For weeks, I'd begged her to say my name. She'd look in my eyes, smile, and say "Da-da." But this time, it was *my* name. I'd listened closely just to make sure.

It's amazing how important it is to hear your name. It made me think of the day I'll stand before Christ, when I'll look in his face and hear Him call out, "Carol Buell Hatcher." Just thinking about it had my heart bursting, and I threw open the door to the nursery.

I ran to the cherub in the baby bed and lifted her up to my face. "Aw, who's got you?" I asked, waiting eagerly to hear my name roll from her baby-soft lips.

"Da-da."

*Lord, I am honored and amazed that
You know me by name.*
—CAROL HATCHER

Day Twenty-Eight

"I will refresh the weary and satisfy the faint."
—JEREMIAH 31:25

~~~~~~~~~~~~

I'm an active mom. Picnics, pools, playgrounds, museums, you name it—we're there. My husband, not so much. He's content to be home watching movies as the baby crawls around looking for something to chew on. It drives me nuts. "They're bored!" I hiss, wishing he'd take the initiative to lug out the double stroller as I do each day. Gary insists the boys are fine, but I know they're not. In my mind they crave adventure as much as I do.

Because I'm a thrill seeker, I was overjoyed to receive an invitation to attend a weekend trapeze workshop. But my excitement was weighed down by guilt. While I'd be flying through the air with the greatest of ease, the boys would most likely be stuck in the apartment watching Elmo. I'd never been away from both of them that long either. After many phone calls to gather opinions, the answer was a resounding "Go!" But the most convincing argument came from my mother-in-law. "The kids will be fine. They're with their daddy," she said, urging me to leave and enjoy. "Gary doesn't do things the way you do, but he's still their father. You need to give him the opportunity to parent, and yourself the opportunity to rest." I'd never thought about it that way.

The weekend did wonders for me, and my babies survived my absence. When I came home, they were all smiles, huddled under a Daddy-tent of blankets and kitchen chairs. Two days of adventure rejuvenated my spirit, but more than that, it gave me permission to let go and let Daddy create a few adventures of his own.

Lord, thank You for opportunities to renew my spirit, and thank You for those who are willing to share their time so I can do so.
—KAREN VALENTIN

Day Twenty-Nine

*In the desert the whole community grumbled
against Moses and Aaron.*
—EXODUS 16:2

I walked into church, carrying my daughter on my hip. As I followed my husband to a pew near the front, I looked around at our grand sanctuary: the high ceilings, the magnificent Italian Renaissance replica painting across the entire back wall, the one-hundred-year-old stained glass windows. Normally I feel overwhelmed with joy and gratitude and the unmistakable presence of the Holy Spirit the moment I walk into this place.

But that day I felt nothing.

Lucy was teething, which meant no one in the house had been sleeping well. She was fussy during the daytime, making it hard for me to get anything done. The house was a wreck and I was too tired to get together with friends. There wasn't enough of me left to feel anything spiritually.

The deacon stood and read from one of the Gospels. I waited for the warm feeling of the presence of God to overwhelm me. It didn't.

I sighed, looked around and suddenly smiled. I'd been so caught up in focusing on *me* that I'd completely forgotten the power of the Word exists regardless of how I feel! The realization was so liberating I was almost moved to tears. In this crazy path of motherhood there will be other times I'm so frazzled I can't sense the Lord's presence. And that's okay. Because He is there nonetheless.

*Lord, thank You for being here with me,
even when I can't sense Your presence.*
—JENNIFER FULWILER

Day Thirty

For now we see in a mirror dimly, but then face to face. . . .
—I CORINTHIANS 13:12

~~~~~~~~~~~~~~~~

I n the city a stroller isn't an accessory; it's a vehicle. Back when I still had functioning brain cells (before they were expelled with the placenta), I spent hours researching different models: how much they weigh, how easily they fold, how far they recline. I wanted something that was durable and could last for miles.

I've since learned that durability is difficult to lug up two flights of stairs, especially with eighteen pounds of baby inside. Durability doesn't fit through the subway turnstile either. But hey—you don't know what you don't know when you're entering motherhood, and I suppose that's a mercy. If I ever fork over another minifortune for a stroller, I'll focus on different features.

Whatever model I choose won't solve my biggest stroller problem, though: When the baby starts screaming, how do you know whether to take her out or keep going?

When Elizabeth was little, it was a no-brainer. If she cried, I picked her up. But now I wonder: Am I spoiling her? Is she manipulating me? Am I a bad mommy for letting her cry, or a good one for getting home before the milk goes bad?

Most days I tend to doubt that Elizabeth's tender psyche will be irreparably damaged by a ten-minute screamfest—as long as she's the one who's hysterical, not me. What gets hurt are my eardrums and nerves. If I can keep the latter calm, I'll probably be fine on the day twenty years hence when Elizabeth tells me she's scarred for life because I didn't stop to console her when we raced home in that thunderstorm when she was ten months old. I'll have a clean conscience: I made the best decision I could with the info I had, with the best of intentions. But I didn't know what I didn't know.

Father, when there's no clear answer on what's right or
wrong, help me be at peace with my decisions.
—JULIA ATTAWAY

Eleventh Month

~~~~~~

Jesus,

What a lesson a mobile child is in how distractible we are! I am good at darting from one item on my agenda to another, without a clear and constant focus on You. Keep my eyes fixed on the cross as I zig and zag through my days, attract my eye to opportunities to praise You, surprise my heart with new ways to serve. Most of all, teach me to love You in all things so that no matter where my mind may wander, it will find You.

Amen.

Tips

» Not getting much Scripture study in? Choose a verse to memorize and make a clapping game out of it to play with your baby.

» Eating supper together is likely to encourage your child to feed himself, because he sees you putting food in your mouth too!

» If you try to be everything to your baby, you're not leaving room for God—or for the love of others.

Day One

*"Do you hear what these children are saying?" they asked
him. "Yes," replied Jesus, "have you never read, 'From the lips
of children and infants you have ordained praise'?"*
—MATTHEW 21:16

Kedar and I were sitting in church one evening. In the middle of the sermon, the unction suddenly hit him to begin clapping and blabbing his favorite word. "*Ah-yoo-yah!*" (Hallelujah!) And whenever he said it, Kedar shouted so loudly it was impossible not to notice.

At first it was cute and funny to hear him talking. After all, adults are used to hearing random outbursts from little ones caught up their own fantasy world. Nothing new there.

But this was different. Kedar let out about seven *Ah-yoo-yahs* in a row. He grew so rowdy I had to leave the sanctuary so others could concentrate on what the pastor had to say. But once we got into a zone where Kedar could freely have a "hallelujah fit," he went silent. Not a single peep.

When we went back into the sanctuary again, his very audible, personal praise session started back up. Obviously my young Mr. Hobbs associated the sanctuary with praise. And he had learned quite well how to imitate what he saw going on around him.

As I sat in the back of the church (just in case I needed to dart out again), one of the elderly greeters walked over to me and said, "You know, baby, you can always tell what these kids are exposed to by what comes out of them. You raising that boy right!"

*Dear Lord, I pray that my child will learn to honor,
love and reverence You by my example.*
—DIANNA HOBBS

Day Two

*But do not forget this one thing, dear friends: With the Lord a day
is like a thousand years, and a thousand years are like a day.*
—II PETER 3:8

We originally met in a grief group to deal with babies we'd never get to
hold. Eventually and thankfully, within an eleven-month span each
of us had a new addition. New friendships continued, and Lunch Bunch was
born.

Nearly each week we gathered, and one lucky mom had the morning off
to do anything she wanted. The rest of us kept the babies, three boys and a
girl, entertained while big-girl talk prevailed. To me, we all had the morning
off. Our times were joyous and greatly educational for me, even as conversations were punctuated with "Uh-oh!" and "Who smells?"

Perhaps because our friendships were born in hard times, I never imagined they'd end. But as my Zach and his buddies grew, the moms' personali-
ties, parenting styles and insecurities grew more distinct. For some, that was
a stumbling block. Others grew edgy over decisions to work, go overseas, or
offer a sip of Diet Coke to a toddler.

Two of those friendships faded, and one deepened. Only time showed me,
and my bruised ego, that God gives us some friends for certain junctures in
our life, others for longer. During our grieving period, one of those women
gave us each a bookmark I have never let leave my refrigerator: "Don't place a
period where God has placed a comma."

Some friendships will end—there *are* periods. But friendships can also be
like the colon: a gateway. Lunch Bunch was a gateway to a better me.

The bonds of motherhood are strong, Lord.
Help me be a worthy, loving friend.
—SUSAN BESZE WALLACE

Day Three

*And now I commend you to God and to the word of his
grace, which is able to build you up and to give you the
inheritance among all those who are sanctified.*
—ACTS 20:32 (ESV)

Solomon's Grandma Sybil is eighty-two years young. Her gorgeous hands lined with life hold Solomon's plump fingers as she taps to the beat of the children's songs that play in the background.

A new song, "Polly Wolly Doodle," fills the room. Solomon dances to the tambourine and shrieks with joy.

Sybil's eyes spark as if seeing an old friend. "Oh! I love this song!" she exclaims. "So many memories! I used to sing this when I was a little girl—it brings me right back. Who would have thought, all those years ago, that I'd get to be this old, with my own grandson on my lap!"

As we munch on the homemade chocolate chip cookies Sybil brought, she tells us stories about growing up, her childhood friends, the one-room schoolhouse that was warmed by a pot-bellied stove. "Oh, it feels like yesterday I was that little girl!" she says.

As Tony helps Sybil gather her things for the drive home, she stops by the window and hums "Polly Wolly Doodle." Our new memories merge with tales of old, and for a moment the past and future come together in a perfect present.

*Dear Lord, thank You for grandmas and
times when the present is perfect.*
—SABRA CIANCANELLI

Day Four

Be kind and compassionate to one another, forgiving
each other, just as in Christ God forgave you.
—EPHESIANS 4:32

When Joshua was eleven months old, I was afraid I'd become a single mom. That's when Flynn was diagnosed with diabetes and high cholesterol. A year before, the doctor had told Flynn he was borderline for both diseases. All he had to do was lose weight to prevent the onset.

But the recommendation came soon after Flynn had had a series of unexplained blackouts while playing basketball. Maybe he didn't exercise because he didn't want to pass out and hit his head. Or maybe he decided to take his chances. I don't know what he was thinking, but *I* was thinking he was selfish for risking his life and leaving me a single mother.

I never put it in words, but he knew. He knew from every look I gave him during the doctor's chastising, from my silence when friends chided him and from my tight lips when his belly told him he needed to go up a shirt size. I continued to be his wife, but I had a funky attitude, dishonoring Flynn for *threatening* to make me a single mom.

I finally stopped when he admitted after a doctor's visit that he should have complied with instructions the first time. "Maybe if I listen, I can get off the medications," he said. I could see the sadness in his eyes, the disappointment, too, that he had in himself.

Right then I knew I didn't want to miss any more pleasant moments with my husband. I was going to aim to love him in all his unsure ways, because I didn't know how long I would have him. I wasn't going to let *my* selfishness get in the way of any day God had given me with my husband.

Lord, help me to have compassion so I can love as I should.
—RHONDA J. SMITH

Day Five

*"Here is a boy with five small barley loaves and two small
fish, but how far will they go among so many?"*
—JOHN 6:9

~~~~~~~~~~~~~~~

S he's beautiful, Francisca!" we whispered, gazing down at the newborn cradled in her arms. It had been three months since I'd first met Francisca in a fast-food restaurant to encourage her in her pregnancy. Now her baby Antonia slept peacefully, swaddled snugly in a white blanket and wearing the obligatory blue-and-pink-striped newborn hat.

"May I hold her?" Jonathan asked.

"Sure," Francisca replied, carefully placing Antonia in Jonathan's arms. She looked more confident than the day I'd met her. Over the past few months we'd kept in contact via telephone. They were short calls, in which I asked how things were progressing and reminded her I was praying for her. Understanding Francisca's broken English over the telephone was difficult. More than a few times I felt guilty for not calling her more often. But it was all I could do right then.

"We brought you a present: just a few things we thought you might need," I explained, happy to pass on some essentials I'd found helpful. It wasn't much, considering how much Francisca needed, but it was as much as we could give.

"Oh, thank you!" she beamed. I wondered if these were the only baby presents she'd receive. Again I felt bad and wished I could be there for Francisca more. But thankfully, God knew my limitations. Although my role in Francisca's life seemed small to me, our God is not small, and He can do great things with little acts of obedience. I can only obey, and pray that He will take whatever I give and use it for His glory.

*Lord, I give You this small offering and
trust You will do the multiplying.*
—LIZ BISSELL

Day Six

~~~~~~~~

Spit-up in the folds of the neck, baby food in the hair, offensive diaper changes—a sweet-smelling baby doesn't happen naturally. The day is a never-ending ritual of baby wipes, clothing changes and spit baths. But just before bedtime my stinky little creatures need a bath. I can't seem to pull shirts and diapers off my boys fast enough as they anxiously wait to get into the tub.

The splashing begins immediately with giggles and belly laughs. The bath is where Brandon made his little brother Tyler laugh for the first time. They play in the bubbly water with cups and squeaky toys, as I sit on the floor getting sprayed with water. It's refreshing. This is a time to breathe: Tyler's not crawling around finding interesting things to put in his mouth; Brandon's not climbing on the furniture. They're happy, they're together, and best of all—they're contained!

One by one I lather them up. It annoys them and interferes with their fun. I wash their faces, hair, bellies, legs, and little by little they become new again. Tyler comes out first. I wrap him in a soft towel and kiss his little wet face. I squeeze him, show him how adorable he is in the mirror and breathe in the sweet fragrance of a clean baby. There's nothing like it in the world. A sprinkle of powder is next, freshly washed pajamas and then it's Brandon's turn. No one goes on the floor after bath time. I can't ruin the perfection and purity of it all with dusty feet. Time enough tomorrow for mud, sand and sticky food. For this moment, they're clean.

*Lord, thank You for the minutes when
everything is right in the world.*
—KAREN VALENTIN

Day Seven

For you were once darkness, but now you are light
in the Lord. Live as children of light.
—EPHESIANS 5:8

*L*iiiiight."

I turned to watch Angelica force the word and its wind through her small lips again. Stunned, I wanted to see it emerge. "Liiiiiiight." She rolls out the *i* long and high, unmistakably saying the word. She is pointing at the fixture I've just turned on in the bedroom. She is saying her first word!

I'm not prepared. I have no video or recorder to document this. Angelica's dark eyes shine as I nod and clap along to encourage her to say it again. I have no treat or gift to offer her as reward for so perfectly pronouncing so beautiful a word. I panic. How will I tell others? What will stand as proof of my daughter's decisive, precocious intellect, her forward-moving mind?

I race to the phone to call someone. But who? Who should be the first I offer this remarkable news?

Angelica watches me, her mouth arranging itself for a new rush of breath and syllable. Her head is cocked, her hands outstretched, her mouth pursed. She is seated, a perfect Buddha-baby, waiting—waiting for me to stop moving to make calls and take photos and find rewards. She is waiting for me to return to *her*. She is patient in her posture, her hands lifted, expectant and watchful.

"*Liiiiiight?*" I ask her, kneeling beside her, opening my arms, basking in her singular radiance and nothing more.

She smacks her gums delightedly and leans in, closing the space between us.

"*Liiiiiight.*"

Lord, what light You have brought into the world!
—DEBRALEE SANTOS

Day Eight

Let us come before him with thanksgiving. . . .
—PSALM 95:2

I walked out the door on Saturday afternoon to meet up with a girlfriend for coffee, feeling good in my new jeans and garage-sale top. I'd even managed a quick swipe of lipstick. *Not half bad*, I said to the mirror before I smooched my baby and my husband good-bye.

I arrived at the coffee shop to see my friend hip as ever—beautiful purse, lovely outfit, not a hair out of place. I hugged her and sat down. And then I noticed. Her eyes kept drifting downward. *Oh no.* I had the strange feeling that all was not well. What? Was my womanhood spilling out? Did I have baby drool on my neck? A little irritated, I excused myself and went to the restroom.

Of course. When I'd kissed Samantha good-bye, she'd managed to land a smear of carrot goo right on the white lace of my top. I tried to remove it, but the stain remained. I caught sight of my frantic eyes in the mirror, took a deep breath and forced a smile. *This is not a big deal*, I said in my brain. *You have a baby; babies have goo. Embrace it.*

I put on a smile, stuck out my chest and went back to my friend.

Lord, parenting is full of messy moments.
This goo is of You, and I'm thankful.
—ELSA KOK COLOPY

Day Nine

For we are God's workmanship, created in Christ Jesus to do good works, which God prepared in advance for us to do.
—EPHESIANS 2:10

My son Joey thrives on messes and noise and chaos. And today was no exception. Joey and I spent twenty minutes making a miniature city out of wooden blocks. And just as I put the final block on top of the tower, *vroom-vroom-vroom* . . . crash! Joey rammed his big yellow dump truck into the city, strewing blocks across the room and obliterating the masterpiece we'd worked so hard to create.

Why would he destroy something we had spent so long making? I just didn't get it. I'm a girly girl to the core; as a child I set up tea parties for my animals and left the perfectly staged scene up for days. I like things pretty and organized and . . . well . . . *quiet.*

But God—in his infinite wisdom—didn't give me a girly girl. He gave me a son who is 100 percent snips and snails and puppy dog tails. A son who will never sit quietly and play tea party while singing "Kumbaya."

But with the assurance that God has never made a mistake—even when he stuck me with a boy who is the living essence of boyness—I can be certain that my son's vibrant, strong and independent personality has a purpose on this earth.

And you can rest assured that Joey's purpose involves messes. And noise. And chaos.

Lord, thank You for creating my son—and creating him with a purpose that will be used to glorify You.
—ERIN MACPHERSON

Day Ten

"Judge not, that ye be not judged."
—MATTHEW 7:1

~~~~~~~~~~

My friend Sarah is a young mom single-handedly raising four children under the age of five. Ben, her youngest, is two years old and hasn't gained weight for a year. He's been diagnosed with GERD (gastroesophogeal reflux disease), which means every time he eats, he suffers the heartburn of a woman in her third trimester of pregnancy. To avoid that misery, he shoves his plate away. Ben's pediatrician told Sarah, "If he'll swallow it, feed it to him." So Sarah searches grocery store shelves for calorie-rich foods that will please Ben's palate enough to help him gain weight. She does whatever it takes: Some days Ben gets pudding for breakfast, and that's all Sarah is lucky enough to get down him.

Ben also has severe asthma. A crying episode can bring on an asthma attack and result in a trip to the ER. So Sarah also has to be careful to keep Ben calm, and that means letting him have his way more often than she cares to.

I wonder, if I didn't know Sarah and the details of her life, what I'd think as I watched Sarah interact with Ben—allowing him to skip the veggies and fill up on ice cream, pacifying him the instant he fusses. I'd be tempted to throw a book or two in her face, books about childhood nutrition and discipline.

And I wonder how many other "Sarahs" I have met and wanted to "bless" with my knowledge, when I was completely void of wisdom.

Lord, help me to listen before I judge.
—FAITH BOGDAN

Day Eleven

"She is clothed with strength and dignity;
she can laugh at the days to come."
—PROVERBS 31:25

I invited Irene and her son over for coffee just before Christmas. They arrived right at the stroke of ten, bursting through my front door in a blinding flurry. Eighteen-month-old Toby ripped off his jacket, mittens and toque in record speed, dropping them in the middle of the kitchen. His boots he left on, of course, leaving a trail of melted snow as he traipsed through my house.

My friend took off her outerwear before following Toby to the living room. I winced as I stepped in a puddle in the hall.

Irene and I tried to carry on a conversation for the next two hours, but we were continually interrupted by Toby's antics. At one point he tried to climb my Christmas tree, and then after a few minutes of suspicious silence, we went to check on him. He had two ornaments in his mouth.

When they finally walked out the door, I was a mess. Trembling at what the future might hold, I called Brian on the phone, "What have we done?" I moaned, as I recounted the morning's events.

Brian laughed and replied, "We have no idea, Ruth!"

"Nope," I said, agreeing. I looked down at Shiloh, who sat quietly on the floor. "But this morning I had a tiny glimpse. Maybe."

Dear Lord, whatever lies ahead, help me love
my child through every stage.
—RUTH BERGEN

Day Twelve

Do not let any unwholesome talk come out of your mouths,
but only what is helpful for building others up according
to their needs, that it may benefit those who listen.

—EPHESIANS 4:29

I sat in a basement playroom in a circle of women, watching our new crawlers scoot about in the center. This group of moms and babies had all been part of a hospital class, and at our "graduation" we decided to continue meeting regularly, rotating houses. Every week I returned, hoping to discover genuine friendships. I'd left behind my closest friends in my cross-country move.

The mom chatter was going when I made a side comment about my husband and his cluelessness in all things mothering. Everyone laughed. Liking the sudden attention, I continued, thinking more about the affirmation I was feeling than the direction of the conversation. The laughs kept coming, further spurring my joke-telling. It felt good to laugh, to have fun. I'd been so lonely the past few months that I relished any moment that felt like a connection.

Later, as I buckled Gabi into her car seat, I started replaying my comments in my head. They had been made in fun, but I started hearing them through the ears of people who didn't know Derek. Would I have used the same words if he'd been in the room? How would my husband have interpreted what I said? I didn't like the answers.

Driving away, I resolved to go into the group the next week with a different attitude. I would set a new tone to the conversation, one of gratitude—especially to my husband, who is doing his best at parenthood.

Lord, may my conversations honor others,
especially my husband.
—ALEXANDRA KUYKENDALL

Day Thirteen

Give thanks to the Lord, for he is good; his love endures forever.
—PSALM 118:1

⁌rownstone apartments have their advantages, but laundry facilities aren't among them. I placed the huge bag of dirty clothes outside the apartment door, put Elizabeth in her winter coat and girded myself for the ordeal. Lock door, drag bag to steps. Exclaim to daughter with (fake) glee as I tumble the laundry bag down the stairs. Pick up my girl and walk down, stroller in hand, to the second-floor landing. Repeat to get to the first floor. Open stroller, insert baby, open door, heave the laundry bag down the stoop and bump the stroller down the steps.

Mercifully, our laundromat was across the street. And thankfully our landlady didn't mind if I left the clean, folded laundry on the first floor for Andrew to bring up when he returned from work. Sometimes I got away with leaving the stroller down there too. The logistics were cumbersome, but the system worked.

Until Elizabeth learned to walk, that is. Her mobility increased the complexity of this stupidly challenging chore exponentially. I'd turn around to put the laundry outside the apartment and find Elizabeth laughingly shutting the door—with my keys inside. Or I'd discover—just before I shoved the clothes bag down the steps—that my monkey had climbed on top of it. The variations on Houdini-like stroller escapes that resulted in a head bonked on stainless-steel dryer doors seemed endless.

So I gave up. The laundry was a zoo on Saturdays, swarming with aggressive city yuppies and bossy grandmas, but Andrew was home to watch Elizabeth. It took me twice as long, and it was irritating and unpleasant. But I got to go *alone*. And while every mom knows that silence is golden, sometimes it's solitude that counts.

Lord, life could always be worse. Thanks that it isn't.
—JULIA ATTAWAY

Day Fourteen

We must pay more careful attention, therefore, to what
we have heard, so that we do not drift away.
—HEBREWS 2:1

⁓⁓⁓⁓⁓⁓

I pressed the last seams of the curtains I'd just sewn, slipped them onto a rod, and hung them across the kitchen window. Perfect. This sunny morning, our kitchen was extra cheery. The door was open to the pretty back garden, and a light breeze carried in wafts of perfume from the bright-colored sweet peas that climbed the brick wall by the door.

As I admired the curtains and enjoyed the charm of our new home in England, Michelle toddled into the room wearing underwear on her head, socks on her arms and cracker crumbs across her sticky, grinning face. I laughed, struck that I had no idea what she'd been doing.

I stepped into the living room and cringed at the scene. Every game, puzzle and deck of cards had been pulled from the cupboard, and the pieces were mixed together in a gigantic mess. *Ugh.* I sat down to sort them, and when it took much longer than I'd have liked, I began to feel slightly put out. There were a number of other things I'd rather be doing.

Little Michelle, who loved being in the midst of things, came to assist me but only complicated the clean-up. I couldn't resist her exuberant willingness, though, and had to admit that I'd recently spent too much time making home cozy. Michelle's easygoing nature was easy to pacify, and rather than mothering attentively, I'd handed her too many snacks and let her play with normally off-limits games so I could sew.

My heart sank. I wanted to be a loving and attentive mother first and foremost. I'd rather do that and tackle projects when I could, even if it meant not doing them at all.

Lord, help me grasp the brevity of babyhood and mother
my child with wholehearted love and attention.
—SUSAN LABOUNTY

Day Fifteen

*God, whom I serve with my whole heart in preaching
the gospel of his Son, is my witness how constantly
I remember you in my prayers at all times. . . .*
—ROMANS 1:9–10

I am *done!*" I snapped as soon as Joe walked in the front door. I dropped Lucy into his hands and ran upstairs to my bedroom. I flopped onto the bed on top of the covers—getting under the sheets required too much energy after a day like this.

I scrolled through the woe-is-me highlight reel of the past ten hours: Lucy had fallen asleep in the car that morning, which meant she wouldn't nap. Overtired and cranky, she threw her bowl of spaghetti against the wall at lunch. I couldn't even make a doctor's appointment because the receptionist couldn't hear me over the wailing in the background.

My moment of self-pity was interrupted when I glanced at a family picture on our dresser. In it my mother-in-law stood next to Joe, and I thought of what days like this must have been like for her. She became a single mother after an unwanted divorce when Joe was still a toddler. With no college education and no established career, making ends meet was hard for her. They were so poor that sometimes they couldn't run the heat in the winter, and they always lived under the threat of losing their home.

And, I realized as I lay on my comfortable bed in my safe home, she had to face days like this—alone. It occurred to me that at that very moment, countless single mothers had had days even worse than mine, yet didn't have the luxury of handing the baby off to someone else and announcing they were "done." I stopped my wallowing and began to pray for single mothers everywhere.

*Lord, pour Your grace out on mothers who are
struggling with parenting alone.*
—JENNIFER FULWILER

Day Sixteen

*Why, you do not even know what will
happen tomorrow. . . .*
—JAMES 4:14

～～～～～～

Tyler looked at my friend's cute baby girl with sad puppy eyes as she whacked him in the face—not just once, but over and over, like an experienced boxer. If she had whacked Brandon, there would have been a fight. Tyler didn't even lift his hands to block his face.

"I'm so sorry," my friend said, before reprimanding her daughter. I've always had to apologize for Brandon, so I completely understood. Being on the receiving end of the aggression, however, was new territory.

Tyler wasn't crying, but I scooped him up anyway and squeezed him tight. He has always been a sweet, gentle baby—qualities I treasure after Brandon's temperamental behavior. At least I could breathe easy with this one, I'd thought. But as I held my peaceful little boy, I wondered if maybe this was worse. For once I wished Tyler had some of his brother's fight. While I'm constantly telling Brandon not to hit, I was secretly rooting for Tyler to throw in a good punch.

How do parents teach their kids to stand up for themselves, I wondered, *without resorting to violence?* I had no idea. My mind fast-forwarded to high school, envisioning Tyler with a "kick me" sign on his back and spitballs in his hair. I squeezed him tighter, but my boy wiggled to get down. I put him back on the picnic blanket. He crawled over to his aggressive little playmate and continued to play with the toys nearby. I shrugged and smiled. I had time to figure out how to raise my boy so he wouldn't be a pushover. But for now, he wasn't stressed out over the bopping and that made me relax about it too.

*Father, I trust You will guide me in my parenting,
one day at a time.*
—KAREN VALENTIN

Day Seventeen

He only is my Rock and my Salvation; He is my Defense
and my Fortress, I shall not be moved.
—PSALM 62:6 (AMP)

~~~~~~~~~~~~~~

Cheerios have invaded my life. They are all over our house, inside the couch, under the kitchen cabinets, wedged into the cracks of our hardwood floors, in our cars, in the lining of Solomon's car seat, even in the bottom of my purse. Yesterday, as I was checking out at the grocery store, I found one in my hair.

Cheerios are Solomon's favorite food, and I read they're great at teaching him to grip with his thumb and forefinger. But as he masters picking them up, he has a habit of dropping one, two or twenty.

I was hauling our heavy vacuum out of the closet when I had a breakdown. "I can't pick up any more of these. It's all I do!" I complained. Not long after, Tony surprised me with an electric broom. It's a lightweight, easy-to-use model with a clear receptacle in the front that gathers dust and dirt—or in my case, Cheerios.

When I first glided it across the living room rug, it formed a perfect tornado of cat hair and cereal. The tornado grew. I kept my eye on the whirl of spinning *O*'s and thought of a quote by Norman Vincent Peale: "A cyclone derives its power from a calm center."

Of course, I thought, *I shouldn't let these tiny annoyances get the better of me.* Cheerios chaos can easily become order with the help of the right core and a good vacuum.

Dear God, You are my center. Thanks for the
glorious calm I find in You.
—SABRA CIANCANELLI

Day Eighteen
A Dad's View

His children become a blessing.
—PSALM 37:26 (ESV)

~~~~~~~~~

"Whoop!" I exclaimed. Hans' eyes grew wide as he smiled. Kids do that when tossed in the air.

"Whoop!" I exclaimed again, as my little boy left my grip, giggling. He dodged the ceiling fan and fell back into my hands.

My wife and I played different roles in Hans' little baby life. When he needed comfort, or nurture, or food—whether solid or liquid—more often than not it was Mama he wanted. I got to be the one who pushed the boundaries, who tried to give him a sense of adventure. I loved helping him walk around the block, wrestling with him, teaching him to kick a soccer ball, helping him pet our aloof cat. And throwing him in the air. . .

"Um . . . what are you doing?" queried Kari, concerned.

Hans left outer orbit and squealed as he landed in the safety of my arms.

"Oh, nothing," I said, feigning nonchalance. "Just teaching our boy to fly. Hold on . . . WHOOP!" I hollered, tossing Hans toward the ceiling as he shrieked with joy.

Kari's countenance turned to alarm, but I caught him, as always. Hans giggled, full of teeth and dimples. We rubbed noses, Daddy now giggling, full of teeth and dimples, as Mommy smiled and understood.

Thank You, Lord, for the delight and joy our child brings.
—LEROY HUIZENGA

Day Nineteen

A gracious woman gains respect. . . .
—PROVERBS 11:16 (NLT)

~~~~~~~~~~~~~

I wasn't prepared for what greeted me behind my mother-in-law's door that evening as Dave and I returned from the restaurant. We'd left Anna in Grandma's care for a couple of hours so we could enjoy an overdue dinner date. In my haste to go, I'd left no rules. Now I faced an eleven-month-old drippy-brown chin and an empty pudding snack on the table. In my absence, the mother of my husband had polluted my baby's insides with a full serving of dyed, preserved and processed poison.

Momentarily, I considered sending Joanne a writ of divorcement attached to a scientific study on the dangers of refined sugar. Deciding instead to install surveillance cameras in her kitchen, I wiped Anna's face and whisked her away to begin detox treatment in the safety of our home.

In time, with Dave's help and a strip of duct tape over my lips, I had the courage to leave Anna once again in Grandma's care. Despite Joanne's tendency toward normal eating habits, she proved to be an exceptional grandmother. She even kept a spanking device handy: a foam-filled pillow attached to a stick labeled "Grandma's paddle." Together she and Anna took regular strolls to the river and skipped rocks, made macaroni and cheese, went swimming and read books.

In some ways she's the grandmother I never had, and she's the only local grandmother my daughter will likely ever know. It's a good thing she's still around, for when we go to relax a while in Joanne's big white farmhouse, I am known to sneak into the kitchen and go looking for an Oreo. But don't tell Grandma.

Dear Lord, help me lighten up! And thank You
for the blessing of grandparents.
—FAITH BOGDAN

Day Twenty

Now as the church submits to Christ, so also wives
should submit to their husbands in everything.
—EPHESIANS 5:24

When my husband asked me to come along for his business trip to the other side of the nation, I knew I needed to say yes. I knew he asked because he wanted to enjoy my company. I wanted to go . . . and yet I didn't want to. My firstborn was eighteen months old before we went away for even one night. My middle child was almost two when we did an overnight without kids. How could I leave my sweet Gracie for five whole days? My heart said, "You can't!" But my head said, "You should!" Sometimes putting my husband first is a struggle.

Alan can somehow separate his sense of self from the children. To me they are like appendages; removal is painful. My loving hubby would never force the issue, though he admitted he was pleasantly surprised when I said yes.

One of the best things I can do for my children is to love and honor their father and keep my marriage healthy. So I packed my bags, left an overly detailed list of instructions for my mother and boarded a plane for San Francisco.

"Hey," Alan squeezed my hand as the plane readied for take-off, "I'm proud of you." I grinned, glanced at the laptop in my carry-on and patted myself on the back for teaching my six-year-old how to video-chat.

Lord, keep this marriage strong. Nudge me to take
time to reconnect with my spouse.
—CAROL HATCHER

Day Twenty-One

". . . To shine on those living in darkness and in the shadow
of death, to guide our feet into the path of peace."
—LUKE 1:79

Zach sat in a high chair making a drum of the tray. My friend Angela and her six-months-older son Sam were over for some playtime and lunch.

Sam, who hadn't been babied much, was always a barometer for my kiddo's development. He'd devoured his lunch while I rattled a spoon through a couple of jars for Zach. "Not sure when he's going to learn to feed himself," I said in a singsong voice to my two-toothed tot.

"Why don't you give him the spoon?" Angela queried.

"He's not ready. He can't do it. He might get . . . messy."

"That's the point. Give him the spoon," she said again.

I debated the merits and downside of letting him slime himself while shoveling in several more bites. Angela, never one to judge, was laughing at me. Finally, I relinquished the Thomas the Train scoop, biting my lip.

Zach was beside himself. He stirred. He slung. He painted his face with baby yogurt. I had a choice: Get the mop or the camera. I hesitated but a moment, and chose the latter.

It wasn't just a spoon I let Zach grip that day, it was a parenting philosophy. Try. Play. Enjoy. Learn. Squish. I'd no idea that moment would echo in my heart for years to come. I wanted my child to experience life, to grab at it. And to know I'd be right there to guide—not spoon-feed. Angela helped get that philosophy of mine from my head to my hands.

Lord, when I want You to spoon-feed me, remind
me You are my guide instead.
—SUSAN BESZE WALLACE

Day Twenty-Two

For out of the overflow of his heart his mouth speaks.

—LUKE 6:45

~~~~~~~~~~~~~

Joey's first word was "tu-down!" Not Mama. Not Dada. Not even dog or cat or cookie. But "tu-down!," said with his arms up in the air in true football-fanatic fashion. It's obvious what was overflowing in our hearts at the time: Texas football fever.

Cute as it was—and it was *really* cute—the fact that my son had picked up on the word touchdown gave me pause. There's nothing wrong with loving the big game—even if you're an Oklahoma fan. But that day I realized I had been so excited (okay, obsessed) with the Longhorn season that my son had heard little else from my mouth.

I decided then and there to be purposeful with my words. My son was only eleven months old, yet he discerned very clearly what my heart desired. And although I didn't mind if he grew up to be a Longhorn fan, what I wanted even more was for him to grow up and be a *Jesus* fan.

That night, while Joey sat in the kitchen banging on pans as I made dinner, I intentionally talked about heavenly things. I told him Bible stories I remembered from my childhood. I chatted about love and kindness and goodness. And I prayed that he would see that my heart was overflowing with love—for him and for Jesus.

Lord, help me to speak to my child with words
that point his heart toward You.

—ERIN MACPHERSON

Day Twenty-Three

Children's children are a crown to the aged, and
parents are the pride of their children.
—PROVERBS 17:6

O-pa!" my girl said as she squeezed my father's face in her hands. "O-pa!"
"Sa-man-ta!" my dad replied in his heavy Dutch accent. "Sa-man-ta!"

The two were sitting on the couch. Samantha sat on his lap, facing him as she smushed his cheeks, and he held her steady so she wouldn't tumble backward.

Dad looked so happy. His blue eyes twinkled as Samantha morphed his face into various positions. He didn't seem to mind a bit.

I was once that little girl, sitting on my daddy's lap. I'm not sure where things went wrong, but for far too many years our relationship had been strained and painful. It may have been the potent mix of my foolish choices and his stoic nature, but whatever it was, my giddy childhood turned into strained adolescence and difficult young-adult years.

But here we were. My dad caught my eye as Samantha pulled on his ears. He smiled and I smiled back. Something had been happening since the birth of my girl—maybe an acknowledgement that I was turning out okay, maybe a mutual decision to put the past behind us.

"She's a firecracker," he said as she groped for his eyelid.

"Just like her Opa," I replied.

Another smile. *Thank You, Lord.*

Thank You, Father, for using my child's joyful abandon to reach
across the generations and tenderly heal relationships.
—ELSA KOK COLOPY

Day Twenty-Four

Kedar had more than his share of challenges—allergies, rickets, slow growth—so we were pleasantly surprised when he turned out to be a very early talker. He had piles of words, some of them intelligible, some of them not. As he began to speak more and more, I could make out less and less of what the little guy was trying to communicate. And quite often, my growing tot was none too pleased with his mother, who seemed hard of hearing. In fact, sometimes our back-and-forth exchanges ended with him crying in frustration.

"I feel horrible," I told Kenya. "I can't figure out what he's saying!" I seemed to play a never-ending guessing game. Typically, every option I threw out there was way off. *You want juice? Are you wet? You want a nap?* The response was usually an emphatic "No!" (which I understood perfectly!) and then more gibberish.

This cycle continued until one day when I was visiting my mom and a few of my young nieces started chatting with my son. They had very little, if any, trouble deciphering Kedar's words.

"How do you know what he's saying?" I asked, desperately hoping these three-foot geniuses could help me. "It's not that hard," my young niece Ayanna said, "Just listen and remember what the sounds mean."

Complex communication challenge solved! Well, not really. But at least I began listening more carefully before tossing out suggestions. And we were both happier for it.

Dear Lord, teach me to listen well—to You and to my child.
—DIANNA HOBBS

Day Twenty-Five

My friend Jessica had color-coded designer bins for her children's toys. Andrea baked cookies with her kids every week. Allison was already teaching letter sounds to her eleven-month-old. And here I was, with the jumbled pile of toys in the corner, my oven untouched for days in favor of the microwave, and not a single educational lesson under way for my baby who was about to turn one.

Instead of getting out the stroller and going for a walk, I sat on the side of my bed, despondent. I'd tried so hard to do all the things my "good mom" friends did, yet I seemed to be failing at every turn.

Just then I caught sight of a plain-looking notebook that sat on my bedside table. It was my diary for my daughter. I was too disorganized to put together a fancy scrapbook, but I'd bought a ninety-nine-cent notebook in which I regularly wrote down reflections from our daily lives together. It would be a gift to Lucy when she was older.

Encouraged by remembering this small success, it occurred to me that I also do other things well. A natural storyteller, I enjoy acting out Bible stories with wild gesticulations. I don't have designer toy bins, but I do maintain a basic level of order that brings peace to my family. I like researching nutrition and I make sure we all eat quality food—even if I do overuse the microwave.

Perhaps I wasn't a failure after all. With joy and relief I realized that holy motherhood might look different for me than it does for other people.

Lord, help me set my sights on Your standards alone.
—JENNIFER FULWILER

Day Twenty-Six

"The eye that mocks a father and scorns to obey a mother will be picked out by the ravens of the valley and eaten by the vultures."
—PROVERBS 30:17 (ESV)

~~~~~~~~~~~~

I returned to work when Joshua was four months old and scrambled to balance my job with marriage, motherhood and ministry. Life became easier when the wonderful aunt who helped raise me agreed to come to my house to babysit.

Trained as a nurse, my aunt had hospital-grade care habits. She was clean. The baby was clean. The dishes were clean. Whatever need Joshua had, my aunt met it. She sang to him. She read to him. She kissed and cuddled him. I knew my baby was completely safe. Then one day she gave Joshua some orange juice.

"Rhonda, I know what you told me, but I gave the baby juice because he seemed like he was catching a little cold."

"But we asked you *not* to give him orange juice, because it gives him diaper rash."

"It will help with his cold. I've been a mother before. I did this with my daughter."

My aunt was unapologetic—and clear that she'd do whatever she believed would help Joshua, regardless of what we instructed. What to do? I love my aunt, and suddenly we were stuck. Joshua was physically safe, but Flynn and I were uncomfortable leaving him in the care of someone who overrode our authority as his parents. We talked; we prayed. And finally, with great regret, we found a new caregiver across town.

Lord, grant me grace to deal graciously with difficult situations and challenging people.
—RHONDA J. SMITH

Day Twenty-Seven

"Please accept the present that was brought to you, for God has been gracious to me and I have all I need". . . .
—GENESIS 33:11

oo-hoo!" I heard Ann's sweet, singsong call through our open front door. I sighed, put down the dishcloth and went to invite Ann inside.

"I've brought crisps for the girls," she said cheerily. Michelle toddled quickly toward Ann and gave her a happy hug. Aimee ran in from the other room. The three of them were delighted to see each other.

"I'll take those for later," I said. "I don't want to spoil dinner."

"All right, then," replied Ann, handing them over.

I put the crisps in a cupboard with a growing stash of treats Ann had brought the girls on previous days. I'd explained to her that although I appreciated her thoughtfulness, I didn't like the girls to have treats often—especially Michelle—but it didn't seem to register. Ann continued to bring them daily, and it began to rankle.

Ann and her husband Colin welcomed us to England the day we moved in across the street from them. They invited us to their cozy home often and always served a delicious pot of tea with chocolate-coated biscuits. They babysat for us anytime we needed someone, and taught us to garden. They'd eased the homesickness we felt upon moving overseas. Right from the start I believed that God had put them in our lives, and I didn't want to begin dreading Ann's visits.

Then it occurred to me that I didn't need to dread her visits; I could continue setting the treats aside and let it go, focusing instead on the many lovely things to appreciate about Ann. And as I did, it dawned on me that the treats weren't the point of Ann's visits at all. They simply made her feel more at ease about popping in to say hello.

Oh, Lord, help me focus on what is lovely in the kind heart of a friend.
—SUSAN LABOUNTY

Day Twenty-Eight

"Through the offspring the Lord gives you by this young woman, may your family be like that of Perez, whom Tamar bore to Judah."

—RUTH 4:12

~~~~~~~~~~~~~~

*T*oday we were cooped up in the apartment all day. Tyler was running a fever, so there were no playdates, no adult conversations. When his fever broke this afternoon, I wanted to treat myself to dinner in a nearby restaurant. I struggled to get the double stroller through the narrow door before I realized the place was packed. People sat in large groups, laughing and eating with family and friends. As I awkwardly backed out of the restaurant, the sound of multiple conversations faded and suddenly I was lonely.

I wandered aimlessly, looking for a place to eat, tears falling uncontrollably, hands too occupied with the stroller to wipe them. I wished I could eat out with the people I love. I wanted my relatives to fight over who held Tyler; I wanted to snuggle into my father's arm and laugh at my cousin's stories. When I was a girl, family was everywhere. I missed the constant affection and commotion I grew up with.

But now everyone was too far away or too busy with their own lives to be part of mine. I wiped my eyes with Tyler's blankie and found an almost-empty BBQ grill. We ordered, and Tyler massaged his gums with corn on the cob, while Brandon ate butter straight from the tiny container. "Yummy," he said in a deep, raspy voice, obviously trying to be funny. Tyler giggled, so Brandon did it again. This time we all cracked up. A glimmer of light pierced my gloom. I wasn't surrounded by the large family I so dearly missed, but as I ate and laughed with this smaller family of my own, the heartache was a little less.

Lord, plant in my child a love of family, both ours here
on earth and Yours throughout the world.

—KAREN VALENTIN

Day Twenty-Nine

"Summing it all up, friends, I'd say you'll do best by filling your minds and meditating on things true, noble, reputable, authentic, compelling, gracious—the best, not the worst; the beautiful, not the ugly; things to praise, not things to curse."

—PHILIPPIANS 4:8 (MSG)

After one month of stay-at-home motherhood, the antsyness started. By five months, I was contemplating part-time work. As we approached the one year mark, a virtual eternity, I was going bonkers. Poor Jonathan had endured more than his fair share of discussions that began with, "Should I go back to work?" or "Why is it so hard to make friends?"

My life had been reduced to *Feed the baby, Change the baby, Go out with the baby.* Philosophically, I felt a strong conviction to be a stay-at-home mom, but emotionally and intellectually I felt unfulfilled. Before motherhood, I'd traveled as a social worker within Manhattan and the Bronx to visit my sixty elderly clients. Now my days were free of deadlines, obligations and a schedule—and it was driving me crazy!

God, why am I so unhappy? I cried out one night. *I know I should be grateful, but I don't feel that way.*

God brought to mind an idea I'd heard of years before. I bought a calendar and wrote down what I was thankful for each day, praising Him for each thing. I wrote down everything: Llewelyn's giggles while we played peekaboo, Jonathan's calls in the middle of the day, and the coffee date with my friend Sue. The next time I started to feel the blues descending, all it took was one look at my calendar of blessings to keep things in perspective.

Father, You schedule blessings into every one of my days. Open my eyes to see them.

—LIZ BISSELL

Day Thirty

*For you created my inmost being; you knit me
together in my mother's womb.*
—PSALM 139:13

~~~~~~~~~~

Samantha and I are very different. I like to read. I like soft music. I like quiet.

Samantha is loud. I never have to question what she is feeling. When she is happy, the laughter spills out in a waterfall of giggles. When she is sad, puddles course down her cheeks and sobs shake her whole body. And when she is mad, oh my . . . when she is mad, that little face turns bright red, her baby fists clench tight and her screams echo through the entire apartment complex.

At first, I spent a lot of time shushing my girl. "Shh, honey, not so loud." "Shh, honey, people are staring." "Shh, honey, my eardrums are going to burst." Nothing worked—not until I realized that my daughter is simply wired to be expressive. She is my living exclamation point. Yes, eventually I'll have to teach her about the times and places to be quiet, but she also needs to express herself the way she was made.

So we go to the park and she squeals outdoors. We laugh wildly in her bedroom, and I've learned to let her sob when she is truly sad. I sometimes shush what needs expressing and sometimes let her express what needs shushing. But in time, with patience, we'll learn to celebrate her unique wiring, together.

Lord, help me bring out the punctuation marks in my child.
—ELSA KOK COLOPY

Twelfth Month

~~~~~~

Father,

Thank You. Thank You for hard times and two-tooth grins, for sleep and unlikely blessings. Thank You for all the ways You've given me to grow this year. It's hard to remember what life was like before, impossible to imagine that I'd never known and experienced all the richness You've poured out on me.

My child is Yours, Lord. I am Yours. Bless her, and bless me, and make Your face shine upon my family, as we continue to strive to serve You.

In Christ, amen.

Tips

» Make a conscious decision about how much screen time you want your baby to have each day. If you don't, he'll end up with more than you think!

» Reconnect with an old friend, preferably one you lost touch with once she had children.

» Practice laughing and shrugging your shoulders. If you won't remember a particular frustration a month from now, let it go right away.

Day One

*"Therefore, if anyone is in Christ, he is a new creation;
the old has gone, the new has come!"*
—II CORINTHIANS 5:17

*E*ach day the itchiness had grown more intense. It had nothing to do with the skin of my big belly bumping against my desk. My heart was ready to leave the office, to trade writing deadlines for diapers, to forgo bouncing around town for bouncing an infant. But my mind and my ego didn't get the memo. And so I did what appeased heart, mind *and* ego: I signed the paperwork for a year's leave. I kept my pager.

But I'd no intention of returning.

I felt guilty at moments but was soothed by the safety I felt when personal and professional contacts asked "the work question." *Extended leave . . . we'll see. . . .*

I knew. And yet for months I clung to the imaginary safety of who I had been: a professional with a title and even a little power. Maybe it helped me feel better when I felt desperate during those early months of parenting. I was sure I wanted to be a mom. I wasn't secure in the world's perception of turning my back on what I'd accomplished with grown-ups.

Time showed me I wasn't giving back a single accomplishment; I was just starting a new chapter. It took too long to realize *I* wasn't the author of anything. God was revealing my story.

The phone call finally came, asking my intentions. I was reading to Zach. It still wasn't easy to cut that cord to my prior life, but it was easier to see who I was becoming.

God, why is my identity so confusing sometimes? I want to serve humbly and love fully. Help me do that with confidence in Your plan for my life.
—SUSAN BESZE WALLACE

Day Two

"Do not fear, for I am with you; do not anxiously look about you,
for I am your God. I will strengthen you, surely I will help you,
surely I will uphold you with My righteous right hand."

—ISAIAH 41:10

I was across the room when I saw Solomon reach for his toy easel. The heavy plastic wobbled back and forth before landing directly on top of him. I ran as fast as I could, bracing myself for what I might see.

Completely aware of the stark silence, I pulled up the easel. Solomon was on his back. He opened his eyes and began to cry. A bump was appearing on his forehead. His beautiful front teeth had gone through his lip.

Frantic, I called the pediatrician and got the next appointment.

As I held an ice pack on his bump in the sterile waiting room, I replayed the accident in my head. *I should have kept the easel out of reach. I should have been right next to him. I should have run faster.*

The doctor checked Solomon's head and mouth. The bump on his head had turned a light shade of eggplant and his lip was swollen. She tickled his ribs. He giggled.

"I feel terrible," I said. "I couldn't get there in time."

"He hit the strongest part on his head. If you have to get a bump, that's exactly where you want one. And lips, well, they're designed as cushions for this exact purpose. I'm sure it did more damage to *your* nerves. He'll be just fine."

Dear God, there will be accidents, bumps and bruises, and I will be
there with prayer, bandages and ice packs. In the meantime, please
give me nerves of steel to match whatever comes my way.

—SABRA CIANCANELLI

Day Three

What matters is not your outer appearance—the styling of your hair, the jewelry you wear, the cut of your clothes—but your inner disposition.
—I PETER 3:3 (MSG)

I walked up the path to Kristen's new house for our weekly mom-baby gathering. *Wow! What would life be like with this kind of budget?* I wondered with a pang of jealousy. I stepped inside to be further impressed by the custom furniture, the kitchen (oh, the kitchen!) and the space. I pictured my own half-remodeled, cramped house.

Familiar faces were already gathering in the playroom. Jen, so sure of herself in her career and her marriage. Megan, who gushed over her baby, totally satisfied in this new job of mothering. Molly, always dressed in the latest trends, with her hair styled instead of thrown into a ponytail like mine. I looked down at my legs in last year's jeans. *Why did I wear these?*

As I placed my diaper bag on the floor and joined the group chatter, I was reminded of other details of these moms' lives. Kristen's husband often traveled for work, leaving her alone for days at a time. Jen's confidence about work didn't overflow into mothering, and Megan struggled with her identity outside of being a wife and mother. I knew these details, but I often forgot them when I let my insecurities have the front-row seats in my brain.

"Alex, you always seem so together," Kristen commented. My shock must have reflected on my face because she continued, "No really. You don't seem to question who you are." If she only knew the inner dialogue I'd been having the past five minutes! It was a great reminder that I needed to look past first impressions—and my own insecurities—to get a full picture of others.

Jesus, give me eyes to see others' hearts.
—ALEXANDRA KUYKENDALL

Day Four

See, I am doing a new thing! Now it springs up; do you not perceive it? I am making a way in the desert and streams in the wasteland.

—ISAIAH 43:19

One blustery fall day, Llewelyn and I went to the library. It was our only outing and my sole opportunity for adult contact before Jonathan was due home from work at 7:00 PM.

The children's librarian was holding a class for toddlers ages sixteen to twenty-four months in an adjoining room. As we passed, the class was singing, "If you're happy and you know it, shout hurray . . . HURRAAAY!" Llewelyn immediately toddled toward the room to see what all the commotion was about. I scrambled to catch her hand, saying, "Sorry, honey, the librarian said you're not old enough . . . not yet. I know. Mommy wants to go in there too."

With no family nearby and only one stay-at-home mom acquaintance, I was desperate for adult conversation and so lonely it hurt. As we waited for the elevator, a mom with a little girl about the same age as Llewelyn walked toward us. After a moment of awkward silence, I decided I had to be assertive. I found myself blurting, "Your daughter is so cute! How old is she? My name is Liz and this is my daughter Llewelyn."

To my utter relief, the other mom nervously smiled back and said, "Hi, I'm Marilyn. And this is Raneth." We chatted for a few minutes and exchanged cell phone numbers. *Hallelujah!* From that first conversation, we arranged a playdate, and then another. And another.

Thank You, God, for new beginnings, and new mom friends and answers to prayer!

—LIZ BISSELL

Day Five

It is God who arms me with strength and makes my way perfect.
—II SAMUEL 22:33

~~~~~~~~~~~~~~

Being a perfectionist makes for an awful mom. I didn't want Joshua to cry. I didn't want him to poop. I didn't want him to get hungry while I was still preparing his milk. I resented when my son interrupted my plans to get him settled so *I* could get settled after a long day. I wanted my life to go on the way it had before. Prayer, work, vacation trips—I was determined to do it all and to do it my way.

I began the day at 4:30 AM with my quiet time; then I prepared Joshua and myself to cross town to get to the sitter. Checklist: breast pump, diaper bag, work bag and what I called my ready-for-the-world bag, which contained the put-together look I used to hide my inner frazzled one.

Finally, one weekend I was able to get away to Notre Dame, Indiana, for a friend's wedding. I was determined to get some refreshment. Rising early, I left Flynn and Joshua sleeping in the hotel and traveled with my journal and Bible across the way to a campus garden. There on a bench among the lilies, ornamental grasses and a shallow pond teeming with splashing fish, I felt at last that I was on vacation. And I was: I was on a break from perfectionism. In that quiet oasis I realized I didn't need to do everything the way I used to. I didn't need to do it all or to add big vacations to my checklist. I already had a daily break, a small getaway with God before the start of each hectic day. I just needed to learn to treasure it.

Jesus, Your will is the definition of perfection, not mine.
—RHONDA J. SMITH

Day Six

I will praise God's name in song and glorify him with thanksgiving.
—PSALM 69:30

We didn't have money for a big Christmas celebration. I'd been home since Samantha's birth and the lack of that second income put us on a tight budget. We had a small Christmas tree, tiny stockings and a string of ancient lights.

I was wholeheartedly disappointed. I knew Jesus was the reason for our celebration, but I longed to have a fancy Christmas party, fun decorations and gifts that spilled out far beyond the tree.

"I don't like this at all," I said to Billy as I stared at our little tree. "It's a stupid tree with droopy limbs and ugly ornaments. Look at that! Half the lights don't even work! What kind of childhood memories are we giving to Samantha? She'll probably be scarred for life. She'll end up just like the Grinch and always hate Christmas."

Billy tried not to smile at my dramatic tirade. "Um . . . Elsa? Who's being the Grinch right now?"

"Not me!" I snapped.

He looked at me with raised eyebrows.

"Well, *maybe* me." I admitted.

"Listen, Samantha isn't old enough to know we don't have a thing. The only thing she'll know is that she has us both home for a day and we're both happy. To her, that'll be the best Christmas ever."

"That's true," I said, though I was still struggling. "So you're saying dump the grinchiness and try something different?"

"Definitely," he laughed, giving me a kiss, "Gratitude is a good start. . . ."

Lord, help me to avoid being a Grinch and go for grateful.
—ELSA KOK COLOPY

Day Seven

Teach me your way, O Lord, and I will walk in your truth. . . .
—PSALM 86:11

~~~~~~~~~~

Grace's tiny body teetered back and forth, her arms stretched out for balance. "Come on, you can do it," I coaxed, a few steps away. Her daddy stood behind her, his hands ready to catch her if she fell.

I grabbed Grace's favorite ball and held it out. Her face, once serious with concentration, lit up when she saw the toy. She babbled and wavered just a few seconds more before she dropped to her knees in a full-scale crawl.

Before I could blink, she was pulling at my pants ready to play. I sighed, plopped down on the floor beside her and drew her in my lap for a kiss.

Grace was more interested in getting the prize than learning the lesson. Why work at walking when she knew a quicker way? Walking is faster, but learning takes time and patience, things Grace hasn't learned yet.

Unfortunately, my daughter gets her preference for the easy path honestly. As soon as I catch sight of a blessing, I do all I can to sidestep the lesson and go straight for the prize. I don't want to embrace challenging situations that can teach me how to walk in faith. I want it all quick and easy. But like my daughter, I am slowly learning to pick up my feet and step out, bit by bit, with baby steps.

God, give me a greater hunger for truth than for rewards.
—CAROL HATCHER

Day Eight

With God we will gain the victory, and he will trample down our enemies.
—PSALM 108:13

*B*uh-bye, buh-bye." Michelle squeezed her hand open and closed to wave, while her big sister Aimee blew kisses until Mike rounded the corner at the top of the street. He was on his way to our English military base, where he would fly to Spain for three weeks with his squadron.

I sighed and took the girls back into the house. Military life was characterized by routine separations, and caring for a toddler and a baby by myself in a foreign country sometimes made me feel isolated.

Mike's trips usually lasted three to six weeks, and the girls didn't put their growth on hold until he came home. Baby Michelle changed daily. When Mike was away, I continually wanted to call across the room to him: "Hey! Michelle just pulled herself to a stand, and look how proud of herself she is!" Or, "Oh my goodness, how did Michelle get up on the kitchen counter?!"

Being so often alone, I knew I could grit my teeth, feel sorry for myself and merely survive Mike's absences, or I could embrace this unchangeable situation and make the best of it. Rather than wasting time wishing things were different, I filled our days with as much loveliness as I could. We played, read countless stories, baked cookies, explored the woods and meadow, walked into our English town for cream scones, enjoyed picnics in the park, and created happy daily routines.

And anyway, God's word assured me that we weren't alone at all. The Lord would be an ever-present help. I prayed that He would walk me through the separations with growing acceptance, strength and joy. That He would give victory over nighttime fears and loneliness. I prayed that He would fill the spaces left empty by Mike's absence, both for me and the girls. He did. Abundantly.

Lord, thank You for strength, peace, and protection,
and for the powerful sense of Your nearness.
—SUSAN LABOUNTY

Day Nine

Jesus Christ is the same yesterday and today and forever.
—HEBREWS 13:8

Wearing a plaid button-down shirt and twelve-month jeans, Zach looked like a little man. Make that a little *old* man. He had a comb-over of the little patch of hair he'd managed to sprout. A giant, mommy-made "1" cake awaited his little hands. Friends crawled everywhere.

Amid the chaos, Zach pulled up on a little rocking chair his buddies had just gifted him with. His Dad goaded, "Come on over, buddy." And without hesitation, he did. One, two, three, four steps and a plop. My baby-no-longer seemed as stunned as I did. A huge milestone just met, and I was across the room, my hands full of hostessing.

It wasn't the way I pictured. Of course, I didn't "picture" it at all, unable to put my hands on the camera in time. I thought the steps would come after a series of failed attempts. Or in the sunshine, on the grass of our backyard. Or as he walked toward *my* voice. Into *my* arms. I was thrilled for him—on the outside. But an unsettled feeling remained within. And it had to stay in. I had twenty people in my home.

Zipped up in footed pajamas that night after we'd cleaned frosting from his nose and ears, Zach seemed as worn out as I felt. We snuggled and rocked in silence for the longest time. I never looked at my watch. I knew it was just a few steps. He wasn't taking off for college the next day. And yet I wanted to scream, "Don't leave me!" Zach's needs were changing, and so was my sense of maternal purpose. He was moving of his own accord, apparently not need-ing me to be next to him. So I wanted to be next to him as long as I could that night, thanking God for baby steps, and thanking Him for my boy.

Father, may Your unchanging love help me
navigate the changes of mothering.
—SUSAN BESZE WALLACE

Day Ten

*Do you not know that your body is a temple of the Holy Spirit, who is
in you, whom you have received from God? You are not your own.*
—I CORINTHIANS 6:19

M y prayer life is terrible," I told Christine. "I haven't been reading my
Bible, and I rarely set aside quiet time to pray. Honestly, I hardly even
think about God!"

Christine was a wise, experienced Christian who was known for her sincere devotion. So when I admitted that my prayer life was in bad shape, I
expected a lecture, or perhaps a list of specific spiritual practices to undertake.
Instead she asked, "Are you getting enough sleep?"

I stumbled over my words. "Well, uh, no. . ." The baby had been sleeping
through the night for a couple of months now, but I was staying up past midnight surfing the Internet. It left me exhausted the next day.

Then she asked, "How's your diet? Are you eating healthy foods?"

"The bag of double-fried, extra-salty chips I ate yesterday said it was
made from real potatoes," I joked.

Christine pointed out that before considering any deep spiritual causes
for my lackluster prayer life, I needed to try taking care of myself. "It's possible
to be close to God in times of physical distress or pain," she explained. "But
if you're sabotaging yourself with attachments to things like the Web or junk
food, it's going to put a block in your prayer life."

That night I tossed the cookies and chips in the trash and set myself a
firm ten o'clock bedtime. The next morning I woke up before the baby and
spent fifteen minutes with God before the day began. It made a difference. I
felt better, in every way possible.

Lord, help me treat my body as Your temple.
—JENNIFER FULWILER

Day Eleven

The Spirit you received does not make you slaves, so that you live in fear again; rather, the Spirit you received brought about your adoption to sonship. And by him we cry, "Abba, Father."

—ROMANS 8:15

Oh, happy day! Double happy day! Lisbet's first birthday coincides with a milestone just as monumental. She becomes legally ours.

Our lawyer travels in from Albany on the train. Dave and I and Lisbet pick him up and drive to the Westchester County Courthouse—the very same building where we had papers notarized years ago when we first filed our application to adopt.

My mother comes too. After her long-ago comment that "adoption is taking on other people's problems," she is now in love with Lisbet.

The five of us walk through the metal detector. I open our diaper bag in the security check. Lisbet is not quite walking yet. I hold her twenty pounds and marvel at her growth.

Family Court is ready for us. The judge admires Lisbet's white flowered dress. We sign papers and are informed of the legal responsibilities of adoption. The judge grants an Order of Adoption, a decree that says we now have the same legal rights over the child that the birth parents had. The court stenographer takes our picture.

We drive back to the train station to drop our lawyer off. On the way, another car T-bones us. The car is totaled, but no one is hurt. There will be no question of fault—after all, we have our lawyer in the car with us! The policeman on the scene is our next-door neighbor. He pokes his head through the car window and gives Lisbet a high five.

The day seems to be a condensed version of the whole first year of motherhood. Rolling with more punches than I ever thought possible. Making more personal connections than ever before. A new sense of what's important. And incredible happiness.

Father, thank You for every second of this experience of motherhood. Thank You.

—LENORE LELAH PERSON

Day Twelve

~~~~~~~~~~

We were celebrating Anjelica's birthday on a frigid Tuesday evening in January, marking the day at my parents' place because our new apartment was still far from ready for a party. While Anjelica busied herself with the architectural possibilities of paper cups, I rummaged in my bag for her tights.

"*Aquí están.*" My mother flourished a new pair of tights. "I picked them up on the way home." She rushed to add, "And I already washed them!"

I stifled the sharp retort that sprang into my throat. Did she think I would have forgotten?

I watched my mother slip the tights on, her dark head touching the top of Anjelica's, their sing-along exchange too soft to discern. She smoothed my daughter's hair, arranged the hem of her dress to keep it from tickling her knees, and readjusted the buckles on her small patent leather shoes. My mother never stopped singing; Anjelica was riveted, as always, by the sound.

I thought of how the same voice probably sang to me on my first birthday, decades ago. I imagined her arranging napkins on a tiny table in a city so far from her childhood home that a passport was required. I wondered how she bought my tights, when she'd barely been in New York a year and still stumbled over words.

I watched my mother dress my little girl much as she would have prepared me in anticipation of my father's arrival from work, awaiting the nearby rumble of the elevated train and the turn of his key. That night the three of us would have gathered around the light of a single candle.

I remember that in Spanish, to give birth is "*dar a luz,*" to give light. I sit beside my mother and my daughter on the bed, tears slick on my face, and lean in close to hear my mother's song.

Father, thank You for mothers: their involvement, their sacrifices, their love.
—DEBRALEE SANTOS

Day Thirteen

If a house is divided against itself, that house cannot stand.
—MARK 3:25 (KJV)

"Lay down Kedar," Kenya said in a deep voice. Somehow, he knows how to sprinkle in just the right amount of bass to send the message that Daddy means business. Usually, Kenya's authoritative tone is enough to keep our strong-willed boy in line. But on this particular day, Kedar didn't want to go to sleep.

Because Daddy wasn't seeing things his way, our early talker moved on to Plan B. "Mommy! *Won dit up, peeez!*" he shouted. Oh, why did he have to ask to get up and say please in the cutest little voice? Kedar knew I was putty in his hands.

"Aw, we should let him up. He's not sleepy." I flashed sad eyes at Kenya, lobbying for Kedar's cause.

But Kenya said, "I already told him no. And if you override that, we'll be teaching him that he can manipulate one of us to get his way." I knew he was right. We needed to present a united front.

"*Mommaaaaay! Mommaaaaay!*" Kedar's calls grew louder and more defiant. I got up and walked into his room. I could tell he was waiting for me, because he was standing up with his arms stretched wide. I slowly walked over to his crib and put my arms around him.

"You have to go night-night," I told him softly.

"*Dit* up," he pleaded pitifully.

"No, no," I said gently but firmly, although everything in me wanted to let him off the hook.

Heavenly Father, help me always to choose the
pathway to peace and unity in my home.
—DIANNA HOBBS

Day Fourteen

B randon kick-boxed in the womb; Tyler stretched. Brandon arrived early; Tyler was late. After having a difficult baby (and now toddler) in Brandon, Tyler was as calm and easy as could be. "Is he always like this?" someone asked, in awe. Tyler was sitting sweet and quiet as his brother ran in circles nearby.

"Yup," I said. "They are both exactly like this."

Early on I put labels on both of them: the hyper one, the calm one; the athlete, the lazy one; the one who will be the busy, careless man who forgets to call his mother, the one to bring me flowers and tell me I look pretty. Perhaps it wasn't just Brandon's speed that made me appreciate Tyler's stillness. It was the speed at which Brandon had grown that made me want Tyler to take his time. I cherished every moment with Tyler, wanting him to stay my baby forever.

As his first birthday approached, I had no party plans. I didn't want to think about it. "We have time," I thought, but Tyler proved me wrong. The little boy I deemed too laid back to walk early like his brother took his first steps. I watched him wobble away from me, no longer my baby or the lazy one I thought he was. And in spite of myself, I smiled.

Father, keep me from making assumptions about
who You intend my child to be.
—KAREN VALENTIN

Day Fifteen

I am the Alpha and the Omega, the First and the
Last, the Beginning and the End.
—REVELATION 22:13

I felt like a celebrity as I wandered through the old folks' home. Every two steps I was forced to stop as wrinkled arms reached toward me, wanting to touch Shiloh. The tired, unexpressive faces lit up as they saw my baby. There was something special Shiloh was imparting to these elderly people.

Thankfully, Shiloh took the extra attention well, cautiously touching hands and even giving the occasional smile. When we finally found Grandma, she sat in the corner in her wheelchair—asleep.

"Hi, Grandma." I gently rubbed her shoulder as she opened her eyes. When she saw Shiloh, her face broke into a huge grin.

"My baby!" Grandma squealed, clearly welcoming our visit.

"How are you doing?" I asked, extra loud so she could hear me.

"What?' she responded, confused. I waved my hand, brushing the question aside. Grandma hugged Shiloh and then start to sing one of my daughter's favorite songs.

"Jesus loves me, this I know. . ." Shiloh started to clap her hands in excitement.

"For the Bible tells me so. . ." Grandma leaned over and gently touched Shiloh's nose.

"Little ones to Him belong. . ." Shiloh wiggled out of my arms, reaching toward Grandma.

"We are weak but He is strong. . ." And there in the midst of a lazy Sunday afternoon sat one who was near the end of her life and one who was just beginning hers, and their hearts connected in an undeniable way. There was no doubt they each understood what the other was trying to say.

Jesus, it is You who unite us from start to finish, beginning
to end. Let me live my entire life in You.
—RUTH BERGEN

Day Sixteen

When pride comes, then comes disgrace, but with humility comes wisdom.
—PROVERBS 11:2

I felt like such a good mom. I took Samantha to the store and she was ab-solutely perfect. No whining, no squirming, no fussing—she just smiled broadly at each person we came across. "What a cute little girl," one woman said to me as she bent close to smile at Samantha.

"Thank you," I replied, taking full responsibility.

As I stood in the checkout line, my heart was bursting with pride: She is cute. And she's so well behaved. I put my shoulders back and glanced around at other people. *See how cute she is? She's mine.*

Within the week I took Samantha on another grocery outing. She squirmed. She fussed. She pounded her little fists on the cart and howled when someone bent to say hello. People glared their disapproval and a flood of shame rushed through me. I tried to comfort her to no avail. *What have I done wrong? Stop crying, Samantha. Please!* I hung my head and didn't dare glance at anyone. I knew what they were thinking: What a horrible mom!

Fortunately, later on God brought the two scenarios to my mind. I felt His tender warning: If I was planning to tie my value to my daughter's behav-ior, I was going to be in for a lot of fall-on-your-face moments. Did I really want to spend Samantha's growing-up years hoping she would make me look good? *Oh, Lord, may it never be so!*

Heavenly Father, please help me to find my value in You,
not in my child's successes or failures.
—ELSA KOK COLOPY

Day Seventeen

Then Jesus said to his disciples, "If anyone would come after me,
he must deny himself and take up his cross and follow me."
—MATTHEW 16:24

nnette called. "I had some bad news yesterday at Tommy's one-year check-up," she said. "He was diagnosed with cerebral palsy."

"Do you want me to come over?" I asked. I packed up Elizabeth in record speed, and went.

We sat on the floor of Annette's third-floor walk-up, the world's largest collection of secondhand toys spread around us. Annette never paid more than two dollars for anything, scouring yard sales for any toy that might strengthen Tommy's muscle tone.

"Did you know this was coming?" I asked.

"Sort of," she replied. "But mostly, no."

"I'm so, so sorry," I said, trying to remember what little I knew about CP. "What are you going to do now?"

"Oh, I've already done it," Annette said. "I cried last night, and now I'm moving on. I've got to find out what I'm up against, and keep going. I already have a call in to Early Intervention. I was on the phone with the insurance company this morning to find out which therapies they'll pay for."

I stared at my friend. Cried *once*? That was it?

"You sure you don't need to cry a bit more?" I asked. "That doesn't sound like enough."

"Oh, I'll cry. I'll cry at night when my dreams of who Tommy could be run into the reality of what we face. But I can't spend all day in tears. I have a son to take care of. He needs me. And I need to focus on what I *can* do, or I'll go insane."

I nodded, slowly. First things first. Pray and cry at night. Focus on what you need to do, and think of the needs of others before thinking of yourself.

It sounds familiar, Jesus.

Lord, when crosses appear in my path, help me embrace
them with courage and a heart to imitate You.
—JULIA ATTAWAY

Day Eighteen

*Whoever finds his life will lose it, and whoever
loses his life for my sake will find it.*
—MATTHEW 10:39

J oe and I sat in the living room, a candle flickering on the table next to us, bowls of strawberry ice cream in our laps. The baby slept quietly upstairs. Out of the corner of my eye I caught a glimpse of unfolded clothes in the laundry basket. I remembered a couple of e-mails that needed replies, and the bill I needed to pay soon. And I went back to eating my ice cream.

I smiled and thought, *So this is what balance is like.*

Overwhelmed by the duties of motherhood, I'd prayed for the Lord to show me how to find balance in my life. What I meant was that I wanted to know how to do all the same stuff I was doing, but without being stressed about it. What I got was a prompting to make my workday end at sundown. So my husband and I began to follow the ancient Judeo-Christian tradition of saying an early-evening prayer to usher in a time of rest. We still needed to get Lucy ready for bed, but we've been avoiding chores and deskwork at night.

I'd thought of balance as a matter of pacing but found it was a matter of sacrifice. I had to give up *should* and *ought* and *must*. I had to surrender some of what I wanted to get done so I could find peace. But those sacrifices led to a routine that left me calm and more in touch with the Lord. Funny how that works: give up a little of myself for Christ and gain more than I could have imagined.

*Lord, give me the grace to make the sacrifices
I need to make my home centered in You.*
—JENNIFER FULWILER

Day Nineteen
A Dad's View

Behold, children are a heritage from the Lord, the fruit of the womb
a reward. Like arrows in the hand of a warrior are the children of
one's youth. Blessed is the man who fills his quiver with them!

—PSALM 127:3–5 (ESV)

ey, Hans, my little bear," I said, getting onto all fours, crouching, tensing, growling.

My son, who had been occupying himself with a set of blocks, turned, giggled and tried to crawl away.

I gave chase. "It's no use, son. Nowhere to run to, nowhere to hide. Daddy's gonna get you, little bear!"

Hans laughed as he made a beeline along his one angle of escape, straight toward the kitchen and the safety of the one we know as Mama Bear.

But it was not to be, for Daddy, although already old, tired and a bit paunchy in his later thirties, still had some rev in the motor when it mattered. Like now.

"I'm gonna getcha!" I roared, as I gently tackled my scooting son, turning him on his back as he shrieked, grinning from ear to ear.

Becoming a father meant giving up a lot of good things. Before Hans, I could go out with the guys to hang out or watch football, or stay up on campus after hours to attend special lectures. Now, I needed to be home more. It wasn't that Kari couldn't handle Hans, but that being home felt right.

"You okay, Daddy?" my wife's voice came from the kitchen. I scooped Hans into my arms and stood up.

"Never been better," I replied. "I love my boy!"

Lord, thank You for the joy I've found in parenthood.
—LEROY HUIZENGA

Day Twenty

*But of the tree of the knowledge of good and evil you shall not
eat, for in the day that you eat of it you shall surely die.*
—GENESIS 2:17 (ESV)

Solomon said his very first word today. We were putting on our jackets to
go for a walk when a single word escaped his lips clear as day.

"Garden," he said. I'd been expecting Mama or Dada.

"Garden?" I asked. "What, honey? What did you say?"

"Gar-den," he said again. "Garrrr-dennn, garrr-dennn."

"Tony!" I yelled. "Come quick; Solomon said his first word!"

Tony ran up the stairs and crouched over Solomon's bouncy seat. "What
did you say, buddy?" he asked.

Solomon widened his eyes and opened his mouth. In a sweet little voice
he said once again, "Garden."

"Did he say garden?" he asked.

"Uh-huh," I said.

"What does he mean?"

I shrugged my shoulders and leaned in closer. For perspective, we aren't
gardeners. We have a postage-stamp of a yard that we've somewhat neglected
while spending all our spare moments with our baby.

"Garden," Solomon said again. "Garden, garden, garden."

We went for our walk, and Tony and I talked about what it could mean.
Was it his first actual word, or just a random babble that happened to be a
word? Was *garden* a hint of the future? Would Solomon be a farmer, a gar-
dener, a florist?

I suppose we'll never know why *garden* came first. I like to think Solomon
was saying something about life, perhaps about reaping what you sow.

*Dear God, help me nurture my child's language, words and
thoughts, so he becomes the person You mean him to be.*
—SABRA CIANCANELLI

Day Twenty-One

"Now I am giving him to the Lord, and he will
belong to the Lord his whole life". . . .
—I SAMUEL 1:28 (NLT)

Not quite a year ago Dave and I walked to the front of our little church in Elmira, New York, and handed our baby back to God. She was dressed in the same satin christening gown Dave had once worn. It was a modest ceremony: John, my "uncle-pastor," lifted the sleeping beauty toward Heaven and said a prayer of dedication. Later we celebrated with family members at a restaurant.

But trusting God with Anna's safekeeping wasn't so simple. My faith was tested the first night we brought her home as I lay awake studying the strange rhythm of a newborn's breathing coming from the foot of my bed. After a few sleepless nights, I had the courage to move the bassinet to my walk-in closet—the "nursery"—and shut the door. *She belongs to You, Lord.* I panicked when Anna couldn't keep her first bowls of rice cereal down for several days and when she nearly choked on a slice of apple. *She belongs to You, Lord.* When I careered around a corner and rolled our white Jetta into a hayfield, I turned a fearful eye to the back seat to see if my baby was still alive. God had graciously given me more time with her. *But she belongs to You, Lord.*

I have a photo of Anna, taken minutes after the baby dedication ceremony. Her little hands are clasped together, as if in prayer. I think she did it as a permanent reminder: *God, please help Mom remember that I am on loan from You.*

Dear Father, thank You for cradling this child
in the palm of Your hand.
—FAITH BOGDAN

Day Twenty-Two

They are brought to their knees and fall,
but we rise up and stand firm.
—PSALM 20:8

~~~~~~~~~

While trying to pull up on a small shelf, Grace tipped it, spilling baskets of toys on her head. I tossed the clothes I was folding and dove to protect her. Grace, looking startled, sagged her bottom lip and let out a scream.

The other shelves in Grace's room are tethered to the wall and stand firm. But Grace pulled up on this one, and it hurt. Because she pulls up on anything above her head, many seemingly harmless objects become dangerous: lamps, tablecloths, books on shelves. We have to watch her constantly.

I have to watch myself too, because sometimes I grab on to things that aren't stable in my walk of faith. After Grace's birth, I was overwhelmed. Taking care of three kids, making dinner, keeping the laundry done and getting a shower everyday were seemingly insurmountable tasks. I tried holding on to sleep but still felt empty. I spent time on the computer and talked with girlfriends, but that left me feeling inadequate. When I finally found time to be alone with God, He was the firm handhold I needed for stability. So I'm learning—slowly, and not for the first time—that I have to be selective about what I'm using to pull myself upright in life.

Lord, help me recognize the things in
my life that aren't tethered to You.
—CAROL HATCHER

Day Twenty-Three

*But about the Son he says, "Your throne, O God, will last for ever
and ever, and righteousness will be the scepter of your kingdom."*
—HEBREWS 1:8

She struts out of the bathroom like royalty, fresh and clean and naked as
Eve, bath towel gathered at her shoulders. Her regal presence is such that
Andrew, standing at the other end of our long hallway, breaks into an off-pitch
rendition of "God Save the Queen." She grins and, eyes aglow, strides with
chubby legs toward her dad. I call out in a deep voice, "Make way for Queen
Elizabeth!"

As she arrives at the end of the hall, Andrew falls to his knee shouting,
"All hail! All hail the clean queen! All hail the queen of the bath!"

"It's a coronation!" I suggest, and Elizabeth—willing to embrace bewil-
dering words if it means Mom and Dad are playing with her—grins wider.
Andrew explains that we will have a ceremony to turn her into a real queen.
He pretends to dub her on each shoulder and places an imaginary crown on
her head. We cheer; she bows. Andrew asks to kiss her hand. She obliges.

*King of heaven, I don't care if she's a queen or a
servant. Just make her part of Your kingdom.*
—JULIA ATTAWAY

Day Twenty-Four

"Meaningless! Meaningless!" says the Teacher. "Utterly meaningless! Everything is meaningless."
—ECCLESIASTES 1:2

*Y*ou've gotta give him a party!" Grandma Rosie said when she heard that we hadn't planned anything. Kenya and I figured Kedar was too small to appreciate a party. But after Grandma's insistence, we folded and did it—for her.

"Happy birthday, dear Kedar. Happy birthday to you!" Fifteen guests stood around the kitchen table singing and applauding. Kedar, however, didn't share the excitement. He was more interested in figuring out how to get that annoying birthday-hat string off from around his chin. "Wanna eat cake? *Mmm* good," I said, rubbing a bit of icing across his lips. No reaction. Then he mutilated the cake and crushed the whole thing to crumbs. Every adult in the room winced; so much for indulging in dessert!

Next came the presents. Family and friends had brought matchbox cars, stuffed animals, clothes, books and expensive electronic toys, but Kedar wasn't interested. He squirmed to get down out of my lap. He was *so over* this lame party. So where was he going? Over to where the empty boxes were stacked.

"Tee!" he said, cracking his first smile of the evening, holding up a small cardboard box.

"Yes, mommy sees!" I said, feigning as much excitement as I could muster. For reasons yet unknown, the undecorated container held his attention for the rest of the night. The box—which didn't cost one red cent—was the biggest hit of the evening.

Father, thank You for using my child to teach me what is—and isn't—meaningful in life.
—DIANNA HOBBS

Day Twenty-Five

But God shows his love for us in that while we were still sinners, Christ died for us.
—ROMANS 5:8 (ESV)

Someone in our family is very defiant. Okay, everyone in our family is very defiant. We are starting to see the rawness of human nature displaying itself in our adorable little girl and in our reactions to her. Sweet as she is, she gets certain traits of disobedience from her father that go all the way back to Adam. The problem does run on my side too.

Now that she's mobile, Geneva is not allowed to touch certain things, such as the strip of foam tape along the edge of the sliding door. She goes up to it, looks straight at me, grins her mischievous grin, extends one finger, hears me say, "Geneva, *no*, don't touch!"—and pulls the foam tape straight up, shaking it in sheer delight.

Even cute little girls can't help but rebel against authority. Big girls too. I hear the Holy Spirit whisper to me to hold my tongue when I want to say something nasty to my husband—and sometimes I go ahead and say it, anyway. But there is grace. I'm certain of it, just as I'm certain that with patience and love and gentle discipline, Geneva will learn to leave that foam tape alone. Most of the time.

I'm sorry, Lord, for not listening when You say no.
—LISA LADWIG

Day Twenty-Six

For the Lord loves the just and will not forsake his
faithful ones. They will be protected forever. . . .
—PSALM 37:28

Joey was cracking me up. He was determined to walk but hadn't quite figured out how to steady himself. His solution was to pull himself up on the coffee table and sprint across the room as fast as he could until he crashed.

Just when I thought he was ready to give up, he pulled himself up one more time and ran toward me. I reached out to grab him up in a giant hug just as he started to tumble. He slipped through my arms, crashing his head into the banister.

I picked him up and immediately felt dizzy. A huge cut ran from his eyebrow up his forehead. It was pulsing blood, and in the center I saw what could only be the shiny, white bone of his skull.

I screamed for my husband, faintheartedly loaded Joey into the car and headed to the ER. My baby got nine stitches straight across his forehead.

In the week that followed, the black stitches were constant reminders of my inadequacy to protect him. *How* had I allowed him to fall? I was right there with my arms held out!

But the stitches fell out. And the scar healed. And my son eventually learned to walk on steady legs. And I learned that as a mom, I can never protect my son from everything. Which is one of those things I already knew, and which I suspect I'll have to learn again and again.

Lord, he truly belongs to You. Protect him when I can't.
—ERIN MACPHERSON

Day Twenty-Seven

For whoever exalts himself will be humbled, and
whoever humbles himself will be exalted.
—MATTHEW 23:12

I was finally starting to feel that I had this motherhood thing down. Confidence felt good, though I didn't notice it was having a terrible effect on my prayer life. I slid smoothly into the attitude that I didn't need much of God's help because I had it all figured out on my own.

Then one evening I attended a party. The builder who developed our neighborhood wanted to foster a sense of community, so he put together a wine and cheese soirée at one of the flagship show homes.

At the event, I struck up a conversation with the neighbors about wine. I regaled my listeners with an erudite explanation of how Pinot Grigio differed from Chardonnay. A small audience developed around me, and the more attentively people listened, the more I began to confuse myself with a wine expert. Confidence does that to you.

I noticed a few glasses of red wine set out in an alcove next to the kitchen, so I led the group over there. "Now, this must be a Cabernet Sauvignon, perhaps a Merlot," I explained. I pointed to the glasses and explained that I could tell a lot about this wine varietal simply by its color and opacity.

I picked up a glass to elaborate further. To my horror, the liquid didn't move. At all. The glasses in the alcove were props—fakes—that the developer had set out as part of the décor. Nobody knew what to say. My audience scattered quickly, while my cheeks turned a nice shade of pinot noir, and I swallowed a large dose of humility.

Lord, keep me from confusing my growing confidence in
being a mom with thinking I can do this without You.
—JENNIFER FULWILER

Day Twenty-Eight

*"For this reason a man will leave his father and mother and be
united to his wife, and the two will become one flesh."*
—MATTHEW 19:5

I line the bottles up on the counter. The washcloths, soft and bright, are stacked high beside the baby tub on the countertop. The water runs from the sink's hose into the basin.

"I want to live/I want to give/I've been a miner/For a heart of gold . . . ," croons Neil Young softly into the bright kitchen light. I shut the water off, a small tuft of steam rising above the surface.

Patrick lifts Anjelica high, her arms and legs kicking fast, and her long form emerges altogether from her towel's cloak. He places her carefully into the white foam, and she murmurs her happy assent with a chorus of babble.

He pours a dollop of soap into his palm. I dip the first washcloth into the water and place it over her to ward off the air's chill. We take turns rubbing soap into the dimples of her knees and the coils of her ears, running warm water continuously over her shoulders, combing out sleek strands of her shampooed hair.

We have done this together, save for one errant instance or another, virtually every night for the past year. We have done it hundreds of times now, in one tub and then another, as her limbs sprouted out and her teeth grew in, as her hair lengthened from wisps to glossy filaments, as the trees at our window heralded spring with dusty pink blossoms and as they were stripped to bare claws bearing white tufts of snow.

"You keep me searching/For a heart of gold. . ."

We move precisely, Patrick and I, the ritual of churning lather and soft strokes now a rhythm born of practice. Side by side, elbow to elbow, together, our best slow dance yet.

*Lord, I love my husband. Thank You for every opportunity
parenting offers us to grow closer together.*
—DEBRALEE SANTOS

Day Twenty-Nine

*Being confident of this, that he who began a good work in you
will carry it on to completion until the day of Christ Jesus.*

—PHILIPPIANS 1:6

Henry was buckled into his high chair, squishing cake in his hands. As at any first birthday party, the guest of honor didn't understand what the celebration was all about. He was attuned to the attention and loved the love. He was happy, we were happy, and he was turning one.

One whole year of life outside the womb! It was a year so rich, so full of unexpected twists and turns, that I can only wonder what lies ahead. Henry will sit, and probably crawl. Maybe he'll walk, maybe not. He might have some words. Maybe he'll dance. Just a little, like babies do. I know he'll open a new door for me in some way. Babies do that.

I never imagined I'd be the mother of a disabled child. But I am. I now know things that I didn't know before. I know that God can't give us the lives He wants for us when we're hanging on to our own priorities. I know that our capacity for love is way less than His. I know we can only imagine what He wants for us—and then we're probably wrong.

I look at Henry on his first birthday, and I think back on this year of questions. Down syndrome raises a lot of them. The main one isn't "What am I going to do about it?" but rather "What am I going to do *with* it?" Will I spend my life apologizing for my son, or advocating for him? Will I spend my life patronizing him or pushing him? Will I accept his limitations or expand his horizons?

Maybe what lies ahead is less about how I'll expand Henry's horizons, and more about his expanding mine. I pray that God will give me the strength and grace to do whatever needs to be done.

Lord, I praise You for what You've taught me this year through this child. I ask for Your guidance as I continue to seek Your will.

—CHRISTY STURM

Day Thirty

*God gave Solomon wisdom and very great insight, and a breadth
of understanding as measureless as the sand on the seashore.*

—I KINGS 4:29

I can't get the picture out of my brain: Samantha toddling down the hallway in her hot-pink sweat suit, pulling a little puppy on wheels behind her. She was laughing and she glanced over her shoulder to make sure I was watching. She rounded the corner to the back hallway and I heard her puppy's squeaky wheel as they made their way through the back rooms of our small apartment. She was relatively new to walking, so I thought about following her but then decided to wait. She appeared again, her bright smile melting my heart. "What are you doing?" I asked.

She giggled, turned awkwardly on her heel and walked the other way. Before she turned the corner again, she gave me another big smile—then she disappeared. She was off on her adventure.

I stood there looking at the empty hallway and thinking, *This is what the next eighteen years will look like. A whole lot of smiles, a whole lot of adventure, a whole lot of letting go as she turns the next corner.*

Sam suddenly appeared, dropped her squeaky puppy and toddled her way to me. "Up!" she said, her arms outstretched.

I scooped her up and nuzzled her neck.

This is also what the next eighteen years would look like. I would have to do a whole lot of letting go . . . but here and there, I'd get to hold on.

*Oh, Lord, grant me wisdom to know what my child needs—when
to stand still and let her walk away and when to hold on tight.*

—ELSA KOK COLOPY

Holidays and Special Occasions

Lord,

This day is special because You made it and have given me the privilege of sharing it with my family. Steer my heart toward thankfulness and away from unrealistic expectations. Help me glorify You as I celebrate with my new child, with joy.

In Jesus' name, amen.

New Year's Day

For this reason I remind you to fan into flame the gift of God. . . .
—II TIMOTHY 1:6

I t was a few days into the New Year, and I hadn't come up with any resolutions. All my friends had filled pages with notes about dramatic changes they'd undertake this year, but I had nothing. I did want to work toward improving my life, but it seemed all the plans I came up with were doomed to failure—after all, my hands were so full keeping up with baby Lucy.

That night I came across a Web site where a mom of many children made a fascinating suggestion: Choose one word as your goal and inspiration for the year. Other women on her site chose words such as *Peace*, *Gratitude* or *Prudence*. Her word was *Joy*.

I prayed and asked the Lord to send me my own word for this year. The response came quickly: *Fortitude*. I typed it up in big bold letters and printed it out to tape onto my desk.

A couple of days later I caught myself in an all-too-typical pattern: The baby hadn't slept well, I had too much to do and was too exhausted to do it. I set Lucy down in her bouncy chair, flopped onto the couch and clicked on the television in defeat. From across the room, the word beckoned to me from my computer: *Fortitude*. I turned off the television. I stood up from the couch. And I approached my day with renewed vigor.

Lord, the simplest spiritual practices often bear the most fruit. Show me ways even a too-busy mom can grow.
—JENNIFER FULWILER

Wedding Anniversary

I [am] my beloved's, and my beloved [is] mine. . . .
—SONG OF SOLOMON 6:3 (KJV)

We sat across from each other silently as the flickering candlelight added warmth and ambiance to the room. The soft music playing in the background made me serene as Kenya and I toasted our anniversary. "*Mmm. . .*" I closed my eyes as I sipped the sweet sparking apple cider out of my black-and-gold wedding goblet with *Bride* inscribed on it.

"Happy Anniversary, honey," Kenya lifted his *Groom* glass and smiled at me. Then he pulled a piece of paper out of his pocket and unfolded it.

"I wrote this for you," he said. And for the next few moments, he swept me away with a poem so breathtakingly beautiful all I could do was wipe away tears. The way my husband expressed his love, appreciation and adoration for me made me feel I was the most special woman in the world.

Just then, we heard a faint cry. It was Kedar, waking up. "Impeccable timing," Kenya said laughing and lifting his brows. We shared a chuckle and turned the bedroom light on. The clock struck twelve, and magically, our romantic hideaway once again transformed into Mommy and Daddy's room.

God, let our marriage bonds and commitment to each other remain strong as we nourish the child You have entrusted to us.
—DIANNA HOBBS

Easter

Because through Christ Jesus the law of the Spirit of
life set me free from the law of sin and death.
—ROMANS 8:2

Elizabeth was unbearably cute in her daisy dress and matching hat. I bumped the stroller up the steps and into church, smiling in the Easter sun. Inside, I unbuckled my daughter and set her free. She immediately toddled down the aisle, white Mary Janes clicking on the hardwood floor, hand upraised to touch the brass numbers on the edge of the old pews.

I stopped to chat with Esperanza and exclaimed happily over the presence of her three-year-old grandson Renato. Spiffy in his jacket and tie, Renato took one look at Elizabeth and was entranced. He approached my daughter, who had never encountered a child his size before, and said something quietly. Elizabeth smiled, reached out, and took his hand. The two walked together down the center aisle.

And there it was: the future. My sweet girl was walking down the aisle with a handsome, dark-haired older man. Sunlight streamed through stained glass, the organist played an interlude, the altar was bedecked with flowers. The two stopped—along with my heart—when they reached the steps leading to the sanctuary. Renato leaned close; Elizabeth looked up at him. And then they laughed the sudden laugh of innocent children, turned, and trotted merrily around the pews, befuddling the glimpse I'd had of life when Elizabeth is grown.

Lord, let me never hold her so close that
I forget that my job is to release her.
—JULIA ATTAWAY

Mother's Day

Do not conform any longer to the pattern of this world, but
be transformed by the renewing of your mind. . . .
—ROMANS 12:2

*C*hurch on Mother's Day used to churn my stomach. Amid the well-coiffed ladies looking forward to brunch and bouquets and a day of appreciation, there I sat. For four Mother's Days I was infertile, fresh from a miscarriage or having just suffered a stillbirth.

My church has a lovely tradition of asking all the moms to stand and then determining who has been a mother the longest, the shortest, and who has the most kids. I resisted the temptation to stand and scream. I ached.

I'd been a mom ten weeks when I finally stood on Mother's Day. I knew the moment was going to light me up like a Fourth of July sky. It did, and I was proud as a peacock holding Zach. But as I rose, I also felt something else. I was thinking about which seat held a yearning womb. And I was thinking about those who would never be mothers, for whatever reason.

Motherhood is the backbone of our culture, and it sometimes involves pain, more often involves pleasure, and is always a privilege. But on my first Mother's Day, I was thankful to find that motherhood was also about looking at the world in a new way and not being so focused on self.

To this day, when I stand on Mother's Day, a piece of me sits with the others.

In my new role, Lord, help me to mature my
thinking and broaden my compassion.
—SUSAN WALLACE

Father's Day

When I was a boy in my father's house, still tender,
and an only child of my mother. . . .
—PROVERBS 4:3

I t was our family's first Father's Day, and I scanned the house for evidence of my husband: a razor in a cup on the bathroom sink, size twelve men's shoes on the closet floor into which I could fit both feet, a basement full of tools ready to continue the do-it-yourself remodel later that day. All clues that someone with a much bigger frame, scratchier face and more testosterone lived here: a man in the house.

As a girl, Father's Day was an annual reminder that a crucial person was missing from my life. It wasn't until I was a teenager and learned about my Heavenly Father's love that I realized a father is defined by much more than a man in residence. It is unconditional love and willingness to sacrifice that change a man into a daddy.

Scanning the house a second time, I looked for evidence of my daughter's *father*. That was harder to identify, but knowing what to look, for I could see it everywhere. The stripes on the nursery wall that Derek had carefully and skillfully painted. The baby carrier straps adjusted to the largest size for a walk to the lake the day before. The enormous flip-flops next to the rocking chair, echoing last evening's bedtime routine. I rejoiced that God had provided my daughter with what I never had: a man with presence, an unconditional love for her and a willingness to sacrifice . . . a father.

Father God, thank You for my child's
earthly father—and bless him.
—ALEXANDRA KUYKENDALL

Thanksgiving

Be strong and take heart, all you who hope in the Lord.
—PSALM 31:24

I was up early to get my turkey in the oven, carefully following the instructions I'd found online. I made Paula Deen's top-rated cornbread stuffing and put it into the oven. I whipped up some homemade cranberry sauce and spiced walnuts. I was ready. It was going to be the perfect Thanksgiving.

I dressed Joey in a pair of supercute tan corduroy overalls I'd bought on sale. I slipped on my favorite jeans and was actually able to get them buttoned. Maybe those morning walks were finally paying off. I was ready. It was going to be the perfect Thanksgiving.

An hour later, my mom arrived with a warm-from-the-oven apple pie. We set the table while Nat King Cole played in the background. I lit the pumpkin-spice candles and arranged the centerpiece I'd made with instructions from Martha Stewart. I was ready. It was going to be the perfect Thanksgiving.

Then, before I took my first bite, my perfect Thanksgiving came crashing down around me. Literally. Joey threw his entire tray of turkey, stuffing and cranberry sauce onto my light tan carpet.

How had my perfectly planned dinner gone so, so wrong, so, so quickly?

Or had it? After all, the food was still warm. My family was sitting around the dining table laughing and talking. No one seemed to notice or care about the carpet. Cleaning could wait. Right now, I had to eat my nearly perfect Thanksgiving dinner.

Lord, help me focus on what really matters
during the busy holiday season.
—ERIN MACPHERSON

Christmas

For behold, from now on all generations will call me blessed.
—LUKE 1:48 (ESV)

⁓⁓⁓⁓⁓⁓⁓

"Leroy, do you see this?"

I looked over. Kari smiled wide as Hans' little arm lay over his cheek, ear and temple as he nursed, the very picture of contentment. Late morning sunlight filled the room, spilling through the window, warming the crisp winter day, as glorious voices sang the classic German hymn "Lo, How a Rose E'er Blooming" on the stereo.

Gazing at Kari gazing at Hans, I heard the voices carol:

> *The Rose which I am singing,*
> *Whereof Isaiah said,*
> *Is from its sweet root springing*
> *In Mary, purest Maid;*
> *Through God's great love and might*
> *The Blessed Babe she bare us*
> *In a cold, cold winter's night.*

Prior to having Hans, I'd thought of Mary's role in the Nativity as merely functional, getting Jesus born. But hearing the song and observing the physical and spiritual bond my wife and Hans shared, I began to see Mary as a real woman. Her job didn't end after she carried baby Jesus in her womb; she nourished and nurtured Him for years. Indeed, as I watched my wife pour love into Hans, it hit me that perhaps some of the compassion Jesus displayed later in his ministry grew from the tender love Mary showed him. Mothers matter.

I must have been staring. "Leroy, what are you thinking?" my wife chuckled, as she got my attention.

"Not much, honey," I dodged, not wanting to reveal my thoughts. "You know, though, there's something about Mary. . . ."

Lord, may we model the love and tenderness
shared by Mary and her Son Jesus.

—LEROY HUIZENGA

Special Concerns

~~~~~~

Jesus,

In this new stage of my life, turn my eyes to You—and give me the grace to ask for (and accept) help from others. Help me be patient and resourceful, open to feedback, and resilient when hurt. Motherhood is a long, rich, wonderful and sometimes difficult road. Grant me the wisdom I will need to travel it at Your side.

Amen.

BABY BLUES OR POSTPARTUM DEPRESSION?

Hormones. Sleep deprivation. Exhaustion. They all mix together to create an emotional roller coaster during the months after pregnancy. You've probably heard of postpartum depression (PPD), but how do you know if what you're feeling is normal or if it's something to worry about?

THE "BABY BLUES" ARE USUALLY SHORT-LIVED. Almost everyone has swings in emotions during the first several weeks after birth. But as your hormones adjust, your moods should too. If your feelings continue to cycle—or deepen—you should consider the possibility that you have postpartum depression. Most women with PPD are diagnosed between two and four months postpartum, but the onset can take place any time during the first year.

PPD IS NOT YOUR FAULT. Depression isn't caused by lack of faith or lack of competence. It's a medical condition—and there's no shame in seeking medical help for it.

PPD IS RELATIVELY COMMON. Mood and anxiety issues are the #1 complication of pregnancy. Approximately 15 percent of mothers become seriously depressed during the first year after giving birth. According to PostPartum. net, an online support site sponsored by Postpartum Support International, major symptoms include:

> » Feelings of anger, irritability or intense anxiety
> » Lack of interest in your baby
> » Appetite and sleep problems
> » Crying and intense sadness
> » Feelings of guilt, shame, worthlessness or hopelessness
> » Loss of interest, joy or pleasure in things you used to enjoy
> » Possible thoughts of harming the baby or yourself

Other, less common disorders to be aware of include PP-OCD (obsessive compulsive disorder), PPP (postpartum psychosis) and PPPTSD (postpartum posttraumatic stress disorder). If you're not depressed but are suffering from intrusive and disturbing thoughts, please seek help.

GET HELP QUICKLY. Studies show that the children of moms whose PPD goes untreated are at higher risk of developing anxiety, disruptive and depressive disorders. The longer you delay in getting help, the more you put yourself—and your child—at risk.

FIND OUT MORE. PostPartum.net has many helpful resources online, including a standard ten-question self-quiz you can fill out and take with you to your doctor.

TAKING YOUR BABY TO CHURCH

Some churches emphasize family worship, while others focus on providing quality nurseries. If you're committed to attending church together as a family, here are some tips to help you manage.

» **OFFER WHAT YOU CAN.** The goal of worship is to give yourself and your praise to God. If all you can manage is get yourself and your family to church, that alone is a huge gift.

» **PLAN YOUR ESCAPE ROUTE.** Expect that you will have to get up and leave periodically; select your seats accordingly. Avoid sitting near loudspeakers that will startle your baby.

» **HAVE A RULE OF THUMB.** Sometimes it's hard to know if your baby is going to calm down or keep crying. If she cries longer than it takes to say the Lord's Prayer, take her out.

» **ROTATE BABY-CALMING DUTY.** Decide with your spouse who will leave to soothe the baby, and when. Trade off weeks, or trade off based on whose emotional needs are deepest that day. Be willing to change your plan periodically.

» **PRACTICE USING A "CHURCH VOICE."** Spend time whispering to your baby outside of church so he gets used to the idea that some times are quiet times. If you can visit church when services aren't in progress, practice there.

» **BRING STRATEGIC ENTERTAINMENT.** Once your baby starts moving, she isn't likely to sit still for the entire service. Keep a bag of "church toys" exclusively for Sundays. Lift-the-flap Bible stories and cloth books are great. In a pinch, sacrifice your wallet to the cause; avoid keys and cell phones, which clatter when dropped.

» **BURN OFF BABY ENERGY AHEAD OF TIME.** Have a tickle-fest, or set an active crawler down to race around for fifteen minutes before the service starts. The more energy she expends beforehand, the less she has available for squirming.

» **FIGURE OUT FOOD.** If your baby doesn't take a bottle, reconnoiter possible locations to nurse before you head into the service. For older babies, you'll need to weigh the advantages (and disadvantages) of food as entertainment. Some families allow snacking; others give a snack just before church begins.

» **DON'T BE EMBARRASSED.** Normal baby noise is acceptable. Yes, at some point someone will give you the hairy eyeball when your baby coos or claps or giggles. It's not your problem; it's theirs. If someone's really snarky, ask him or her—gently—to pray for you.

» **PRAY.** After the service is over, take turns with your spouse so you each have a few minutes alone with God. Better yet, take advantage of the supply of eager arms willing to babysit, and pray together.

PREVENTING (OR OVERCOMING) LONELINESS

Life as a mom can be isolating, an endless cycle of baby needs and baby talk. Building a support network for this time of your life is a worthwhile investment in keeping yourself sane.

GET OUTSIDE. There's no one new to meet within your own four walls. Fresh air and exercise will lift your spirits . . . and might put you in the path of other moms hoping to make new friends!

FIND SUPPORT. Reach out to older moms you know and find out where they found encouragement at this stage of life. Check the bulletin board at your church, grocery store, library and community center for new-mom groups. Call friends; visit the library and the park.

FIND EVEN MORE COMPANIONSHIP. See if MOPS International (www .MOPS.org) has a branch near you. MOPS is a community of moms who understand the unique joys and challenges of mothering, and is a great place to find friendship, encouragement and spiritual growth.

KEEP YOUR MIND ACTIVE. Read a magazine or listen to a book or lecture on your MP3. You'll be a better mom if your brain's engaged—at least occasionally—in grown-up pursuits.

AVOID OVERUSING THE COMPUTER AND TV. Distraction doesn't make loneliness go away. Join that online chat group, but set a goal of spending at least as much time seeking in-real-life friends who can come over for a cup of tea.

JOIN A MOMMY-AND-BABY CLASS. Consider a class an investment in your social life as well as a benefit to your baby. Check your local gym or Y for postnatal yoga, kiddy music or baby gym classes.

ENCOURAGE YOURSELF. Your self-talk can lift you up—or bring you down. Build yourself up by making a conscious effort to be open to others, and remember your successes. Try not to ruminate on the negatives.

PRAY! You may feel alone, but you're oh-so-not. Enlist God's help in finding companionship and support. Ask your spouse, your friends, your parents to pray for you too!

KEEPING YOUR MARRIAGE HEALTHY

Is it possible to do everything a mom has to do and still be a loving wife? Maybe not at first. But figuring out how to balance two sets of needs is hard enough when you're rested, so don't expect to get it all right at once.

WORK THROUGH PROBLEMS TOGETHER. Long-term research at the Becoming a Family Institute shows that how couples handle decision-making is the #1 factor affecting happiness in marriage. And the top conflict new parents face (surprise!) is who's in charge of doing what.

TIPS:

» Make a plan for responsibilities, and revise it whenever you're feeling overwhelmed.
» Discuss problems when you're not already angry or over-tired.
» Show respect for your spouse's opinions.
» Hold your tongue. Listen for content; discount the emotion. Don't play the blame game.
» Apologize honestly when you've said or done something hurtful.

KEEP YOUR SPOUSE IN THE AFFECTION LOOP. Tally up how many kisses you give your baby in a day and compare that to how many you give your hubby. You don't have to go for a one-to-one match, but a good smooch makes up for a lot!

BE HONEST. If you want to snuggle but are afraid it will lead to more romance than you can handle, talk to your husband about it. He will probably appreciate your candor, and you can work together to find ways of showing affection that are comfortable for both of you.

SHOW INTEREST. Too exhausted to hear about your husband's day? Listen anyway. It will keep you connected to his world and shift your mind away from diapers for a while. Remember to ask how he's feeling about being a dad; moms aren't the only ones who sometimes feel marginalized, isolated, resentful or exhausted.

SPEND TIME TOGETHER. Even if you can't afford a sitter and don't have family nearby, develop a plan for daily conversation with your honey. Set a family rule of no TV after 9:00 PM, or reserve fifteen minutes in the morning or at night to talk. If all else fails, call your honey during the baby's nap (before you conk out). Healthy marriages require interaction.

SPEND TIME ALONE. Both of you need time to follow your own interests or just to take a walk in silence. Carve out an hour or two a week you can "give" as a gift to your spouse. Ask him to do the same for you. You'll each be grateful for the breathing room.

SHOW HIM IN LITTLE WAYS HOW YOU LOVE HIM. Give him a real kiss instead of a peck on the cheek. Put the baby in a carrier instead of the stroller so you can hold hands with him. Text him to say you're crazy about him.

PRAY FOR YOUR HUSBAND—AND YOUR MARRIAGE. God joined you together as husband and wife, and He will help you stay together. Ask Him daily to bless your hubby and your union and to keep your heart open to change as you grow into your new role as wife *and* mother.

PRAYING FOR YOUR CHILD

If you don't pray for your child, who will? Start now, when it's easy to get in the habit. Regular prayer helps you stay committed to your child's spiritual as well as emotional and physical needs.

» **BE FOCUSED.** Ask for specific blessings, especially for character qualities you hope to see in your child. Honesty, kindness, obedience and courage are all valid requests and are more concrete than a vague "Bless Suzie."

» **BE BOLD.** Don't be shy about requesting a lot. Go ahead and ask God to make your child a missionary, a pastor, a world-changer. He might say *no*—but it doesn't hurt to ask!

» **FOCUS ON RELATIONSHIPS.** Pray that your child will develop a rich, strong relationship with God and that you will be given the grace to guide her in faith.

» **DON'T FORGET TO PRAY FOR SPIRITUAL PROTECTION.** Your child's physical well-being is important, but so too are fortitude and the ability to discern good from evil.

» **THINK AHEAD.** Ask God to send good role models into your child's life: caring teachers, humble leaders, pure and responsible friends. Even if you don't see the shadow of darkness now, get in the habit of praying for protection.

» **CONSIDER YOUR OWN WEAKNESSES.** If you struggle with finding contentment, have a bad temper or forgive others only grudgingly, ask God to protect your child from suffering because of your sins.

» **PRAY WHEN YOU CAN.** Long quiet times with God are great, but it's equally valid to pray in snippets throughout the day. Post a prayer for your child above your sink for when you wash dishes; whisper thanks when you whisper "good night."

LOOKING AHEAD

As the toddler years approach, fear not! Our contributors wish you well with a few parting words of advice.

When things get rough, remember the rotten truth: *Someone* has to act like a grown-up . . . and it's probably got to be you. **JULIA ATTAWAY**

Instead of figuring out how to fit your baby into your busy world, sit down and join her in her uncomplicated one. **RUTH BERGEN**

Focus on how you respond to your child instead of on how she is misbehaving. **LIZ BISSELL**

Keep regular date nights with your husband, bearing in mind that the word "sitter" does not mean a high chair at McDonald's. **FAITH BOGDAN**

Keep a journal and try to jot something down every day. Even something as simple as "He licked the cat!" can bring back priceless memories.

SABRA CIANCANELLI

This is the only time in life when slobbery kisses and gooey fingers will bring a smile to your face. **ELSA KOK COLOPY**

I've saved my sanity many a day by taking a ride in the car, because car seats are the one legal way to strap your children down. **JENNIFER FULWILER**

When you're out in the public eye and your child does something outrageous and you're tempted to scream, that's the time to pull out snacks.

CAROL HATCHER

Whenever you feel frustrated, squeeze your adult-sized feet into their little shoes and let compassion guide your steps. **DIANNA HOBBS**

Channeling a child's desires in other directions works better than simply saying no. If he wants to bang on the piano, suggest something quieter, such as kicking a foam soccer ball. **LEROY HUIZENGA**

Find a mothering mentor whose parenting style you admire, someone you can ask questions of and who can help offer some perspective.
ALEXANDRA KUYKENDALL

Chesterton wrote, "Angels fly because they take themselves lightly." Our kids are funny and our foibles inevitable, so we might as well take ourselves lightly and laugh. SUSAN LABOUNTY

Make the choice each day to have fun with your child by finding ways to include her in what you're doing and by joining her as she plays. LISA LADWIG

Be prepared: The terrible twos can begin at around eighteen months!
DONNA MAY LYONS

Your kid will survive if he only eats cheese and Cheerios for an entire year. Some days, the broccoli fight just isn't worth it. ERIN MACPHERSON

Resist marketing. Don't buy big plastic farms; go to a real one.
LENORE LELAH PERSON

To be a mother is to traffic in the small. Find joy in the journey and the practice: in quick naps, short stories, tiny fingers. DEBRALEE SANTOS

Be consistent with your discipline or your child will consistently rule you.
RHONDA J. SMITH

Never take anything for granted—every step is a miracle! CHRISTY STURM

Listening to your toddler is like watching a foreign film without the subtitles. Sometimes you're the one who needs a time out. KAREN VALENTIN

Write it down! What you think you'll always remember, you won't, and what you think you won't want to remember, you truly will!
SUSAN BESZE WALLACE

OLD TESTAMENT

A

abundance, 200

acceptance, 148

   of accidents, 356

   of change, 210, 220, 355, 363

   of grandparents' behavior, 181

   of life, 263

   of limitations, 22, 191

   of mistakes, 244

   of other moms, 168

   of others' choices, 285, 318

   of who people are, 273

accidental phone call, 266

accidents, 209. *see also* falls

   acceptance of, 356

   in the cot, 250

   eating bugs, 271

   locking baby in car, 308

   needing stitches, 380

adapting to change, 99

adoption, 20, 365

   bonding after, 166

   telling people about, 166

   termination of rights, 77

adventurous baby, 306

advice, 94, 183

allergic reaction, 174

anger, 75, 151, 169

   letting go of, 285

   words spoken in, 207

anxiety, 12

appreciation, 26, 31. *see also* thankfulness

   for being a dad, 373

   for being a mom, 145, 254

   of choices, 218, 228

   of the day, 235, 249, 252

   for family, 221, 249

   for God's Creations, 212, 279

   for God's Guidance, 31

   for grandparents. *see also* grandparents

   for help offered, 243

   for husband, 45, 60, 134, 177, 250, 305

   of life, 335, 337

   for mother in-law, 195

   for new discoveries, 269

   of surroundings, 229

   of who you are, 86

   of wonder of life, 149, 200, 212, 266

assumptions, 368

Attaway, Julia

   advice from, 402

   devotionals, 11, 27, 36, 63, 73, 91, 101, 114, 127, 139, 149, 159, 168, 177, 188, 201, 212, 218, 224, 234, 265, 284, 309, 320, 335, 371, 377, 388

   life details, v

attentive mothering, 336

awareness of others, 141

B

baby blues, 64, 394–395

baby monitor, 69

babysitters, 96, 140, 201

   grandparents as, 67

   unsatisfactory, 251, 348

bad day, 36

bathtime, 234, 328, 381

behavior, 213

   biting other babies, 283

   grandparents', acceptance of, 181

   misinterpreted, 213

   misplaced values in, 370

belly buttons, 7

Bergen, Ruth

   advice from, 402

   devotionals, 4, 16, 46, 57, 71, 95, 106, 123, 135, 146, 155, 173, 176, 208, 233, 278, 287, 292, 302, 333, 369

   life details, v

Daily Guideposts: Reflections for a Faith-Filled Life

Daily Guideposts: Your First Year of Motherhood is just one of the resources Guideposts offers to help you make the most of your devotional time. Others include:

DAILY GUIDEPOSTS 2011

Now in its thirty-fifth annual edition, America's favorite devotional has helped millions of readers to a closer walk with God and a richer, fuller life. For every day of 2011, you'll find a short Scripture verse, a first-person story and a brief prayer. It's available in regular-print jacketed hardcover and deluxe faux-leather with gilded edges (432 pages) and large-print paperback (624 pages). For more information, visit www.dailyguideposts.org.

DAILY GUIDEPOSTS JOURNAL: A YEAR OF REFLECTION

Discover a beautiful way to maintain a positive outlook. This brand-new journal features a short Scripture to focus your thoughts, a brief prayer to set the tone for your day, space to list your prayer requests and to note prayers that have been answered, and room to keep track of God's marvelous gifts in your own life. A perfect way to step back from the cares of everyday life, commit your deepest thoughts to paper and reflect on your journey with God, it's available in hardcover, 256 pages.

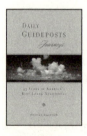

DAILY GUIDEPOSTS JOURNEYS

This special collection of more than one hundred devotionals brings together the best of thirty-five years of *Daily Guideposts*, enriched with a year-by-year history of the *Daily Guideposts* family and the events that have shaped us all. It's available in jacketed hardcover, 304 pages.

ALL OF THESE BOOKS ARE AVAILABLE AT YOUR LOCAL BOOKSELLER OR DIRECT FROM GUIDEPOSTS AT WWW.SHOPGUIDEPOSTS.COM.